COZY POLITICS

COZY POLITICS

Political Parties, Campaign Finance, and Compromised Governance

PETER KOBRAK

LYNNE
RIENNER
PUBLISHERS

BOULDER
LONDON

Published in the United States of America in 2002 by
Lynne Rienner Publishers, Inc.
1800 30th Street, Boulder, Colorado 80301
www.rienner.com

and in the United Kingdom by
Lynne Rienner Publishers, Inc.
3 Henrietta Street, Covent Garden, London WC2E 8LU

Library of Congress Cataloging-in-Publication Data
Kobrak, Peter
   Cozy politics : political parties, campaign finance, and compromised governance / by
Peter Kobrak.
   Includes bibliographical references and index.
   ISBN 1-58826-023-2 (alk. paper)
   ISBN 1-58826-067-4 (pb, alk. paper)
   1. Politics, Practical—United States.   2. Political parties—United States.
3. Campaign funds—United States.   I. Title.
JK1764.K66   2002
324.7'0973—dc21

                                                                    2001048640

British Cataloguing in Publication Data
A Cataloguing in Publication record for this book
is available from the British Library.

Printed and bound in the United States of America

⊗   The paper used in this publication meets the requirements
     of the American National Standard for Permanence of
     Paper for Printed Library Materials Z39.48-1984.

   5   4   3   2   1

To my sons—George, Mark, and Harry

Contents

Tables and Figures

Tables

Figures

Acknowledgments

N umerous individuals have contributed over the past three years to the writing of this book. Western Michigan University librarians Michael McDonnell, Hardy Carroll, and David Isaacson frequently steered me in the right direction. Vernon Jacob has provided numerous lessons in political economy over the years. Warren Gregory was generous in sharing his considerable knowledge on using census and other federal agency data. James Schneider provided excellent suggestions on cutting and focusing the material. Juleen Audrey Eichinger exhibited her formidable skills in preparing the manuscript for publication. Dan Eades and Leanne Anderson at Lynne Rienner Publishers proved congenial editors in transforming the manuscript into the final product. Dennis Marshall was a helpful and constructive copyeditor. Jackie Van'tZelfde provided her usual knowledgeable clerical assistance, and Yolanda Jones saved valuable time, thanks to her efficiency and good-natured cooperation. Finally, as always, thanks to my wife, Barbara, for her meticulous editing, steady encouragement, and patience.

Introduction

M ore and larger grassroots and Washington-based interest groups, fewer voters, reduced party impact on elections, and increasingly expensive campaign technologies . . . it is small wonder that nervous politicians are engaged in a frenzied pursuit of money. As citizen involvement in elections and participation in politics slowly lessens, cash and single-purpose interest groups are filling that political vacuum. The resulting cozy politics has had an appreciable impact on how Congress makes decisions, how agency missions are compromised by public/private partnerships, and how political "reinventors" have altered the very functions of the federal bureaucracy. Cozy politics contributes to the increasing erosion of civic confidence and citizen participation, the warping of political parties, the denigration of politicians, and the compromise of federal administrative agencies.

Over the years, it has been fashionable among worldly journalists and cosmopolitan political scientists to shrug when reformers complain about financial excesses that benefit the few at the expense of the many. After all, financial hanky-panky is nothing new, and hardly unique to the United States: during the Jacksonian and post–Civil War periods, pork-barrel practices were widespread;[1] and the director of the Bureau of the Budget testified in the 1960s that in one three-month period, he received two hundred requests from members of Congress advocating projects for their districts;[2] and in the wider world, Paul Starobin was able to identify terms for pork (in its use as political metaphor) in Japanese *(buta)*, German *(schweinfleisch)*, French *(charcuterie)*, Mexican *(puerco)*, Italian *(maiale)*, Egyptian *(khanzir)*, Hebrew *(chazir)*, and Icelandic *(svinakjot)*.[3]

But pork-barreling and cozy politics are different. Cozy politics includes a broader array of financial misbehaviors—ones that directly impact the very *nature* of the political system and the relationship of citizens to their government. Cozy politics is particularly serious today because many citizens have become distanced from their national government by their economic and social circumstances as well as by their relationship to the political system. This distance is reflected in our use of the term *democratic capitalism* to describe the nation's successful current system, whereas in the old days we celebrated the virtues of our democracy and our capitalist system separately.

There is much to celebrate in the dynamism of our economic system and its triumph over communism. And our political system continues to meet the ultimate democratic tests—citizens cast their ballots in comparatively, though not entirely, honest elections in which the candidate with the most votes wins.[4] Power is surrendered peacefully by losing incumbents to the winning candidates, and the government bureaucracy subsequently is responsive to the newly elected power holders.[5]

However, much as we have assessed Russian society in terms of its democratic and economic reforms *(glasnost* and *perestroika)*, so is there much to be gained from thinking separately and distinctly about our own economic and political systems. A number of our corporate stocks have remained comparatively high historically despite the 2001 recession. Meanwhile, the stock of our political system is nearing a performance low in the eyes of its citizens. To be sure, it still holds much of its value, and citizens will rally to our democracy when national security requires patriotism, as the aftermath of the terrorist surprise attack on September 11, 2001, demonstrated. Nonetheless, we must take a hard look at our political system now in order to be prepared if and when the economy takes more than a cyclical downturn and regional global events require an even larger and more sustained U.S. response. Furthermore, effective governance requires a political system able to respond not only to domestic or foreign emergencies but also to such looming long-term problems as the solvency of social security and medicare, the overall coverage of the nation's health care system, environmental degradation, reducing the size of our prison system without endagering the citzenry, and educating a higher proportion of Americans to compete globally. Such a response requires a political system that stimulates the development of an active and thereby well-informed citizenry that influences its elected officials to act. In short, such a citizenry must bring the same zeal to sustaining a healthy American political system that it brings to introducing the continual changes necessary for a flourishing capitalism.

This book is about how our political system, slowly but surely, is being corroded by the way that we conduct our political affairs. Business analogies used throughout this discussion seem ironically appropriate because that is increasingly how we view our world. There is no magic way to reverse our political direction. The antidote to cozy politics is widespread citizen participation. *Cozy Politics,* therefore, takes the radical position that the dangers of the current course can be overcome only through an extensive redesign of our political parties and a more modest reworking of our government. This would encourage broader citizen involvement, which in and of itself would do much to counter the current political excesses and promote the broader interests over the special interests.

Traditional Pork vs. Cozy Politics

The meaning of *pork* and *pork-barreling* is sometimes unclear, and its critics rarely pause to define it. Journalists, porkaphobes, and others of that persuasion plunge directly into the juicy details of how a politician, corporation, or interest group has "done it again" to the average Joe or Josie. Waste and the triumph of political interference over programmatic purpose figure prominently in such discussions.

More sympathetic political scientists and journalists often justify what I term *traditional pork* as a time-honored system for building legislative coalitions and gaining reelection. Veteran reporters of *Congressional Quarterly* capture the spirit of this definition: "Since the first Congress convened two centuries ago, lawmakers have ladled [political pork] out to home constituencies in the form of cash for roads, bridges, and sundry other civic projects. It is a safe bet that the distribution of such largesse will continue for at least as long into the future." In "obtaining 'pork' by raiding the pork barrel (the state or national treasury), the representative is likely to improve his or her chances for re-election."[6] To win reelection, members of Congress, therefore, engage in logrolling and "usually do not question each other's pet projects for fear that their own may be voted down. . . . 'You scratch my back and I'll scratch yours.'"[7] In this sense, pork-barreling is "functional" for the political system.

Furthermore, pork-barrel politics historically has served as a means for geographically based constituents to get what they want. After all, it is only fair that if those concerned about the "big picture" are winning on an issue important to them, in exchange, constituents in other jurisdictions should get the little things that they want too—little lighthouses, little marinas, and the not-so-little dams or highway extensions.

Political scientists devote little attention to whether such pork is an accurate translation of local district or state preferences. The justification for pork lies in its being "the necessary glue that holds political coalitions together."[8] For example, congressional and senatorial votes to pass the landmark Tax Reform Act of 1986 were collected partly through "transition rules," which catered to district concerns and enabled members of Congress to justify their votes on the bigger and more controversial issue of tax reform.[9]

Pork-barrel politics also brings some welcome humor to politics. In the unlikely event that the carping killjoys win, there would be no more $250,000 grants included in the appropriation process to "help Alaskan natives hunt polar bears, sea otters and walruses."[10] And how then in 1989 could the U.S. Navy have arrived at a strategically sound decision about stationing its four recommissioned battleships? Frantic competition among states and cities ensued in allocating cash and exercising political clout, much as it would for any economic development project. Of the four ships, one went to Staten Island at a cost of $250 million, largely thanks to $20 million in cash contributions from the New York Port Authority and the city. Critics termed the exercise "homeporking."[11] After Operation Desert Storm, though, the navy decommissioned those ships: like crime, pork does not always pay in the long run.

So, what's the big deal about the triumph of political influence over programmatic purpose? It hastens the feeling of alienation from politics for large portions of our country's population and, thereby, contributes to a political system that is less responsive to the general needs of the populace. And it does so by stealth.

For a number of reasons, only some of which stem from money, the nature of our political system has profoundly changed since the 1960s. We seem to be a nation quick to embrace technology but slow to recognize political changes. As a nation, we simply do not pay attention to political change. Although writers in think tanks, university faculties, and public-interest groups have sounded the alarm, they typically are scorned as "policy wonks" and "talking heads." Citizens are all too willing to ignore the telltale signs of political trouble identified by these modern Paul Reveres.

Ironically, as the world becomes more global and the stake that most U.S. citizens hold in the federal government thereby grows more significant, the public devotes less attention to politics and political economy. The intellect certainly is not lacking. The same reading public that shuns politics—many of them the opinion leaders of today or tomorrow—turns on to such intellectually engaging subjects as Eastern philosophy, psychology, and military history. There seems to be a sense that an individual can do little to affect the high-stakes politics dominated today by wealthy individuals, special interests, and distant bureaucracies. There is a striking contrast between our economic confidence and our political pessimism.

It is tempting to engage in wholesale condemnation of politics and politicians, and people in the United States are doing so in large numbers. The temptation is particularly strong because political behavior appears to reflect an increase in what is termed here *cozy politics*. Politics is "cozy" when political decisions are driven primarily by who benefits along the way rather than by the purpose of the program or regulation. Tort trial lawyers, for example, were Bill Clinton's largest presidential-campaign contributors in 1992, and 94 percent of their contributions went to Democrats in 1994. Congressional legislation that would have capped most product liability lawsuits at $250,000 was vetoed by Clinton—a veto he sugarcoated with the rationale that such a ceiling on jury awards would restrict consumer rights. The ultimate beneficiaries then became the politicians and those implementing the congressional or presidential decisions rather than the alleged clients or the public interest. Such cozy arrangements may benefit a specific geographical area or they may enable companies, interest groups, professionals, or nonprofit agencies to win public-agency contracts through political influence rather than technical competence. Cozy politics is also larger than traditional pork in the proportion of federal resources that it absorbs and in its impact on the political system.

Cozy Politics and Compromised Governance

The stark presence and systemic consequences of cozy politics are nothing new. History is replete with examples of the dire consequences that follow when citizens fall asleep at the political switch. During Roman times, the rise of a "politics of interest" eroded the society's moral fabric. The problem was not that ambitious politicians and their allies clashed while pursuing their goals but, rather, that the competition of interests was gradually reduced to the pursuit of self-interests unaccompanied by any aspiration to serve society-wide material and cultural needs or by generally accepted and controlling standards of obligation. One result was the decline of popular participation in the polity; the people came to be "governed by a power organization rather than a political association." Power no longer served as the means to direct and coordinate human activities; it had now become the central political fact.[12]

Institutions other than the state can fall prey to cozy politics, too. In the Middle Ages, popes issued indulgences, although "with a certain restraint and [they] conscientiously applied the financial returns to approved Christian ends." During the Renaissance, however, sale of the papal certificates came to be viewed as merely "a device for raising taxes . . . and was consigned to licensed vendors who offered them to the public."[13] The sale of papal indulgences furthered the pope's financial interests rather than the buyer's spiritual welfare. The Vatican's political executives, by entering into what became pervasive and sizable cozy political arrangements, had opened to question the church's integrity and the legitimacy of its religious mission.

When cozy political arrangements become endemic and widespread, they can compromise governance. While the institutional and political arrangements that have contributed significantly to our greatness still remain in place, the United States is well on its way to substituting cozy political arrangements for our political and constitutional rules of the game.

Our political processes and institutions are besieged by cozy political pressures, as money that talks and the passionate voices of political, single-purpose interest groups increasingly drown out the preferences of other citizens in the political system.

The Boundaries of Cozy Politics

When does pork stop being the relatively harmless glue that seals political bargains and become the gunk that subverts the system? Traditionally, members of Congress have justified road projects, waterway improvements, and even funds earmarked for a particular company in a member's district on the grounds that one person's pork barrel is another person's economic development. When cozy politics extends into numerous issue areas where it rarely appeared previously, however, and when its financial commitments are frequently extensive, cozy politics becomes dangerous. Over the past two decades, cozy politics has produced more arrangements long on political expediency and short on purpose. What economic justification is there for providing 90 percent of our agricultural subsidies to just two dozen of the four hundred classified farm commodities—particularly when 80 percent of the money goes to farmers with a net worth of more than half a million dollars?[14] Or providing oil-depletion allowances that can total more than the original investment cost?[15]

The Impact of Cozy Politics on Federal Administrative Agencies

While traditional pork-barrel logrolling involving small economic-development projects can be justified as the political grease for achieving agreement on larger issues, the newer cozy political arrangements often involve much larger appropriations and affect the missions of far more administrative agencies. For example, in 1996 the Department of Energy wanted to eliminate its $39-million Advanced Light Water Reactor (ALWR) program, which had been launched in the 1970s to combat the energy crisis. The program, designed to assist the nuclear-power industry, persisted even though every order for a U.S. nuclear reactor in the last twenty-three years eventually had been canceled. Congress insisted on continuing the program, even though, as one Bear Stearns stock analyst speculated, the next U.S. nuclear reactor would be built "when Jimmy Hoffa is found alive and well."[16] The continuance of such an appropriation—or rather misappropriation—affects the fundamental purpose of this agency, namely, anticipating and meeting the nation's energy needs. The future effectiveness of an energy agency is largely affected by the quality of its research.

On occasion, Congress has forced the military to adopt a large-scale change opposed by the Pentagon, such as the Goldwater-Nichols reorganization of the Department of Defense in 1986.[17] In the 1990s, however, cozy politics rather than strategic requirements often seemed to drive legislative initiatives concerning the Pentagon. Congress forced the military to extend some weapons systems and disallowed downsizing efforts supported by the Pentagon. Every year, Congress appropriates funds for weapons that the military does not want. In 1995, for example, Congress pushed through a total of $7 billion in weapons systems for which the Pentagon had requested either no funds at all or less money than Congress appropriated; two years later, such "add-ons" came to $3.8 billion.[18] This figure does not address those weapons systems that Congress sometimes adds after careful deliberation, nor does it include the larger weapons-systems dollar figure of dubious projects on which Congress and the Pentagon agree for political reasons. Such cozy political bargains on occasion have undercut the ability of administrative and regulatory agencies to perform functions previously regarded as central to effective government.

Compromised Governance

Discussions of *government* entail descriptions of how government works. For its part, *governance* refers not only to the constitutional framework and political behavior of government but also to the challenge of political and administrative leadership. Governance thus is defined here as national leadership by elected and appointed officials in constructing the broad coalitions necessary to pursue fundamental public goals and legitimate strategies. These coalitions may include, depending on the issue, the congressional, presidential, and judicial branches, the several levels of government in our federal system, and interest groups, elites, or public opinion.

Democratic governance requires decisionmaking by elected and appointed officials that is made in accord with the constitutional rules of the game. The means as well as the ends of the intended outcomes must be, without straining credulity, framed in accord with the public interest. The reputation of the democratic regime thus stands behind the implementation as well as the formulation of its public policies.

Compromised democratic governance occurs when the political and constitutional rules of the game in a democracy are violated. Such compromise may result from the overthrow of a democratic regime by illegitimate internal forces, such as military or other unelected factions, or as a result of war or other external forces. More subtly, it can also occur through the triumph of *cozy politics*; that is, when such arrangements undercut agency missions.

It is encouraging, though not surprising, that U.S. governance seems less compromised on the *grand issues* confronting us. Where sufficient numbers of citizens are informed, issues are salient, and the press is vigilant, politicians remain more likely to act responsibly. Congress, for example, ultimately did reduce defense spending appreciably when the Cold War ended and curbed discretionary budget deficits in the 1990s. But even on these issues, the system is besieged, thanks largely to changes in the political landscape that have so adversely affected normal governance.

Plan of the Book

This book is divided into three parts. Part 1 addresses the changing economic and political conditions that have contributed to the expansion of cozy politics and discusses the performance and promise of political parties in light of those conditions. Part 2 is concerned with the consequences of spiraling campaign finances for the political system and the penetration of cozy politics into all four pathways of congressional decisionmaking. Part 3 shows not only that cozy politics has influenced how Congress and the president make public policy but also how administrative agencies implement policy. It also provides some suggestions for reinventing political parties and thereby reinventing citizen-based politics.

Political Economy and Political Parties

Part 1, Chapter 1 explores the economic circumstances that have enabled "free marketeers" to revel in the longest period of prosperity in U.S. peacetime history, even while "interventionists" complained about the differential impact on people at different income levels. Such analyses usually focus on differences between the rich and poor; however, I argue that three-fifths of people in the United States, while they benefited from a number of economic trends during the 1990s, are disconnected economically from critical parts of this progress. In addition to noting the differential impact in who gets what assets and income, this chapter develops a future "Opportunity Cost Index" (OCI). Despite unprecedented prosperity in the 1990s, this index records a prosperity where health-care costs rose while health insurance coverage declined, educational costs increased twice as fast as did the Consumer Price Index, and savings sank dramatically.

Meanwhile, the connection between citizens and political system has become ever more tenuous because many people—even those still participating in the system—mistrust it. This has resulted in decreased voter turnout, weaker political parties, and a decline in citizen participation in politics. Fully three-fifths of U.S. citizens are absent without leave from their political system.

The Importance of Being a Political Party

Selling political parties these days is a little like trying to sell dinosaurs. Few would argue that well-functioning parties are what is missing in federal, state, and local politics. There is, however, no substitute for parties (as they might be reconstituted) in our political system. No other organization possesses the potential to—or, indeed, can even pretend to care about—reconnecting citizens to their political system. Furthermore, parties are the only institution that can harness the power of numbers within the political process. Parties, where they work well, are the only institution that can organize citizens to address a range of issues larger than single-issue areas and can serve as the antidote to cozy politics. Campaign reforms can help, but only an aroused citizenry, exercising the countervailing clout of numbers through their reconstituted party instrument, can counter the greater wealth, organizational strength, and other resources of better-off elites, and thus restore democracy's balance.

Parties Still Count

The importance of parties can be seen in the functions they *should* perform for a democracy. Chapter 2 describes how failure to perform these tasks creates a power vacuum. The media and interest groups—particularly grassroots interest groups that represent some, but never all, of the people—have filled that vacuum. Nonetheless, these organizations operate under their own limitations in performing what previously were party functions. Perhaps their most serious offense against the political system is their willingness to talk "political trash," rather than engage in a dialogue meaningful to citizens both during the campaign and during the policymaking process.

The importance of political parties for democracy is the unique way in which their grassroots workers mobilize voters. Who votes is determined more by such mobilization efforts than is generally appreciated in some states and counties. Social networks as well as media networks still count in those areas. Such mobilization, however, is limited today in most states; too often, political consultants simply ignore politically passive citizens.

But are political parties really any different from these other organizations? The answer is yes and no. Activists working in the parties are devoted to certain principles. Chapter 3 probes this partisan concern about the issues, while showing that activists want to win, too. Winning, in turn, involves listening to the voters. Party leaders usually, though not always, try to move their organizations toward popular sentiment. Political-party organizations have had their ups and downs over the nation's history, and, like successful corporations, they periodically have had to reinvent themselves. If they now are to stage a comeback, parties must learn from the private sector and adopt a modified version of the decentralized, participatory model of the global corporation capable of engaging in integrated, rather than traditional, marketing. A relatively vigorous party organizational base still exists on which to build a reconstituted party system.

No such strong parties serve today as a powerful ally for candidates and elected officials. As a result, confronted with low electoral turnout, a disengaged electorate, and mounting campaign bills, candidates have come to rely on TV, direct mail, and other expensive technologies. Candidates are thus even more dependent on the various resources that only wealthy individuals and interest groups can provide.

Faced with this situation, the president and members of Congress seeking election can take advantage of two options. One is the escalation of cozy politics. When cozy politics extends across contact with numerous campaign contributors and interest groups, elected officials often exercise their political influence to alter agency policies, procedures, and activities. The other option is to increase their chance of reelection by undercutting campaign-finance reform. This enhances the chances of reelection for those members choosing to run and entrenches well-established politicians and their wealthy individual, corporate, and interest-group allies in enduring and mutually beneficial relationships. As a result, these allies are in a particularly advantageous position to influence public-policy making.

The Growth of Cozy Politics

Part 2 traces an escalation of cozy politics that, not coincidentally, has paralleled the decline in citizen participation. As seen in Chapter 4, *cozy politics,* the rule of the few, increasingly is displacing *citizen politics,* or rule of the people. It is reflected in the growth in the number of interest groups, trade associations, and lawyers. The currency of these political actors is money and information, and this currency is supplied to candidates and political decision makers in ample quantities.

Out of the resulting cozy political arrangements has come a comparatively new term, the *second constituency,* which presidents and members of Congress represent along with the citizens in their geographical constituencies. The "Washington lawyers" serving this second constituency are masters at manipulating multiple sources of money. While these political actors are often described as members of an "interest group society," individual fat cats are also back. And none too soon, because anxious politicians must look in the most unlikely places to feed the increasingly voracious campaign money machine.

Money and Political Decisionmaking

The influence of these campaign antics is more widespread than is commonly appreciated. Chapter 5 argues that there are four pathways to congressional decisionmaking. The four pathways relate to (1) the geographical district or state to which elected officials are constitutionally and politically accountable; (2) the elected officials, interests, and agencies involved in the comparatively small policy subsystems that make many decisions in specialized issue areas; (3) demands from the second constituencies; and (4) the decisions made on large public programs and regulations by the president and Congress as a whole. Each may be characterized by a growing amount of its own type of pork. Such traditional pork as lighthouses was around at the time of our founding fathers and continues today. Policy subsystems yield pet programs, and campaign-fund inducements encourage second-constituency support. Supporters find it easy to attach expensive riders to bills that authorize and appropriate large new public programs and regulations or to amendments to major existing laws.

The Consequences of Compromised Governance

Chapter 6 is concerned with the relationship of cozy politics to the implementation of public policy. Cozy politics extends its tentacles to what administrative agencies do and how they do it. The widespread exercise of this political influence has weakened the capacity to govern.

Cozy political arrangements interfere with agency missions, reducing public confidence in agencies precisely when budgetary constraints militate against such administrative waste and political irresponsibility. A pattern of cozy politics activity may be seen where politicians and their interest-group allies succeed in achieving agency compromise or agency capture or where pieces of an agency mission are traded to achieve a viable political coalition. Agency program changes appear to have resulted from political contributions to elected officials, and such *apparent* quid pro quos have contaminated agency reputations.

Privatization and Cozy Politics

The greater acceptance of privatization in contracting out has provided numerous opportunities for politicians to reward faithful supporters. In Chapter 6, a distinction is drawn between privatization and pseudoprivatization. *Privatization* involves contracting out on the basis of open competition carefully monitored by public agencies vested with the power to protect their mission. *Pseudoprivatization* involves contracts allocated to a politically well-connected sole bidder whose actions are relatively unchecked by agencies—agencies that have inadequate monitoring capability and insufficient insulation from politics. Contracting out is not the best policy alternative as often as it is good politics. Privatization can operate honestly and effectively, but pseudoprivatization has ushered in some blatant cases of political corruption. The Department of Housing and Urban Development (HUD) in the 1980s remains the most notorious such case, and its implications are examined in some detail.

Revitalizing Politics

The concluding chapter provides modest proposals to reduce the instance of cozy politics. The idea is not to eliminate politics, since agencies work at the behest of the people and their representatives, but rather to improve the quality of our political campaigns and policy process. First, a lawsuit is needed to compel candidates and political organizations to spend "soft money" on strengthening grassroots parties. Citizen politics could then once again face off more evenly against cozy politics.

Second, Congress and the president must provide the U.S. Post Office and major television networks with regulatory concessions in return for reduced-rate political mailings and reduced-rate television time. Such adjustments would limit the need for so much campaign money; at the same time it would provide insurgent candidates with the opportunity to gain greater visibility at a lower cost.

Third, political parties must build on their existing organizational base by mobilizing more activists and citizens and engaging them in public discussion and political action. Such changes are needed if U.S. citizens are to reconnect with their political system, lift the siege on our administrative agencies, and restore effective governance. An active citizenry, aroused through do-it-yourself involvement in decentralized political parties, is the prescription for countering the cozy few. Such cozy political arrangements today bear little relation to the quaint pork-barrel-politics ancestors that traditionally greased political action.

PART I

THE CHANGING POLITICAL ENVIRONMENT

I

Three-Fifths of the United States

I n 1999, W. Michael Cox, a Federal Reserve official, and Richard Alm, a business reporter, contended that "the U.S. free-enterprise system continues to deliver prosperity. Living standards are steadily improving for all segments of society."[1] Yet in 1998, Robert Reich, a former secretary of labor, contended that "the disintegration of the social compact . . . even threatens economic growth. Those who bear a disproportionate share of the burdens and risks of growth but enjoy few if any of the benefits will not passively accept their fates."[2]

Disagreement in interpreting economic data is hardly unusual, but for these responsible observers and others in the camps of what might be called, respectively, the *free marketeers* and the *inclusivists* to disagree so profoundly after six consecutive years of economic growth underscored the crosscurrents confronting the U.S. political economy. The disagreement can be explained partly by the inclusion of politics in Reich's analysis, while Cox and Alm focus exclusively on economics. Even in the case of economics, however, it is not just a matter of optimists and pessimists looking at the same half-full/half-empty glass of water. As they develop two disparate visions of just what U.S. prosperity means, these free marketeers and inclusivists emphasize different economic indicators and interpret the same data differently.

This chapter argues that free-market economics and democratic politics cannot be artificially separated in assessing how well the people of the United States are doing. Many analysts prefer to dwell on the wonders of a bountiful capitalist system and view government as an unavoidable nuisance. Our political problems, however, now threaten capitalism, just as some stubborn economic problems may have serious consequences for our democratic system. The connection between our economics and politics looms particularly large now because three-fifths of our people, while they benefited from a number of economic trends during the 1990s, are disconnected economically as well as politically from critical parts of this progress. While analysts have used a variety of *a* words to characterize the electorate—*angry, alienated*—people more often seem to be, rather than

15

emotionally engaged, *removed*. Deteriorating economic times could widen this disconnect, with potentially serious political consequences.

U.S. Prosperity in the 1990s

The starting point in gauging economic progress commonly is the real median income for all wage earners in a household. The U.S. Census Bureau defines a household unit as including not only family members but also lodgers, foster children, wards, and employees. In 1997, median household income rose 1.9 percent, to $37,005, and thereby returned to the 1989 peak preceding the early 1990s recession. Under the umbrella of household income are clustered unmarried males, unmarried females, and three types of families whose income differs markedly: married couples, males living without their spouses, and females living without their spouses. The old adage that two can live as cheaply as one may or may not be true, but there is no doubt that married couples fare better than single people: their median income is $51,591, while that of single-family males is $32,960, and for single-family females it is $21,023.[3]

These figures worry inclusivists because they reflect disturbing trends. Married families have achieved their above-average income largely thanks to the entry of more women into the labor force. Between 1970 and 1995, the proportion of women in the labor force increased from 41 percent to 61 percent.[4] This strategy for expanding family income is self-limiting. Furthermore, the typical family by 1997 was working sixty-four hours a week, 4 percent more than at the beginning of the decade.[5] In addition, married couples represented 76.6 percent of all families; 17.9 percent of the families were headed by single females, and 5.5 percent by single males.[6] So there is relatively little slack in a system where families are working longer hours, and most families—particularly those earning less money— no longer have a spouse in reserve to throw into the battle to sustain the family income level.

Wider Distribution of Private Goods and Services

While the income gain in 1997 was only 2 percent over 1996, the improvement could be seen in most sections of the country and in communities of all sizes. The gains were similar in 1998, and free marketeers emphasized that these gains were somewhat better than they looked. Real wages do not include employer health-care contributions, pension costs, and other fringe benefits. When such "nonwage compensation" is added to wages, real total compensation increased by 8 percent between 1974 and 1997.[7] In addition, there were improvements in the quality and reduced cost in real terms in what people could buy. Homes were on average 40 percent larger than in 1970; more than three-quarters of all households owned a clothes' washer and dryer; 98 percent owned a color TV, and 89 percent already owned the videocassette recorder to go with it.[8]

There are other measures besides income in gauging economic progress, and they show a long-term leveling between the rich and the non-rich. Those omnipresent TV sets allow everyone to view more or less the same programs; we are retiring earlier and living longer; and there is an impressive array of information available to those choosing to take advantage of it.[9] Herbert Stein points also to a remarkable "lifetime of progress," including an average of 1.7 cars per household and the invention of nylon as an example of the many products that are shared by everyone in the society. Where duchesses previously wore silk and their maids cotton, now all purchase the same nylon stockings.[10]

The Resurgence of U.S. Business

This lifetime of progress was accompanied in the 1990s by a resurgence of U.S. industry so vigorous that it surpassed the expectations of all but a handful of free marketeers, as well as the inclusivists. Mainstream economists have argued that annual growth in the sum of all goods and services (gross domestic product, or GDP) could not for long exceed 2.5 percent, particularly if accompanied by low unemployment and low productivity, without overheating an economy that then would bid up the price of labor, thereby leading to inflation. After a more muted growth in the mid-1990s, GDP increased by 3.4 percent in 1996; this was followed by three years of even more robust expansion. Productivity growth increased at a rate that took most economists by surprise and in 1999 compelled them to increase their economic projections, though it slowed during the 2001 recession.[11]

"The Business of America Is Business"

U.S. corporations during the 1990s also benefited from the more powerful position that they had already in the 1980s begun to establish in relation both to organized labor and to their own employees. Besieged by strong corporate competitors from abroad, U.S. companies modernized their facilities, shuttered unprofitable operations, and, where necessary, moved operations offshore for competitive or strategic reasons. The proportion of manufacturing jobs in the labor force shrank from 23.4 percent in 1979 to 18 percent in 1989, to 14 percent in 2001.[12] Furthermore, in the early 1960s, one-third of the U.S. labor force belonged to unions, including many working in the better-paying manufacturing jobs. These powerful manufacturing unions had negotiated with the corporations from a strong competitive position. But while unions represented one-third of U.S. workers in 1960, by 1999 union membership had sunk to 14 percent, and there having been growth in unionization of the government sector, in the private sector only 9.4 percent of workers were unionized.[13] Most workers in the U.S. workforce were unrepresented.

By the late 1990s, U.S. corporations largely had achieved the ability to compete globally, but investor and manager expectations had changed as to what constituted acceptable profit levels. In order to maintain growth in size and profits, management stuck it to labor much as labor had stuck it to management in the 1960s. The consequences for labor of these altered rules are captured by economist Edward M. Kerchner and his colleagues in their description of the relationship between the global corporations and their employees: "Virtually no major U.S. corporations offer 'lifetime employment.' Today, when profits are squeezed, payrolls are cut. When corporations merge, redundant employees lose their jobs."[14]

Despite these changes, workers rarely turned to populism or other forms of political resistance. They often blamed the remote forces of global capitalism for the waves of corporate downsizing and doubted that employers could protect them. They also were fatalistic about technological change. One autoworker explained, "Well, they didn't ask the horse about the tractor."[15] Workers also had nowhere to turn politically, since the "new Democrats" as well as Republicans had placed their bets on strengthening the more competitive U.S. global corporations and fostering a high rate of technological change. Consequently, the corporations were able to use both their political and economic power to raise profits from a low point of 5.5 percent in the early 1980s to 10 percent of GDP by the end of the 1990s.[16]

The surprisingly high labor force participation rate during this period may have softened the blow of the rapid technological change, even if the apparent scarcity of labor by the 1990s did not increase wages appreciably. The deterioration in the 1990s was somewhat greater in the middle than at the bottom, as the economic upturn and some federal funding assisted those at the bottom. There were enough good, full-time, full-benefit jobs for the highly skilled and/or well-educated 40 percent of the workforce in the 1990s, but not for the 60 percent who lacked either a four-year college education or those specialized skills that happened to be in demand at the moment.[17]

If jobs did not pay as much for this 60 percent of the labor force, at least they were plentiful. The unemployment rate fell to a level not seen since the halcyon days of the late 1960s. These jobs helped U.S. workers absorb the shock of moving from declining "sunset" to emerging "sunrise" industries. Furthermore, those highly skilled new and replacement jobs in the new economy held out the possibility that more workers, if they pursued the necessary training and education, could improve their lot.

Discouraged people no longer in the labor force might also be encouraged to try again.

Accumulating Wealth in the New Economy

While free marketeers enthusiastically tout this remarkable job machine and the dramatic comeback of U.S. industry, they hesitate when questioned about what happened to all those profits. It is not that the free marketeers, good capitalists to the core, feel apologetic about what the 1990s have done for the rich. Profits, after all, drive the system. But not everyone sees such a dramatic accumulation of wealth so benignly. Neither the amassing of wealth and the distribution of income nor worker downsizing became hot campaign topics in the 1990s, despite the shift of so much money into the hands of so comparatively few people.[18] How and why did 60 percent of the population miss out on this bonanza of financial assets—the most significant form of wealth in the new economy?

Where the Stock Market Wealth Goes

No financial trend stirred more media excitement in the late 1990s than the remarkable stock-market run. Wealth grew in all forms during this period, but the main action was in household financial assets—pension funds, stocks, and bank deposits. These rose from $12 trillion in 1987 to $26 trillion in 1997.[19] Household wealth of other kinds increased as well. The number of home owners increased to two-thirds of all U.S. families, and the value of that real estate grew. Nevertheless, the increase in financial assets was so great that between 1990 and 1997, real estate shrank from 33 percent to 27 percent of total household wealth.[20]

Meanwhile, Federal Reserve Board researchers found that the proportion of U.S. families owning stock directly—through a mutual fund, retirement account, trust, or other type of managed investment account—grew steadily from 32 percent in 1989 to 49 percent in 1998.[21] The authors of a book felicitously entitled *The Millionaire Next Door* estimated that, by 1997, 3.5 million individuals possessed a net worth of at least $1 million. One of the book's reviewers speculated that "the implication of the book— and this may explain its popularity—is that nearly anybody with a steady job can amass a tidy fortune by living below his means and investing soundly."[22]

This growth in stock ownership stands as an impressive achievement and has led to considerable hyperbole about the American Dream and the coming together of Main Street and Wall Street, but for most of us, millionaire status remains a pipedream. In a nation where real median income has shown comparatively little growth even when calculated in terms of total compensation, there are limits to how widespread wealth accumulation can be. Roughly one-half of U.S. families held no stock whatsoever. Table 1.1 shows that the financial assets of those in the top "quintile"—the 20 percent of the U.S. population with the most such assets—possessed 84.3 percent of all wealth in 1997. Those in the lowest three quintiles—the 60 percent with comparatively fewer such assets—possessed 4.9 percent. Indeed, for 20 percent of people, savings went *down* in 1997.

While the increase in stock ownership is appreciable compared with earlier times, it is the increase in their *home equity* stake, rather than their *stock equity*, that contributed most to the average person's wealth. Median household net worth grew from 1995 to 1998 by 18 percent to $71,600.[23] Lower interest rates led to lower mortgage rates, easier borrowing, and rising home values. These higher home values helped to create a "wealth effect," as economists call it, and bolstered consumer confidence, as the nation's gross domestic product in the late 1990s grew by $2 trillion.

The Impact of Productivity on Wages

While most companies, like most individuals, have benefited from this increased wealth, larger companies grew disproportionately in size and wealth. The explanation for this increase lies in their generally often rapid rate of productivity growth. Paul Krugman has observed that "productivity

Table 1.1   Shares of Wealth Held by the Top 1 Percent and by Income Quintile, 1962–1997

Wealth Class	1962	1983	1989	1995	1997
Top 1%	33.4%	33.8%	37.4%	37.8%	39.1%
Top Fifth quintile	81.0	81.3	83.5	83.7	84.3
Fourth quintile	13.4	12.6	12.3	11.5	10.8
Middle quintile	5.4	5.2	4.8	4.5	4.4
Second quintile	0.9	1.2	0.8	0.9	1.0
Lowest quintile	–0.7	–0.3	–1.5	–0.7	–0.5
Bottom four-fifths	19.0	18.7	16.5	16.3	15.7

Source: U.S. Bureau of Census: *Distribution of Wealth in the United States,* various years.

isn't everything, but in the long run it is almost everything."[24] Firms must in one way or another raise their output per worker, and the larger companies on average have done so far more than the smaller ones.

Productivity gauges how efficiently the economy turns workers' labor into goods and services. If workers can produce more goods and services for each hour of work, employers can afford to raise wages and benefits without raising prices or squeezing profits. So productivity is a key indicator for measuring living standards as well.[25] Rapidly growing companies can afford to raise wages more easily than slow-growing ones.

Large companies tended to increase their productivity more dramatically, but they were careful to hire proportionally fewer new employees. Using Bureau of Labor Statistics productivity figures, economist Edward McKeon found that the productivity of the industries in the Standard and Poors 500, weighted by their market capitalization, grew 3.9 percent— more than tripling the 1.1 percent in productivity growth for the economy as a whole.[26] Some of these rapidly growing companies—the Microsofts, Dells, and Compaqs—increased the size of their labor forces, but many others limited hiring, preferring to contract out to other firms with lower overhead. One way that small and medium-sized firms can limit their overhead is to pay lower wages and fringe benefits.

The comparably slow increases in wages of most U.S. workers thus become understandable, since hirings are increasingly made by small and medium-sized companies and the nonprofit sector, both of which are characterized by slower economic growth. It defies the laws of economics to argue that companies averaging a low rate of productivity growth will pay high wages.[27] To be sure, some companies, such as Home Depot or McDonald's, manage considerably higher sales per employee than their competition, but they pay the prevailing wage for most jobs in their industries, bidding higher only for that comparatively smaller number of jobs where they can gain a competitive advantage by hiring better-qualified employees.

It is thus the rate of productivity growth that, as always, drives the size of wage increases, rather than the distinction between manufacturing and service industries. There are numerous well-paying service jobs in the professions and for those providing skilled information and personal services that are in demand. But productivity growth within service industries for the most part is slower than in the large manufacturing companies. In projecting job growth between 1998 and 2008, the Bureau of Labor Statistics predicts that manufacturers will maintain their share of output, even while there will be 89,000 fewer jobs. Service-producing jobs will, therefore, account for virtually all of the nation's predicted 14 percent job growth.[28]

Personal Saving vs. National Saving

The cost of living well in a nation with slowly increasing real wages can be seen in part—but only in part—from the declining savings rate for most people. That personal savings rate sank from roughly 7 percent in the 1960s, 1970s, and 1980s to less than 1 percent in 1998 and turned negative in 1999.

A number of economists argue that only a doomsayer would worry about the low personal savings that accompanied the extraordinary 1990s boom; it is, after all, normal for savings to go down during good times, when lower interest rates provide less incentive to save, as well as less income, when capital gains accumulate on financial assets, and when good times reduce the sense of urgency to save. It is also true that financial assets rise most in periods of low inflation and high prosperity. High inflation appears to "improve" wealth inequality "because it raises the value of real assets, such as housing, that are mainly held by the middle class, relative to financial assets mainly held by the wealthy."[29] Furthermore, in the late 1990s the federal government ran a budgetary surplus for the first time since 1969; business savings rose dramatically in the form of accumulated capital gains; and foreigners continued to invest their savings in attractive U.S. opportunities. The result of this strong economy was that in 1998, both gross national savings and investment actually increased faster than economic activity. Gross national savings, for example, constituted 17.4 percent of GDP in 1998, up from 16.7 percent in 1989.[30] Who in their right mind wants to return to bad times just because the personal savings rate looks better when capital gains and home equity shrink, interest rates rise, and intimidated consumers hunker down?

The progress in the government and business savings segments was certainly heartening, but personal savings matter, too, both because of the low aggregate savings figure and the distribution of those savings within the population. Economist Edward Wolff estimates that even most middle-class people save so little that their assets would sustain their lifestyles and consumption habits for only three months.[31] While of little concern when times are good, these are paltry sums to sustain families when economic times turn bad.

Just why people in the United States save less than their counterparts in Europe or Japan is unclear. Some would argue that by failing to include capital gains, we understate the aggregate personal savings. While that seems true, the distribution of those gains among the population is such that it would not provide a transfusion for the anemic savings rate of most Americans. Economist Maury Harris analyzed tax return data compiled by the U.S. Internal Revenue Service in 1996. He found that around 78 percent of reported net capital gains were on six-figure tax returns. There were 3.9

million such returns, and 6.5 million returns accounted for another 11 percent; in other words, around nine out of every ten dollars in realized capital gains was reported on only 8.6 percent of all returns.[32]

Prosperity Without Personal Savings

Indeed, only 18.2 percent of all returns reported *any* capital gains. More frequently, homeowners tapped into their home equity even while refinancing to take advantage of the lowest mortgage rates in three decades.[33] The category of homeowners includes numerous better-off people, but in the 1995 Federal Reserve Bank Survey of Consumer Finances, only 61 percent reported saving over the previous year; the comparable figure for renters was 44 percent.[34] Furthermore, even as interest rates kept falling, consumer bankruptcies continued at a record pace.[35]

Small wonder that a *Wall Street Journal*/NBC poll of working adults found that only 42 percent were confident of having enough money to live comfortably in retirement—and only 18 percent felt strongly that they were prepared.[36] From this fragmentary evidence, we know that a relatively small number of people have accumulated a significant amount of financial assets and other savings, while roughly three-fifths of the population lacked the wherewithal, motivation, or both to save much at all during the prosperous 1990s.

The Distribution of Income

One would think that the distribution of income—the classic question of who gets what, when, and how economically—would have attracted great attention over the years. It has not, largely because for decades the distribution of income in this country did not change. Economist Henry Aaron observed that following the slow changes in the income distribution "was like watching the grass grow."[37] How did he reach this conclusion, and how do we measure the distribution of household income? To determine the degree of income inequality, economists and demographers often divide the population into fifths, or quintiles, and then see what proportion of all household income falls into each quintile (see table 1.1). The share that goes to the poorest one-fifth of all households becomes the bottom quintile; the next one-fifth in income is labeled the second quintile, and so forth.

By the mid-1980s, the Census Bureau found that the top quintile in household income had begun to separate from all the others. While it had received a traditional proportion of roughly 43 percent in 1967 and 1977, by 1987, during the Reagan economic good times, the proportion of all household income in the top quintile had grown to 46 percent.[38] The top quintile made these gains at the expense of all four of the other quintiles. From 1977 to 1989, real income for the bottom two quintiles actually shrank, while the middle quintile gained only about 5 percent.[39] These trends persisted, as Table 1.2 shows, in the 1990s. In 1996, the top quintile's income had increased to 46.8 percent—and for the first time since World War II, it was more than 150 percent above the combined income of 60 percent of the population.

But quintiles, at least so far as inclusivists were concerned, no longer told the whole story, and they began looking further upward. After all, as economist Paul Krugman observed, it took only $59,550 in 1989 to put a family in the top quintile, and $98,963 for it to be in the top 5 percent, so "the implication is that we are essentially a middle-class society, with only an insignificant handful of people rich enough to excite any concern about ill-gotten gains."[40] However, the average income (before taxes) of four-person families in the top 1 percent was about $800,000, and this small but dramatically more wealthy group more than doubled its income between 1977 and 1989.

This increasing disparity might have faded as just another relic of the remarkable Teflon Reagan presidency if this stubborn trend had not persisted into the 1990s. Between 1975 and 1995, the wealth of households in the richest 5 percent grew 54.1 percent, and the top quintile grew 35.4 percent, whereas the increase for the bottom three quintiles—60 percent of the total—ranged from 1.5 to 6.7 percent. So although everyone gained, the top one-fifth did eight times better than even the middle fifth. The disparity, though, did not figure in the 1996 election, even though political scientist Gerald Pomper stressed at the time that, "while the most affluent

Table 1.2   Share of Aggregate Family Income for Each Quintile and the Top 5 Percent of Families

Year	1st Quintile (poorest)	2nd Quintile	3rd Quintile	4th Quintile	5th Quintile (richest)	Top 5 Percent[a]
1947	5.0%	11.9%	17.0%	23.1%	43.0%	17.5%
1949	4.5	11.9	17.3	23.5	42.7	16.9
1959	4.9	12.3	17.9	23.8	41.1	15.9
1969	5.6	12.4	17.7	23.7	40.6	15.6
1979	5.4	11.6	17.5	24.1	41.4	15.3
1989	4.6	10.6	16.5	23.7	44.6	17.9
1996	4.2	10.0	15.8	22.1	46.8	20.3

Source: U.S. Department of Commerce, Census Bureau, *Current Population Reports*, various years, as reported in Levy, Frank, *The New Dollars and Dreams* (New York: Sage, 1998), appendix, p. 199.

Note: a. Top 5 percent is contained in the fifth quintile.

Americans (the top 5 percent) have seen an average growth of 38 percent in their real incomes since 1979, most Americans *(the bottom 60 percent)* have endured a decrease of 2.5 percent in their paychecks."[41] While in the late 1990s real income eventually turned upward somewhat for the population as a whole, the gap in relative wealth continued to grow.

Education and the American Dream

The disparity between the top two quintiles and the remaining three in income earned and wealth accumulated would seem less disturbing if it were not increasingly associated with a better education and more highly developed skills (inheriting wealth also helps, but this is often associated with more education). The increasing importance of education in obtaining better-paying jobs is underscored by census figures showing that in real 1997 dollars, income for those with a college education or a postgraduate degree had increased from $38,496 to $47,126, while income for those with high school degrees, grade school degrees, and grade school dropouts since 1979 had declined to $25,453, $16,818, and $12,157, respectively.[42] Men with college degrees thus were earning roughly twice the amount received by those with high-school diplomas, and grade-school dropouts were earning half of what high-school graduates made. The median income for all educational groups without a college degree actually had declined in real terms since 1963.

Political scientist Andrew Hacker underscored the close relationship between level of education and income by studying men at the time of their peak earning power between ages thirty-five and forty-four. He found some mobility. For example, 20.1 percent of the high-school graduates were making more than $40,000; 12.7 percent were making more than $75,000. Then again, some—12.8 percent of the high-school graduates, along with 28.8 percent of the college graduates and 29.4 percent of those with graduate degrees—were downwardly mobile. So there is some movement between quintiles, but not much.

Whatever the other virtues of a liberal arts education, thanks to changing job descriptions, college and graduate school are now a better deal economically than ever before. Gone are most of the higher-paying manufacturing jobs with fringe benefits that required little skill or sometimes not even a high-school education. While such jobs were often physically demanding, men (and sometimes women) with limited backgrounds could achieve instant middle-class status by taking them. Today, the higher-paying technical and business service-industry jobs for the most part also require advanced training or education.

One can certainly argue that educational determinism is not so bad. After all, once one moves beyond a handful of comparatively elite colleges and universities in each state, numerous other higher education institutions stand eager and ready to accept candidates with seemingly every level of intellectual competence. But there are barriers. College expenses have exceeded the inflation rate in recent decades, as parents and students (who almost always pay some or all of their college expenses) well know.

There is also what some have termed a "digital divide." The Census Bureau found in a survey of 48,000 families in 1997 that minorities, poor people, seniors, and those living in rural areas were much less likely to have computers and were thus among the "least connected" members of society. Conversely, college graduates were nearly ten times more likely to own a computer than those without a high-school education.[43] While this divide is usually couched in racial and ethnic terms, a 1998 report found that only 41 percent of white families owned a computer,[44] again suggesting that income level and education are the decisive factors.

This digital divide is a manifestation of the broader *intellectual* divide that separates the upper two quintiles of well-educated people from the other three quintiles. Word processing or negotiating the Internet do not indicate sufficient computer proficiency for advanced jobs. Participants in a more sophisticated economy need to use specialized professional software, work with computer networks, and overcome the technical problems involved in transferring data between different programs or operating systems.

This gap between quintiles of the haves and the have-nots, however, should not obscure the progress made in this area. Raising educational attainment is a slow process, but a U.S. Census Bureau study found that by 1996, 82 percent of the population had a high-school degree, compared with 33 percent in 1950, and 23.6 percent had a college degree, compared with 6.2 percent in 1950.[45] The mushrooming of "super bookstores" on and off the Internet reflects a growth in book sales from 430 million in 1982 to 1.7 billion in 1995. The challenge is to expand the size of the reading audience so that the lower quintiles, too, benefit from what remains the most critical pathway to knowledge and can position themselves to take advantage of our increasingly "wealthy, worldly, and wired" society.

What Should the Distribution of Income Be?

Given the coexistence of significant prosperity and some disturbing inequities in the distribution of income—then what? Virtually no one argues today for equality of income or anything near such a situation. Gilbert and Sullivan reproachfully reminded the Gondoliers, as they strove to build a utopia:

> When every one is somebodee,
> Then no one's anybody![46]

The truth is that nobody knows how much U.S. distribution of income can be skewed before it affects the political process. As Lester Thurow observed in 1995, "These are unchartered waters for American democracy. Since accurate data have been kept, beginning in 1929, America has never experienced falling real wages for a majority of its workforce while its per-capita GDP was rising."[47] Though these real wages subsequently turned slightly upward, still the possibility that inflation could undercut these gains remains real to many. Interestingly, while hardly militant about it, most of us in the United States are well aware of who came out ahead in the 1990s. In a *Wall Street Journal*/NBC Poll, 81 percent agreed that the strong economy mostly has benefited the top wage earners and that "more needs to be done to close the gap between the rich and the poor."[48]

So the populace has a sense of the increasing gap in wealth and income over a quarter of a century, and no backlash has occurred. The nation's lack of class consciousness may help to explain this seemingly benign attitude toward the wealthy. In any event, Thurow may be right in arguing that this is a dubious social experiment: "Perhaps our society could move much farther along the continuum toward inequality; perhaps not. But it is a stupid society that runs an experiment to see where its breaking points are."[49]

Interestingly, a number of wealthy conservatives may now have, consciously or unconsciously, come to agree. The top-priority Bush tax cut in 2001 was given a relatively cool reception by some of the wealthy. After all, the top 25 percent of taxpayers, ranked by income, made 65 percent of total 1997 adjusted gross income and paid about 82 percent of total federal individual income taxes.[50] Perhaps these upper-middle and upper-class citizens realize that, as their extraordinary wealth continues to accumulate at an extraordinary rate, they have far more to lose than people in the "lower quintiles." Unlike other social-science experiments, this one has consequences. Besides, to succeed, the better-off need a strong middle class—and not just so that it can buy cars.

Political philosophers and historians through the centuries have noted the importance of a strong middle class for a successful society. Most prominently, Aristotle favored a state in which citizens have "moderate and sufficient property." Otherwise the impoverished majority may tyrannize the better-off through "extreme democracy." Conversely, where the better-off feel exploited by the many, they may seek to form a government characterized by rule of the few (or "oligarchy"). Both extreme democracy and oligarchy thus are inherently unstable.[51]

The Importance of a Middle Class

Sociologist Seymour Martin Lipset perhaps best drove home the significance of a strong middle class for modern democracies. He found that the presence of "economic development, producing increased income, greater economic security, and widespread higher education largely determined the form of the 'class struggle' by permitting those in the lower strata to develop longer time perspectives and more complex and gradualist views of politics."[52] Kevin Phillips, too, has provided persuasive evidence of the integral connection between the golden age of such great powers as Holland, the United Kingdom, and Spain and the presence of a confident, creative, growing middle class. When elites subsequently exercised greater power and thereby stifled their middle classes, there followed periods of national decline.[53]

There was little evidence in the 1990s that the 60 percent of people less connected to the economic system even identified, much less felt abused, as a class. Conservative Irving Kristol attributed the presence of income inequality without class conflict to people's attitudes and an intuitive understanding of the conditions favoring economic growth. People also possess "a willingness to undergo the personal stresses and strains associated with such growth." Furthermore, we are a society where "income *inequality* tends to be swamped by even greater social *equality*" in such matters as where we eat, how we dress, and how we travel.[54] As political scientist Hugh Heclo has observed, "Today, as always, it remains politically easier to engender resentment against the weak than against the powerful."[55] Most middle-income people thus showed more enthusiasm in the 1990s for reducing the income of "cheaters on the dole" through welfare reform than indignation at the disproportionate incomes of CEOs.

Social Equality

But does social equality continue to characterize this society? The 1990 U.S. census marked the first time that more of us lived in the suburbs than in central cities. While some suburbs contain members of all income strata, more are now segregated by income than by race. The abolition of the type of draft found in World War II that touched people from all communities in the United States, the income segregation of most schools, and the clustering of housing by income make it likely that fewer individuals will come to know those from other income strata. Robert Reich seems on firm ground in contending that the bottom half now are more separated "geographically, economically and culturally."[56] We do not yet know the full implications of this division, but they are unlikely to be favorable. "A high degree of inequality causes the comfortable to disavow the needy," wrote economist

James K. Galbraith. "It increases the psychological distance separating these groups, making it easier to imagine that defects of character or differences of culture, rather than an unpleasant turn in the larger schemes of economic history, lie behind the separation."[57] Such separation matters less when times are good. It is when times are bad that the question of how best to hold together the strata of society becomes more compelling.

Income Redistribution

The sensible course from the standpoint of all income strata is to act when times are good—to take steps to improve the lot of the 60 percent during a period of prosperity, when such redistribution would be relatively painless for the better-off and would be most likely to contribute to social stability. Unfortunately, it is as difficult to attract support for enhancing social stability as for expanding preventive health care. Until a calamity occurs, the problem does not seem pressing, but once the problem has occurred, the less expensive preventive measures no longer are an option.

Dealing with income redistribution during good times is particularly important because there are limits in a capitalist society to what can be done. The proposals of inclusivists—mostly economists—reveal that they are hardly revolutionaries. Karl Marx would feel lonely at an American Economics Association Conference. Robert Eisner pointed in 1998 to the extraordinary opportunity to push for an even higher growth rate and to sustain the 4 percent unemployment rate, heretofore only a distant goal, envisioned in the Full Employment Act of 1946. Thanks to the combination of high employment and low inflation, rising real wages at the turn of the century made work available and attractive for many on welfare and millions of others often removed from the workforce. Most critical in sustaining this trend will be to "pursue monetary and fiscal policies that keep purchasing power high and maintain incentives to invest and grow at all levels."[58] George Stiglitz, as a member of the Council of Economic Advisors' (CEA), while cautioning in 1996 that spurring growth is difficult, pointed approvingly to Clinton administration efforts to improve education and work training and infrastructure.[59]

The nation has taken some promising steps—more toward helping the poor than those in the second and middle quintiles. Increases in the minimum wage and the earned income tax credit, along with the availability of more jobs and the development of more day-care facilities, certainly contributed to the increased real income of those in the poorest quintile. In addition, upper-income taxpayers now have shouldered a larger share of the federal income-tax burden.[60] Thanks to the strong economy, those earning more than $100,000 per year (the wealthiest one-tenth of the population) paid 62 percent of all federal income taxes in 1998. This figure, up 5 percent from the previous year, reflected the larger share of total income received by this group. Conversely, 47.8 million people owed no federal taxes at all, thanks to a variety of exclusions, deductions, and credits.[61] Those in the lower quintiles, however, shouldered more of the burden in the case of the more regressive state and local taxes (such as sales and property taxes), and paid proportionally more of their income in social-security FICA taxes, which in 2000 were paid—except for the 1.45 percent Medicare payment—only on the initial $76,200 of income.

The Future Opportunity Index

Income distribution is perhaps too abstract to become an election issue, but the same may not be true of the things that money can buy—particularly those viewed as central to the American Dream. In dealing with the income-distribution problem, perhaps the most philosophically and politically acceptable step from the standpoint of those in the top two quintiles and the most encouraging step for the other three-fifths of the population would be to focus on solving those issues that offer hope for the future— namely, strengthening Social Security, health care, and education and training programs, and bolstering savings incentives. Politically, this approach is palatable because there is a rough consensus that all those *working* in the society deserve to achieve some part of the American Dream. That hope is difficult to provide for those in the lower three quintiles, since due to demographic trends and technological change, the cost in real dollars of the resources necessary for such opportunity has risen markedly. Ironically, pieces of the American Dream continued to fade despite the enhanced prosperity of the 1990s.

Economic Security

One such piece—future economic security in the form of a comfortable retirement—underscores the cost of opportunity and the limitations on government actions. The scope of this problem can be seen in the failure of the proportion of the population that is covered by pensions to rise during a period of prosperity (between 1992 and 1995, it remained fairly constant at approximately 40 percent) and by the number of people who now are working under a defined benefit plan, rather than one with a guaranteed contribution.[62] In the 1970s, most corporations promised a "defined benefit"—a specific amount of money each month. But that promise proved too costly to keep once corporate profit margins fell in the 1980s, so corporations have shifted to "defined contribution" plans—mainly 401(k) plans, where the worker and employer pay in a specific amount each, and the worker takes responsibility for investing the money.[63]

Participation in 401(k) plans and the like is voluntary. In 1995, one-fourth of family heads eligible to participate in such a plan did not do so. The choice depended largely on their income. Heads of families with incomes of less than $25,000 were less likely to participate than others.[64] The proportion of families at other income levels owning such individual retirement accounts rose impressively—though there was a striking contrast between the median personal pension holdings of those families earning less than $100,000 and those earning more.[65]

Even the most activist government cannot reconstruct the pension systems of so many people in the lower three quintiles that have disappeared partially or wholly. Management and labor (organized or unorganized) will bargain the terms of their wages and total compensation. While as a society we cannot shoulder the burden of retirement saving for all, we can agree as a people to continue to preserve and protect Social Security. Though intended historically as a supplement to other retirement income, it has come to serve as a lifeline for those in all five quintiles who could not or would not save.

Health Care

We can also confront the skyrocketing cost of health care for many people. Free marketeers rightly argue that the improved quality of health care partly accounts for the higher costs, and there is no stemming the tide of medical advances. New medical technology has enabled us to improve and prolong millions of lives in this country through expensive continuing treatment. But nearly 40 percent of all money spent on the average person is consumed in the final year of life, and fraud, high profit margins for drug and medical supply companies, excessive testing, and overly generous legal awards continue to undercut the medical system. We will eventually have to come to grips with these issues, whether we like it or not, and impose some cost limitations.

Furthermore, the free marketeers do not tell the whole story of health-care costs. These costs continue to rise both for those who have incurred serious illnesses and for those seeking to prevent or ameliorate such illness. The consumer price index (CPI) shows that between 1970 and 1997 the cost of medical care as a whole, as indicated in Table 1.3, increased 590.6 percent—almost twice as fast as the cost of living.

Prescription drugs, an item not covered by health insurance for many people, increased even more rapidly. Prices for the fifty prescriptions most frequently used by older people increased on average by 25.2 percent

Table 1.3   **Opportunity Cost Index, Using CPI Data for 1970–1997
(1982–1984 = 100)**

Year	All Items	Medical Care	Tuition/Fees	Educational Books/Supplies
1970	25.5	34.0	34.7	38.8
1975	42.1	47.5	46.9	50.3
1980	86.0	74.9	71.2	71.4
1985	101.6	113.6	119.7	118.2
1990	102.9	163.0	175.7	171.3
1995	105.4	220.7	253.8	214.4
1997	111.5	234.8	280.4	238.4
Percentage Change	337.3%	590.6%	708.1%	514.4%

Source: CPI: U.S. City Average; All Items, Medical Care, Tuition, and Educational Books and Supplies

between 1994 and 1999, a period of relatively low inflation, when 12.8 percent was the rise for the overall Consumer Price Index (CPI).[66] Meanwhile, according to *Consumer Reports,* "the average prescription price for branded drugs introduced in 1998 was $71, compared with $30 for existing drugs."[67] The cost problem, though, is also a result of the rapid increase in the number of people using more and better drugs. Between 1992 and 1998, according to the National Association of Chain Drug Stores, the number of retail prescriptions dispensed each year increased from 2.0 to 2.73 billion.[68] This figure is expected to increase to about 4 billion by 2005, thanks to an aging population, reliance on drug therapy as a less costly alternative to surgery or psychiatry, and the availability of new "lifestyle" drugs designed, for example, to increase hair growth or sexual potency.[69]

The cost of health care becomes particularly important for those without any health coverage—and that proportion increased throughout the 1990s. In 1987, 75.5 percent of those working in the private sector were covered by insurance—a figure that declined to 70.2 percent by 1997.[70] The number without health insurance is also higher because the size of the labor force grew by 14 million during this period.[71] Government coverage partly offset this private-sector decrease, but by 1997 roughly 3 percent fewer people were covered either by employment-based or government programs.[72] An estimated 43.4 million people were without health coverage in 1997, according to the U.S. Census Bureau, including one out of every seven children.

Most of those without coverage fell within the lowest three quintiles. It is scarcely surprising that those employees worth more to companies are likely to receive more fringe benefits as well as income. Of those earning $50,000 or more, only one in ten had no health coverage, while one in four earning between $25,000 and $49,999, and almost one in two earning $25,000 or less faced this problem.[73] Much of the health-care coverage debate has centered around the poor, but the percentage of the nonpoor—those who earn more than twice the federal poverty level of $16,700 for a family of four—increased from about 40 percent of the uninsured in 1994 to nearly 46 percent in 1998. Those who are not poor are likely to figure even more prominently if the Health Insurance Association of America is correct in predicting that the number of uninsured by 2008 will grow to 55 million—more than 22 percent of the nonelderly population—or to 60 million if the economy falters.[74]

Access to Technical and Higher Education

Hope for the future also must include opportunities for people of all ages—including those displaced by the new economy and their children—to obtain high-quality technical training or to attend junior college or college. Table 1.3 shows, however, that the average increase in tuition and fees at four-year colleges rose between 1970 and 1997 by 708.1 percent, and the cost of educational books and supplements rose by 514.4 percent—both increases considerably more than the 337.3 percent change in the CPI as a whole.

More quality *technical* training would also enhance the range of opportunities for many in the lower three quintiles—particularly for those less enamored with "book learning." The nation seemingly no longer has the confidence in such training that it had in 1962, when the Manpower Development and Training Act (MDTA) passed unanimously in the House of Representatives. More controversial employability programs designed to reach the underclass, efforts to move recipients off welfare, and expensive job creation programs in the public and nonprofit sectors largely eclipsed the initial MDTA intent. However, by the 1980s, the nation had come full circle when a similar, modestly funded effort, the Job Training Partnership Act (JTPA) of 1982, was "launched at a time of renewed concerns about international competition, adjusting the skills of the workforce to economic change, and expanding economic opportunity."[75] During this debate, though, only a determined Congress with a Democratic majority overcame Reagan administration opposition to what was viewed as yet another activist government initiative, despite the act's core of a public/private-sector partnership.

The U.S. Bureau of Labor Statistics predicts that employment in all education and training categories that require an associate degree or more education will grow faster than the rate of job growth. Occupations generally requiring an associate degree are expected to grow 31 percent—faster than all other education categories between now and 2008.[76] Other post–

high school opportunities also hold out the possibility of better wages. Earners of high wages often can develop needed skills not only through associate-degree programs but also through government employment and training programs, college courses, postsecondary vocational schools and technical institutes, apprenticeships or other formal employer training, informal on-the-job training, and experience in the armed forces. Access to a variety of educational opportunities is thus a vital piece in the future opportunity index.

"A Penny Saved Is a Penny Earned"

Finally, the federal government can join with concerned private and non-profit groups in mounting a national campaign to provide us with more information about saving. We know far more as a nation about how to shop than how to save. While many invest through mutual funds and indirectly through pension systems managed by others, a nation better informed about investments presumably would have a greater incentive to save, and its investors would have the knowledge to defend themselves against those opportunistic brokers and other financial experts willing to play games with others' hard-earned savings.

The Investor Protection Trust, a nonprofit organization created in 1996 by several states to educate people about personal finance, tested the knowledge of 1,001 actual investors. It found that 32 percent of them could not answer half of eight questions dealing with such issues as whether diversification among stocks increases or decreases the risk of losing money, what usually happens to the price of bonds when interest rates go up, and whether the Securities Investor Protection Corporation protects investors from losses if the stock market goes down.[77] As people are compelled increasingly to manage their own pension plans, more knowledge about savings seems a prerequisite not only to providing greater motivation to save but also to enabling more people to profit from financial assets.

Gauging Future Opportunity

To gain a sense of how optimistically the U.S. population can be expected to view the future, items dealing with health, education, and savings are combined here into an opportunity cost index (OCI). This index is designed primarily to assist wage earners in viewing their future with realistic expectations—much as the Dow Jones Industrial Average and other such indices purport to do for wealth accumulators. The OCI could be published monthly by the Department of Labor—the agency responsible in part for helping workers to help themselves. Figure 1.1 combines these costs of upward

Figure 1.1 Opportunity Cost Index Increase, 1970-1997

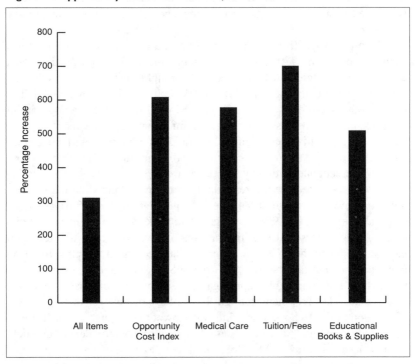

mobility over the last three decades and compares the costs of these necessities for future gain to the rise in the overall consumer price index (CPI). In doing so, the OCI measures the size of the burden imposed on the populace by the sum of net personal savings, medical expenses, and training and higher educational expenses, in comparison with the sum of all CPI items.

Although taxes remain a large CPI item, they are not included here for two reasons. First, the OCI focuses on increasing the opportunities for those in the three lower quintiles (those with incomes in the lower 60 percent). The largest tax paid by these citizens is social insurance, which increased twelvefold between 1970 and 1997. In the same period, income-tax payments stayed constant at 40 percent of all tax payments.[78] Since it is social security and Medicare that face a long-term fiscal crisis, neither Congress nor the president is likely to enact any significant tax relief for this 60 percent of taxpayers. Most tax-reform initiatives now focus on the income tax, where the better-off 40 percent of the nation's taxpayers pay a disproportionate share. As President George W. Bush has demonstrated, tax reform is a set of schemes where the comparatively better-off are likely to become the even-better-off when the tinkering is over. If greater opportunity for the lower quintiles is to occur, it must be achieved by focusing on the OCI items.

Second, proportionally, the increases on consumer spending items show that between 1970 and 1994, the total amount spent on federal, state, and local taxes increased by 623 percent—roughly parallel to the 626 percent increase in consumer spending on taxes plus the items in the OCI. The total amount spent on taxes was sizable, $1.6 billion, but the amount spent on taxes plus health plus tuition plus the amount in savings came to a hefty $2.2 billion, and it is in examining the other OCI components that one finds the explanation for the *higher costs of opportunity* today. Health costs rose by 1,067 percent and tuition by 930 percent.[79]

Savings also represent a resource for improving one's lot and protecting economic security. In 1984, the U.S. population saved 8.6 percent of disposable income; by 1998, that figure had sunk to 0.5 percent.[80] This disturbingly low personal savings rate—the lowest among all industrial nations—reduced the OCI. The argument has been made that this low savings rate does not accurately reflect the U.S. rate of savings, since it does not include the remarkable capital gains made on financial assets over the last decade. That argument, though, has little relevance for the 60 percent of the population whose stock and bond ownership ranges from little to none. Indeed, many U.S. families at all income levels sank deeper into debt during the prosperous 1990s. Household debt, as a percentage of personal income, rose from 76 percent in 1989 to an estimated 85 percent in 1997. Total credit-card debt more than doubled between 1989 and 1997. Like most debtors throughout history, these credit-card holders paid through the nose, as they forked over an average of $1,000 per year in interest and fees.[81]

The OCI is not intended to serve as a "doom and gloom" indicator, however; rather, it has the potential to function not only as a warning sign when opportunity is waning but also as a benchmark for celebrating gains in opportunity. When progress is made, it can stand as a beacon for those tough-minded politicians seeking to make more opportunity a reality—devoid of mushy and misleading political rhetoric—and as encouragement for those citizens earning comparatively less in our society but working hard to create a better future for themselves and their children. Three-fifths of the nation would then have a more accurate measure for determining whether they can reasonably look forward to building their own personal savings for their retirement (rather than relying too heavily on Social Security), possessing good health care in the intervening years as well as during their retirement, and pursuing the education necessary to connect more closely with their fellow citizens.

The Tenuous Connection of
Many Citizens to the U.S. Political System

While opinions vary markedly on the extent of the capitalist connection of many in this nation, there is considerable agreement that the link between many people and their political system has grown more tenuous. In one sense, suspicion and distrust of government are not new; these attitudes are deeply lodged in our history and culture. We have inherited them, much as we have inherited other parts of the national creed such as the Protestant ethic, loyalty to the market mechanism, and ambivalence about sex. But there is a difference between healthy skepticism and destructive cynicism, and a disturbing number of people have crossed that line.

Lack of Political Trust and Confidence in Government

The steep decline in political trust from 1960 through 1997 is well documented. From 1958 through 1997, the American Enterprise Institute/Roper Center reported that the percentage of the population believing that you "can trust the government in Washington to do what is right" sank from 77 percent to 22 percent.[82] The Pew Research Center similarly found that fewer than half as many people expressed confidence in government during that period. In 1964, 78 percent felt that "the government in Washington can be trusted to do the right thing usually or just about always," whereas in 1997 only 38 percent agreed with that statement.[83] This dissatisfaction has grown largely as a result of disillusioning events that reflect political, social, and economic changes that have shaken and shifted our demands on and expectations of the federal government and political system (see Table 1.4).

One might argue that an impressive list of confidence-building events during the last twenty-five years could also be compiled. This would include glasnost and perestroika, the resurgence of global U.S. firms, a remarkable period of job creation, the breaking of the Mideast oil cartel, and a reduction in violent crime. Such social and economic confidence-building events, though, have not lent their luster to the political scene. After World War II and until the 1970s, government and society in the United States enjoyed historically unprecedented prosperity, idealism, confidence, and cultural, social, and educational development—marred only by the Vietnam War division and the 1960s culture wars. A confluence of disillusioning events then materialized in rapid succession. While initially unrelated, they have combined since then, and multiplied, thereby contributing to the present politics of frustration. Partly due to what happened then and partly to what followed, 1973 emerges—at least in retrospect—as a water-

Table 1.4 Disillusioning Events Since the Watershed Year of 1973

1973

- Kissinger and Le Duc Tho reach agreement; the last U.S. troops leave Vietnam.
- Vice President Spiro Agnew resigns.
- *The poverty rate reaches an all-time low at 11 percent and then begins another upward climb.*
- Middle Eastern nations form an oil cartel that quadruples prices and causes a gas shortage.

1974

- House Judiciary Committee opens presidential impeachment hearings; Nixon resigns.
- *The number of events initiated by the civil-rights movement sinks to the level of the 1950s.*
- *The passage of FECA amendments launches a rapid increase in the number of PACs.*
- *The last year in which discretionary spending equaled half of the federal budget.*

1974–1975

- Recession and the emergence of "stagflation."

1975

- U.S. ambassador Graham Martin flees Vietnam by helicopter as Saigon falls to the Communists.

1979–1982

- A second oil crisis contributes to double-digit inflation and unemployment.

1979–1981

- Fifty-two U.S. hostages held by Iran for 444 days.

1981

- Over the next fifteen years, partisan conflict over domestic vs. defense priorities results in a quintupling of U.S. debt.
- *The S&L industry is deregulated, leading to the largest financial scandal in U.S. history.*

1982

- *Reagan proposes a reduction in Social Security cost-of-living increases; a furious public compels him to withdraw the initiative.*

1984

- *Walter Mondale refuses to say that he will not raise taxes to balance the budget; he loses the election.*

1985

- *Gramm-Rudman Act passes, but in the ensuing years there is still a failure to balance the budget.*

1986–1987

- The White House sells arms to Iran, hoping it can gain the release of U.S. hostages in Lebanon; it illegally diverts the profits to help Nicaraguan contras.

1988

- Stalemate: an allegedly temporary congressional "continuing resolution" continues throughout FY1987, when Congress cannot agree on an annual budget.
- *Voter turnout in the 1988 presidential election sinks to 50 percent.*

(continues)

Table 1.4   (continued)

1988–1990
- *U.S. prison population reaches 426 per 100,000 (vs. 74 in the other Big-7 nations).*

1989
- Scandals at HUD dating throughout the 1980s become a matter of public record.

1990–1992
- A recession is prolonged by what has become a slow-growth economy.

1990
- Bush assigns a higher priority to bipartisan agreement on deficit reductions than he gives to his "no new taxes" pledge; he loses the 1992 election.

1991
- *U.S. savings rate sinks to 2.4 percent, its lowest point since the end of World War II.*

1993
- Omnibus Budget and Reconciliation Act reduces the deficit but scars Clinton politically.

1994
- Voters reject an incumbent Congress and opt overwhelmingly for "neocon-servatives."
- *Roughly 40 percent of all children in the nation now do not live with their fathers.*
- Clinton and Congress deadlock on health-care reform.

1995
- House Speaker Gingrich's "Contract with America" further undercuts confidence in the government.

1996–1999
- Sex and money scandals shower the administration.

1998–1999
- The "Year of Monica" and impeachment of Clinton.

---

shed year. It was quite a year. The United States completed negotiations with the enemy and the last U.S. troops left South Vietnam. The United States had lost its first war. On the home front, a cartel of Middle Eastern nations precipitated a gas shortage that left drivers haplessly sitting in their cars in long lines before gas pumps. Meanwhile, the U.S. vice president was compelled to leave office for accepting bribes delivered directly to him in the White House—the first VP ever to have had to quit office in such a way.

The populace might have shrugged off these events had they not been quickly followed by the 1974 Watergate burglary and cover-up. That event was the first to drive a president from office prior to completion of his term. Next came a serious recession, memorable for "stagflation," which uncharacteristically combined high inflation and declining real economic growth. In 1975, the nation watched the spectacle on television of a U.S. ambassador and his entourage fleeing Saigon by helicopter while thousands of terrified South Vietnamese allies remained locked outside the embassy gates to cope with the victorious northerners. A number of these disillusioning events impacted on the U.S. midlevel population personally and directly. A second oil crisis in 1979, for example, resulted in double-digit inflation and double-digit unemployment by the early 1980s. Then in 1982, President Ronald Reagan proposed cuts in Social Security, which most older people viewed as an untouchable insurance program. The resulting public outcry scuttled the proposal but left a sense of unease in its wake.

A number of what might be termed *seminal* events also occurred in the 1970s. These events represented either the beginning of disturbing trends or the end of promising trends whose significance was not recognized until many years later. The trends are italicized in table 1.4. In 1973, for example, the poverty rate began moving upward again, thereby presaging another lost war—the War on Poverty. In 1975, the percentage of black high-school students enrolling in college peaked; disturbing numbers of blacks were beginning to give up on the white mainstream. Other events would impact the society as a whole. Passage of the Congressional Budget Act of 1974 signaled growing congressional awareness that it must move to stem a budget edging out of control. In turn, 1975 marked the final year in which real income increased for the majority of the middle class until more than two decades later. In 1981, Congress deregulated the Savings and Loan industry, which several years later led to the largest financial scandal in U.S. history. Evidence of dismaying events and political disarray continued to unfold through the 1990s. By mid-decade, citizens could point to events signifying an economic comeback, but no such events signaled a *political* comeback, and voters could find little solace in the actions of either political party. While voters eventually rejected the conservative Republican no-holds-barred attack on government in 1994, then Speaker Newt Gingrich's "Contract with America" conveyed a negative tone that further sapped confidence in government. Meanwhile, the alleged and substantiated sex and money scandals following the 1996 election tarred the administration and the Democratic Party, culminating in the feeding frenzy by the media that accompanied the coming out of Monica Lewinsky and the impeachment of President Bill Clinton.

The Voting Decision

One expects lack of trust in the government to be expressed partly by individuals not voting. However, those casting ballots express as much lack of confidence in government as the nonvoters. Restoring confidence thus cannot be achieved simply through involving more voters in casting their ballots. Nor is it the case that nonvoters and voters necessarily feel differently about the candidates and issues.

Nonvoters and Excluded Alternatives

But there may be less to the apparent issue agreement between voters and nonvoters than meets the eye. Political scientist Martin P. Wattenberg found that President Bill Clinton's two most visible policy failures—the 1993 economic-stimulus package and the 1994 effort to establish universal health care—attracted their strongest backing from people who were not even registered to vote.[84] And such polls usually address those issues under consideration on the public agenda and by those candidates who gained visibility partly by making the necessary concessions to the better-off "investors" who fund much of their campaigns. There may well then be issues of concern to nonvoters, such as those under the rubric of economic security, that do not make it to the public agenda but instead are relegated to the "politics of excluded alternatives."[85]

The exclusion of some political economy issues from the campaign agenda is not the result of collusion among wealthy contributors, but simply a logical extension of the privileged and influential position held by medium- and large-sized corporations where democratic capitalism prevails. Citizens and the state realize that their economic well-being depends on business success. Where corporate interests conflict or the need for government regulation is palpable, business interests may come into play. But where there is consensus among business and professional interests on political economy issues, they constitute a formidable political force. The safest course for members of Congress and even presidents, then, is to prevent such issues from entering the public dialogue. Economist Charles Lindblom thus points to the privileged position of business in explaining the absence from the political agenda of such "grand issues" as maintaining close contact between business and government, protection of the status quo on distribution of income and wealth, and restriction of union demands to those consistent with business profitability.[86] The exclusion of such economic security issues does not require collusion—only that business executives and professionals share the same views. The increasing need for corporate campaign contributions strengthens this already privileged position. In the political calculus of candidate-centered politics, money needed for reelection outweighs the need to raise economic security issues pertinent to three-fifths of the voters. If lower turnout results from excluding such alternatives, that is a problem for the League of Women Voters.

Whatever their views on issues and trust in government, nonvoters differ from voters in their assessment of the political system. When the 1996

National Election Study asked people to rate their satisfaction with how democracy works in the United States, nonvoters responded less positively than voters.[87] There may be candidates in the wings who—if they can assemble the necessary resources—might galvanize support among these nonvoters by addressing their concerns. Third-party candidate Ross Perot garnered 19 percent of the presidential vote—the highest proportion since Teddy Roosevelt—even though he mixed his populist message with a heavy emphasis on deficit reduction.

Differences Between Voters and Nonvoters

While voters and nonvoters may possess a number of similar attitudes on issues, their backgrounds—and the skills and attitudes they acquire through those experiences—differ significantly. The single most important criterion determining the decision to vote is the person's level of education.[88] The higher a person ascends the educational ladder, the more likely that she or he will vote. A 1996 Census Bureau survey thus found that 30 percent of those with less than a high-school education voted; 34 percent of those with some high school, 49 percent of the high-school graduates, 60 percent with some college, and 73 percent of the college graduates.[89] This association between educational attainment and electoral turnout makes sense: more highly educated voters tend to know more about politics, are better able to acquire more political information, and are more likely to feel that citizens should vote and that they can influence the political process.[90]

To some extent, voter turnout thus stems from a stronger sense of civic duty often absorbed through the socialization process that accompanies higher education. Such civic duty is reflected in feelings that those living in our democracy have a responsibility to vote.[91] The reduced sense of civic duty among those with less education can be seen in responses on the need for more civic education in the schools. When asked in a John Doble Research Associates poll whether more civic education was needed, 72 percent of those with college or advanced degrees favored a greater emphasis on "getting involved" politically and in civic activities, while only 39 percent of those with a high-school diploma or less agreed.[92]

While education is more important than income level in the decision to vote, because the changing job structure increasingly requires greater knowledge and capacity for analytical work for better-paying positions, it is not surprising that those with higher incomes also vote disproportionately in terms of their numbers. Actually, those with higher incomes are able to vote twice—once by casting a ballot and once with their checkbooks. The checkbook vote carries more clout than in earlier years, and according to the Citizen Participation Study, candidates now more eagerly seek citizen money than time. In the 1990s, 23 percent of the voters contributed to presidential or midterm elections, but two-thirds of these citizens who donated their time or money to political campaigns limited their involvement to writing checks.[93]

How a citizen feels about his or her relationship to the political system is also associated with the decision to vote.[94] This attitude consists partly of feelings of personal efficacy. This feeling of control over oneself and the environment, Robert Lane found, is nurtured in childhood and reinforced— or inhibited—by society. The individual then generalizes these feelings into a sense of political effectiveness. A strong sense of political effectiveness leads people to "become more alert to their political environment, more informed and partisan in their views, and more active in the political process."[95] Better-off individuals tend to have greater feelings of such effectiveness, thanks partly to their more successful experiences in their personal lives and partly to a realistic assessment of their effectiveness in translating their greater resources and personal confidence into political effectiveness. It is the latter "external" sense of efficacy—the confidence that one's political activities can actually influence what the government does—that is more significant politically, even though it is often integrally related to one's personal feelings of competence to understand and partici- pate in politics. One reason for differentiating internal from external feel- ings of efficacy is that individuals from less advantaged backgrounds and income groups can gain confidence in their ability to have an impact on government and society through their involvement with social movements, interest groups, and informal social groupings.

The Importance of Party Identification

In addition to a sense of political efficacy, the strength of a person's party identification also comes into play in determining not only how but also whether citizens vote. Most voters neither maintain a formal membership with one party nor work with the party organization; rather they feel a sense of attachment to a political party.[96] Such identification does not mean that voters will always opt for their preferred party, but it is their "standing decision" under normal conditions. The voter has confidence in the party's political stance. The party thus serves here as a "reference" group with which the voter identifies on political matters—much as the person might identify with another group (or institution) on religious matters. In both cases, as Warren Miller has shown, the group is important in defining the relationship between the person and those religious or political matters that have a social significance for that person—"Indeed, the existence of the group, with acknowledged leaders who articulate the group's values and interpret the group's interest in the stream of public affairs, is crucial to the group member's ability to relate to the larger world."[97] Party identification thus orients an individual's political attitudes much as a religious denomination orients its members on religious matters.

While it is sometimes argued that such support of a party is a poor substitute for making an independent decision in each election about the candidates and issues, party leaders interpret party loyalties as based largely on people's evaluations of each party's past and current performance.[98] For example, voters respond most strongly to income growth and pay attention to recent experience at the expense of the more distant past.[99] However, in gauging inflation, those with at least a college degree form accurate forecasts of inflation, while citizens with less education prove less able to make such predictions and are more likely to be fooled by policymakers.[100] An example is the federal government's frequent reliance on allowing unemployment to rise in order to curb inflationary growth. Those marginally attached to the labor force, who are most likely to lose their jobs as a result of this policy trade-off—the victims—often do not understand the connection between this federal action and the likely consequences for them.[101]

Therefore, if one party more often represents a particular individual and the groups with whom she or he identifies, it may make sense to take cues on candidates and issues from the party's leaders. Comparatively few voters have the time or inclination to develop the relatively sophisticated belief system necessary to organize their thoughts about the numerous, sometimes complex political issues raised in an election year, particularly in terms of how those thoughts relate to their particular interests and concerns. Better to rely on the party to protect their interests, and ultimately, if it fails to do so, support alternative candidates or the other party.

The role of the political party as prime motivator and educator of the electorate has come under question in recent decades. Voters certainly do not flock to the polls with the same spirit and unquestioning loyalty as in the old days. Even those identifying with one party often now show little hesitancy in voting for the candidate from another. This can be seen in the dramatically increased incidence of split-ticket voting in recent times.[102] While individual choices and split-ticket voting may appear more rational to the voter—judging the person rather than "unthinkingly" pulling a party-label lever—the overall result is greater partisan conflict and less capacity to govern. Voters note the resulting discord with frustration, without seeing it as the result of how they cast their ballots.

The Decline of Partisanship

There is ample evidence that the proportion of those identifying strongly with the party has declined and that the proportion of the electorate lacking partisan feelings for either political party has increased. The problem is not that people dislike political parties but rather that they simply ignore them or no longer find them significant for the governmental process. One study in 1994 found that 29 percent of the electorate could think of nothing they liked or disliked about either party. Only 10 percent of the voters in the 1952 election responded in this detached fashion.[103] For three times as many voters today, parties are no longer a psychological anchoring point for their political attitudes. The parties could well identify with Amos, in the John Kander and Fred Ebb musical *Chicago*, who laments that cellophane, Mr. Cellophane, "should have been my name, cause you can look right through me, walk right by me, and never know I'm there."[104]

The Unaffiliated Independent Voter

The expanding number of voters without partisan leanings would provide little cause for worry if this unaffiliated voter truly met expectations of such a model citizen. This person is supposedly well informed and interested in government and politics, possesses a healthy respect for the nation's rulers and rule of law, and readily detects and sides with the public interest rather than seeking grants, services, and entitlements through the medium of interest groups.

Unfortunately, the evidence suggests that such unattached voters, when compared with partisan voters, are less likely to vote, less informed, and more prone to short-term influences. To be sure, people in the United States generally have a weak knowledge base about politics. A 1996 Harvard University study showed that 54 percent could not name either U.S. senator from their state, and 58 percent thought that more of the federal budget was spent on foreign aid [1%] than Medicare [19%]. Such less politically informed citizens—regardless of whether they were Republicans or Democrats—were more fearful of war and more likely to believe that it would be better for the United States to stay out of world affairs. Similarly, those who knew the least about the relative economic positions of blacks and whites were far more likely to see no need for special efforts by either government or the private sector to help minorities.

The unaffiliated and nonvoters, however, were more likely to be poorly informed, and more inclined to believe that the country is in decline. They were more likely than better-informed people to believe that, even where progress has been made on issues such as water and air pollution, problems were becoming worse, and that federal government involvement invariably makes every problem worse. This level of rigid cynicism differed from the views of better-informed voters across the political spectrum.[105]

Besides the amount of information possessed by a citizen, there is also the question of how well the citizen can use that information. Most nonvoters in 1992 and 1996 surveys were independents, but some proved so lacking in political consciousness that they were classified as nonpolitical. Forty percent could not place themselves on a seven-point ideology scale ranging from very liberal to very conservative. This inability to classify themselves as liberals or conservatives—the basic stuff of political debate in this country—stems partly from their lack of association with either political party: 20 percent of these nonvoters—compared with fewer than 10 percent of voters—denied any affinity for either political party.[106]

Minnesota's unaffiliated and nonvoters may have provided a preview of coming attractions in the 1998 gubernatorial election when they selected Jesse "the Body" Ventura, the ceremonial mayor of Brooklyn Park, Minnesota, over Democratic attorney general Skip Humphrey and Saint Paul mayor Norm Coleman, two well-known and generally respected party candidates. Ventura is a classic populist candidate with a roguish charm, a shrewd sense of humor, and an antipolitician stance. More instructive is how he won. The polls indicate that he tapped into the growing number of voters who do not belong to a political party, and—since Minnesota allows voters to register and vote on the same day—attracted three of four voters who registered on election day, including thousands of hitherto uninvolved young people and disaffected citizens.[107]

Such increased participation is important, but the Ventura phenomenon also underscores the political impact that can result when a growing number of nonvoters—primarily unaffiliated independents who are unable to assess candidates in terms of their views on a range of issues and their belief system—emerge from the woodwork. When times are comparatively good, such short-term influences (as posed by Ventura) may pose relatively little danger to the body politic. However, when times are bad, the story may be less amusing. Where a segment of the population comes to suffer under the pressure of social, political, or economic dislocations, bad times may generate both "an elite which wishes to organize a movement and a public which is restive." Stoked by seed money and organization, such short-term influences are then more likely to take the form of "flash" parties and "candidate-centered" demagogues with access to big money and the media.[108] Nobody knows how susceptible these independents will be to such mass appeals. However, just as the wise capitalist saves money for a rainy day, it seems prudent also to strengthen the political system while its stability remains high.

But the U.S. populace has never been particularly well-informed. While polls continue to demonstrate that the public has a poor grasp of proper names and figures that they cannot relate to their concerns, these same individuals emerge as a far more rational public when one examines their policy preferences over time.[109] Survey data may show that only one-quarter of the voters is well-informed, but we may well ask what portion of the electorate needs to be informed for our democracy to perform adequately.[110] That is difficult to say, but both parties in 1999 seemed to bet on the electorate's limited capacity to make a connection between issues. The

Democrats bragged that they had reduced the number of federal bureaucrats, even while proposing additional federal programs, and the Republicans promised extensive tax cuts combined with long-term balanced budgets.

Certainly the information is available if independents, nonvoters, and other less-informed citizens decide to seek it from such now national newspapers as the *Wall Street Journal* and the *New York Times*, from such television stations as Cable News Network (CNN), Cable National Broadcasting Company (CNBC), or C-SPAN, or from the Internet. We are an information-rich society with increasingly less-informed and less-concerned voters.

Symbolic vs. Substantive Politics

One problem is that the same media and political consultants who address informed voters on the issues through these sophisticated sources have also become much more adept at addressing less motivated and uninformed voters through *symbolic politics*. Political campaigns thus are waged in a two-front war. For less knowledgeable voters, politics is reduced to a diet of candidates portrayed as heroes and villains, and complex policy debates are caricatured as clashes of good and evil. The resulting polarization leaves elements of the public less accepting of compromise, more mistrustful, and less tolerant of attempts to compromise with the demonized opposition.[111] Political independence breeds isolation; isolation in turn creates emotional vulnerability; and that vulnerability then opens individuals to such methods of strategic communication as marketing, image-shaping through focus groups, and advertising.[112] Independents, nonpoliticals, and those only tangentially linked to the parties or other political groups are particularly vulnerable to such messages because they lack the enduring identifications with parties, leaders, and political programs that would provide the stable frame of reference and psychological cues that encourage citizens to trust government and tolerate politicians.

Politics as a Social Act

There is a tendency to think about the electoral decision as an autonomous act occurring in the voting booth, but it is usually also a social act. Citizens often make their voting decisions after interacting with trusted friends and co-workers. Such informal interactions provide occasions to test ideas and take cues from those who may be better informed on an issue or candidate. Similarly, citizens are creatures of the groups that comprise their demographic background, their voluntary group affiliations, and the interest groups to which they may belong. Such characteristics as religion, sex, and race can influence one's political views—particularly when one becomes

involved with a politically active church denomination, the women's movement (or female groups opposed to parts of that movement), a Jesse
Jackson Rainbow Coalition or Louis Farrakhan's Million Man March on
Washington. These affiliations stem from a shared ethnic, gender, racial, or
religious background but may then evolve into extensive interest-group
activity or full-fledged social movements. Interest groups may attempt to
influence the government on issues as diverse as support for the arts, the
right to bear arms, or campaign reform. They also emerge from business,
labor, trade association, or other shared interests stemming from the production of goods and services; social movements arise from concern about
causes such as control of nuclear energy, the environment, or civil rights.

By far the most extensive and expensive interest-group activity
revolves around the business and commercial concerns of industries and
professions. Interest-group activity surged during the 1960s and 1970s; in
1985, 76 percent of these groups pertained to business and commerce.[113]
Sometimes these business-related interest groups pose little threat because
they are competing for political influence.[114] But such groups share in common a strong ideological commitment to unfettered capitalism, a collective
allergy to taxes, and a firm conviction that the business of the United States
is business. Furthermore, they are rarely bashful in seeking to permeate
these views throughout the national policy process both directly themselves
and indirectly by funding think tanks, academicians, and other participants
in the marketplace of ideas.

Political Networking by the Better-off Two-Fifths

Such proactive political stances distance the disconnected three-fifths further from the political system because these interest groups are disproportionately representing precisely those same highly educated and high-
income citizens who are already overrepresented elsewhere in the political
system. Comparatively less-educated and less-wealthy citizens, therefore,
must seek their group support and the basis for their participation elsewhere
in the society.

The people of the United States have historically drawn on what
Robert Putnam terms their social capital in seeking to engage actively in
community affairs. This effective means of influencing government and
other powerful social institutions consists of the networks, norms, and trust
that enable participants in a voluntary organization to develop and practice
the skills necessary to work together effectively. Citizens can then draw on
these leadership and other group skills, as well as the social trust built
through such civic involvement with others, in becoming active politically.
These activities, though, occur in separate spheres. Social capital con-

tributes to civic engagement—one's connection generally with community life through activity in bowling leagues, hobby and garden groups, sports groups, or the numerous other kinds of clubs and organizations that together constitute community life.[115]

Social Networking and Electoral Turnout

The importance of social networking in stimulating political participation led the League of Women Voters in the 1990s to alter its strategy for encouraging voter turnout. The league, according to its 1998 president, Becky Cain, had assumed that disillusionment and cynicism were responsible for the sinking electoral turnout. A survey sponsored by the league, however, revealed that voters were no less cynical than nonvoters—instead, it was far-stronger social networks that distinguished the two groups. Since then, the league has devoted more time to talking with citizens about the importance of community involvement and about how voting impacts their economic, educational, and health-care concerns.[116]

The existence of such a network is particularly important for the numerous citizens whose lack of interest-group affiliations, high-status jobs, and education more frequently prevent them from voting and participating in other political activities. Such social networks can help these less engaged citizens overcome some of the attitudinal and experiential barriers reducing the likelihood of their participation. Participation in these networks, for example, contributes to an enhanced sense of political efficacy, particularly for those with comparatively less formal schooling.[117]

While they may share distrust of government and views on some issues, their attitudes toward voting and more intensive forms of political participation and the extent of their social networking strongly differentiate voters from nonvoters in the society. Those failing to vote, not surprisingly, are also less likely to participate in other ways. These activities are particularly significant in the United States, where citizens vote less but engage in other political activities more often than citizens in other countries.[118]

The age-old formula in a democracy for coping with the limitations of income distribution is by countering wealth with numbers. The vote is critical in maintaining that equation. Turnout is thus important not only because it is a "good thing" to vote but also because it is the only weapon in the hands of the *majority* to temper corporate and elite power. This is particularly important because those in the top two quintiles parlay their money and educational know-how into political power through greater interest-group activity, bigger contributions, and higher electoral turnout rates. The only countervailing power consists of widespread participation that conveys a wider range of concerns to the political system. Democracy is thus "neither a consumer good nor a spectator sport, but rather the work of free citizens, engaged in shared civic enterprises."[119]

Who Votes and Who Doesn't

The differing turnout rates over the last three decades underscore that far from redressing the political balance by voting in large numbers, those less connected to the society economically are also less likely to vote. The proportion of eligible voters going to the polls in presidential election years has steadily declined with the exception of a brief upward blip in the early 1980s. By 1998, when voters were asked to select the Congress that would represent them, 72 million showed up, while 119 million eligible voters stayed away. Only 36 percent voted—the lowest percentage since 1942 during World War II. Thus, many members of Congress "won their seats by securing the support of fewer than 20 percent of the eligible voters in their districts. It is often said that Congress is the voice of the people. More accurately, it has become the voice of one in five people."[120] The 1998 election was not, however, unusual. Since 1974, more than three-fifths of the eligible voters have not taken the trouble to vote in an off-year election.[121]

The Disconnected Three-Fifths

This deterioration in the body politic can also be seen in terms of who votes. In 1994, people with no college education constituted 53 percent of the population but only 42 percent of the voters.[122] And while the turnout rate among college graduates held steady between 1968 and 1992, the turnout rate of those who never finished high school declined by about one-third.[123] The shrunken electorate is thus not only smaller but also less representative of all eligible voters.

Some degree of economic inequality is presumably desirable in a free-market system anxious to reward the pursuit of excellence, hard work, and the assumption of risk. A democracy, however, requires political equality. Ideally, everyone's voice should be heard some of the time even though everyone's voice cannot be heeded all of the time. The difficulty in reaching all citizens is underscored by the conditions necessary to encourage political participation. These include organizational and communication civic skills, citizenship (with its eligibility to vote), institutional affiliation (job level, nonpolitical organization membership, and religious attendance), and political engagement that can enable citizens to gain increased political interest, more political information, and attitudes of greater political efficacy and partisan strength. Other items contributing to participation, however, are less tractable; namely, educational attainment and English proficiency, income level, and, most importantly, resources.[124] In the case of the poor, "time, money, and skills provide the wherewithal without which engagement is meaningless. It is not sufficient to know and care about politics. If wishes were resources, then beggars would participate. Political engagement, however, does not produce resources, and the resource-poor are less politically active than those who are better endowed with resources."[125]

The ranks of the disconnected, however, now extend well into the middle class. Judging by their backgrounds, a number could parlay their educational level and job experience into the skills necessary for political participation if they were to change their negative view of politics and government. Too often, though, these nonparticipants do not appear to think strategically in terms of their relationship to political power. So they do not recognize that political activity is more important for them than for those who possess greater resources and hence alternative means of access to power. These political dropouts see less relevance, and so, election by election since the 1970s, their political activity has become less relevant. As one such disconnected citizen admitted to political scientist David Mathews, "It's like a snowball effect—you don't feel that you can have a voice; therefore, you don't participate, and you get farther and farther apart from your representative."[126] Hence, representative democracy becomes caught in a vicious downward spiral of neglect—neglect of these citizens by their democratic representatives and neglect by these citizens of their democracy.

Just how and where to break this spiral of neglect is a puzzle. The disconnect of the many simultaneously enables the comparatively few to rule less responsibly and reduces the likelihood that the remaining active citizens can sustain a depleted democracy. In viewing this problem, though, it is important to note that it is not, as it is frequently portrayed, simply a participation gap between two extremes, the rich and the poor. Instead, three-fifths of a nation is now drifting toward political disengagement.

A citizen majority possesses strategic advantages in a democracy. In addition to numbers, another underutilized resource that these citizens possess in as much abundance as the better-off is time. The Citizen Participation Study demonstrated that free time is unrelated to income or education but depends instead on such life circumstances as having a job, a spouse who works, or young children.[127] People have the time to spend on political participation, if they so choose. Sweat equity is a valuable democratic resource that is widely available.

Political equality, then, hinges partly on reversing the current trend toward more writing of checks and less direct political involvement through voting and more intensive forms of participation. People must be asked to engage in the political process. While this idea may sound wild-eyed in an age of couch potatoes and political consultants, the evidence, as we shall see in the next chapter, shows that personal contact remains a potent form of influence and political mobilization. The trick is that citizens blossom through personal contact, and such an effort requires leadership and organization. To be more specific, this frequently entails organization by a political party.

Such party mobilization involves both reaching out to citizens and structuring campaigns so that they involve competitive electoral races that address critical issues. These issues often emerge in response to events. We have seen since the 1970s, rightly or wrongly, it is disillusioning events that voters have associated with politics and government. By contrast, in the minds of voters, the economic vitality of the 1990s seemingly occurred thanks to a free-market mechanism functioning in existential loneliness—in spite of, rather than in accord with, political and governmental involvement. With the notable exceptions of national defense and public safety, government is all too often seen as an unalloyed impediment to progress. This spirit is captured by the attitude of those Internet devotees determined to protect the World Wide Web from any form of government incursion. Like impassioned free-market advocates, those defending an unfettered information universe, unburdened by government regulation, maintain that "things are great the way they are."

Rebuilding Citizen Trust Through Crisis Management

Reversing the trend of downward citizen participation in light of such negativism toward the political system and government is a daunting task. But considerable evidence exists that how the leaders of political institutions and political candidates respond to events often can have a marked impact on how such leaders are viewed by the electorate.

Perhaps the most dramatic example of such change occurred in the aftermath of the September 11, 2001, terrorist attack. Until then, a number of citizens regarded the president's election in 2000 as illegitimate in light of voting irregularities, particularly in Florida. After the terrorist attack, and Mr. Bush's vigorous response, the electoral controversy was set aside as citizens closed ranks behind their president. Only time would tell whether such a patriotic response could form a base on which to build more widespread citizen support on other issues and for the political system, but the citizen response did demonstrate the power of events in influencing public sentiment.

Political trust is thus neither an attitude established early in life that perseveres in the face of dismaying events, nor is it necessarily a permanent condition. Hence, James Wright found that the level of public trust in politics rises and falls in response to events, and Gregory Markus similarly found that "a capacity for lifelong political learning exists, and historical occurrences may influence basic political attitudes throughout the life cycle."[128] William Mayer showed that external events changed public attitudes: the Tet offensive changed attitudes toward Vietnam; publicized strip-mining incidents altered environmental views; and the Three Mile Island accident reversed attitudes about nuclear power.[129]

How well or how poorly its leaders respond to such events partly shapes the public's reaction to the political system. In his classic study, Richard Neustadt showed that presidents exercise power by effectively dealing with those events that condition public attention. The challenge for presidents is to persuade those inside and outside the beltway by making choices in response to events that enhance one's professional reputation and public prestige. Educating, and thereby persuading, the public is rendered more difficult because it is instruction "aimed at students who, by definition, are habitually inattentive to the teacher." These students pay attention only when they notice public trouble in their lives—hence the significance of events—and the public's interpretation of such events may differ from the president's. Not surprisingly, then, the president "teaches less by telling than by doing (or not doing) in the context that his students have established in their minds." Past events also figure in the equation, since part of that context consists of what the president "has previously said and done."[130]

Some writers have come to view public dissatisfaction with government as a response to events, and to the perception of events, primarily in the political sphere.[131] This approach distinguishes those political and social events that build *political* trust from the economic events that often decide a particular election. Political scientist Garry Orren also found in the mid-1990s that bad citizen reviews of government performance were "largely a response to a litany of dramatic and highly visible international misadventures and domestic shocks."[132] Table 1.4 similarly lists a number of dismaying political events that persisted well into the 1990s. The lesson conveyed by this body of research is that how the political system responds to upcoming events—rather than hardened attitudes or societal forces beyond our control—will largely determine whether citizen trust and confidence rise or plummet still further.

Conclusion

While it rarely springs to mind among the electorate, the only voluntary organization with the size, the incentive, *and the potential* to mobilize the politically inactive majority of the nation and respond to such disillusioning events is the political party. In the next chapter we turn to identifying the organizational tasks of democracy previously performed by parties and now so often preempted by other institutions; analyzing the limited effectiveness of political parties today; and examining why transformed parties may represent the only realistic hope for involving the other three-fifths of the United States in its political system.

2

Why Parties Matter

P olitical parties are unique and vital institutions in our history—the support system of democracy—and yet they can neither return to how they once worked nor continue on their present course. Their significance lies in the political tasks that only they can perform for a democracy; the vital, unanswered question is whether they can reconstitute themselves to perform those tasks more effectively in the future.

The far-flung pieces comprising a party operate semi-autonomously—often with surprisingly little coordination—as grassroots party organizations at the state and local level, congressional party caucuses, presidential parties, and as Republican and Democratic National Committees. At election time, "groups and individuals come together in association almost as accidentally and irrationally as molecules of gas come together in a chamber. The result of the multilayered local, state, and national elections are determined in large part by the effectiveness of the ephemeral relationships that are built up by hundreds of thousands of separate and discrete campaign organizations."[1] While parties engage in numerous tangible activities, it is their partisan identification, images, and symbols in the minds of voters and party activists that make them important. The elephant and donkey even today remain an important political cue for millions of card-carrying party members. The parties' *potential* significance in drawing together the disparate elements of a growing and heterogeneous nation ironically has increased even while other institutions, such as the media, interest groups, and social movements, have successfully encroached on their turf.

This chapter begins with a discussion that emphasizes societal functions of political parties—underappreciated in the public's eyes—and indicates the serious interest-group and media incursions on those roles. It then discusses the persistent and promising activities of the party organizations and their workers (or activists), as they relate to the voters. The chapter concludes with some comments on how parties may be able to build on their strengths and learn how to adapt to changed conditions.

Party Functions

Parties are perhaps best visualized as "three-headed political giants." Each giant interacts with "party leaders and officials and the thousands of anonymous activists who work for candidates and party causes, the people who vote for the party's candidates, and the men and women elected to office on the party's label. As political structures, they can be thought of as the somewhat unwieldy combination of a party organization, a party in office, and a party in the electorate."[2] All three segments of this party system influence each other, particularly during elections, when they are mutually interdependent. Furthermore, thanks to their decentralized nature, the interactions of these three structures differ greatly. For example, in some states, party organizations dominate the party in government, while in others, those controlling the government dominate their party.[3]

Each of these structures has a separate and distinct core, and these differ markedly in the current state of their organizational health. On the one hand, there are some generally positive reviews of the state of political parties; these come from those political scientists who focus on the party organization. On the other hand, if a Broadway show received critical reviews such as those that these days are aimed at the party as it relates to the electorate, it would not survive a week. The biggest disappointment about contemporary political parties is their inability to serve as an electoral link between the millions of disconnected citizens and their national government.

The importance of involving the political party in creating such an electoral link is perhaps best understood by contrasting parties with other organizations that have now largely subverted their role as intermediaries in the political process. The party, unlike interest groups, professional and business elites, societal factions, social movements, and such basically nonpolitical groups as the corporation, is "an agency for the organization of political power characterized by *exclusively* political functions, by a *stable* structure, and *inclusive* membership, and by the ability to dominate the contesting of elections."[4] The party is stable in that it persists beyond a single election or cause. In doing so, it gradually acquires traditions, clienteles, and ideologies that live on beyond the policy issue in vogue or any particular politician. This long-term commitment also means that the parties in theory must be answerable for the quality of their decisions in coming years, and thereby increases the likelihood that they will seek solutions closer to the public interest. However, as one experienced political operative observed, "the pursuit of short-term interests [now] is what is killing us."[5] The party is inclusive in that it constantly entices newcomers to support its goals, candidates, and symbols. It must continually broaden and solidify its base. By remaining inclusive, parties also serve as an obstacle to factional domination of government. Because the major parties include all kinds of interests, in theory, they are not free to cater to a single interest or a small cluster of interests to the exclusion of others.[6]

When functioning ideally, a party thus constitutes the only voluntary organization in the United States that aspires to accept everyone in its membership, attempts to make decisions designed to withstand the test of time, and plays the critical governance role of sustaining the election period, the transfer of power, and the making of public policy. No other institution has ever sought to perform all of these ambitious roles on such a broad scale.

Direct Party Functions

Their supporters and critics view parties differently in part because these organizations vary dramatically in how well they perform a wide range of functions. Parties perform these tasks in seeking to control the struggle for power in order to dominate the contesting of elections. Historian Clinton Rossiter noted in 1960 that "it is the great purpose of political parties . . . to bring the struggle under control: to institutionalize it with organization, . . . [and] above all to stabilize [it] in the form of that traditional quadrille in which the Ins and Outs change places from time to time on a signal from the voters."[7] Furthermore, while the direct primary has largely undercut the party's ability to control the nomination of candidates, the parties persist in playing a role, when possible, in the sifting of candidates for elective office, promoting those candidates during the campaign, manning the polls and counting the votes on election day, and suggesting men and women for political appointments.

Few citizens view political parties as the support system of democracy today, and yet the parties' efforts continue to promote a more open, less bitter contest among factions and interests seeking power. They thus facilitate the peaceful surrender of power when insurgent candidates defeat incumbents—the acid test that distinguishes a democratic from an autocratic form of government. Parties also cannot afford the luxury of hating individuals and groups if they are to amass a majority of the voters. Indeed, the fundamental value of parties in the United States lies in their "pulling together an immensely varied mass of social groups, economic constituencies, racial stocks, and local and sectional interests for the purpose of governing by consent."[8] The parties have, with some notable historical exceptions, led efforts to alleviate tensions based on race, religion, or ethnicity. They seek to bridge such differences in order to build a winning coalition.

Such a winning coalition starts with the groups traditionally associated with a particular party. The Democratic Party's New Deal coalition—while merely a shadow of its former self—still persists. Some members have departed (particularly in the case of southerners and blue-collar workers), while others—such as teachers' unions, women's groups, and organizations representing blacks, Hispanics, gays and lesbians, and environmentalists—have been added. The remnants of this "coalition of minorities" no longer being able to win an election alone, the Democrats must seek additional allies. Similarly the Republican Party includes Wall Street and Main Street fiscal conservatives, Westerners anxious to shed government interference with their lives and lands, and social conservatives, such as pro-life groups and fundamentalist Christians who, in contrast to Democratic groups, reject a government proactive in economic affairs but seek active government on social issues.[9] Like their Democratic Party foes, however, the Republicans, too, must seek support from members of groups affiliated with the other party as well as from unaffiliated groups and voters.

David Broder captures the meaning of coalition building for governance in arguing that we cannot "go on electing people on the promise that each of them will create his or her own majority for his or her own program by his or her own communion with the people." Instead, we need people in federal, state, and local government "who have demonstrated the skills of negotiation and compromise, the insights, the articulateness and the boldness to overcome the centrifugal forces tugging at government in this hyper-pluralistic age."[10] Parties alone are now "weak reeds" for building such grand peace-time coalitions, so partisans must build coalitions that extend beyond their own party and its constituent groups. But party leaders operate in a political environment that assigns a high priority to coalition building. The political party remains one of the few institutions where officials must hone this art of leadership and from which such master coalition builders can be recruited. Sadly, the importance of this greatest coalition of them all—and the political parties that make it possible—is least appreciated by the three-fifths of our citizens who benefit from it most. And yet, political parties with all their well-known shortcomings serve as the only device that "can, with some effectiveness, generate countervailing collective power on behalf of the many individually powerless against the relatively few who are individually or organizationally powerful."[11]

Parties also represent the views of their activists and members—and those citizens whom they seek to bring into the fold—in order to assist them in gaining access to their officeholders. In representing their members, the parties are thus *mobilizing and linking citizens to government*, whether it be at the local, state, or federal level. The party thereby provides a particularly important channel of access to the federal government, which is often a long distance from the citizens, both geographically and psychologically.

This linkage between governing elites and broad electoral coalitions ideally works in both directions: it provides an opportunity for voters to express their preferences through their party intermediaries, and it allows the elites to explain and—particularly where they find it necessary to depart from majority views—justify their policy stands to the citizens. The party, as intermediary, fulfills a vital need for organization within our democracy and a linkage mechanism through which popular priorities can be translated for the political system.[12] For Edmund Burke, this linkage was the party's ultimate justification. The party "is a body of men united for promoting by their joint endeavors the national interest upon some particular principle in which they are all agreed."[13]

The strength of this citizen-government linkage depends on whether parties can mobilize voters and on the nature and extent of that mobilization. For mobilization to work, parties must reach many voters and develop a sustained relationship with them. Romancing the voters must involve not merely a one-night stand—the activation that today represents most of what is called "mobilization." Real mobilization addresses the need for organized and continuing efforts to build support among large numbers of citizens around the same general approach to political issues, and to persuade them to work and vote together to achieve common goals.[14]

While U.S. political parties are often criticized for being out of touch with citizens, they remain an important source of public-policy ideas. Their task is to convert needs and demands into coherent and acceptable policies. Both individual candidates and parties through their platforms seek to win the contest of ideas that remains central to promoting those policies important to party workers, partisans, and voters and to winning an election. Furthermore, party leaders, interest-group representatives, and other presidential convention delegates would not become embroiled in such bitter platform debates if the resulting party stands did not convey significance as policy positions and symbols.

With the advent of the direct primary and candidate-centered congressional contests, parties no longer control the recruitment of candidates for office and the selection of political appointees following the election. The parties still are involved in recruiting some congressional candidates and numerous candidates for state and local offices—particularly when the draftees face an uphill battle.[15] Furthermore, only between 5 percent and 30 percent of the electorate vote in the presidential primaries; hence, in many states, even while candidates lean heavily on TV and radio ads, they also must cultivate the party activists and their leaders who under these circumstances constitute a higher proportion of the electorate.

Indirect Party Functions

In order to achieve their goals, parties must engage in not only direct functions but also indirect functions that similarly contribute to a democratic society. For example, to promote their ideas and platforms successfully, parties must persuade citizens on the merit of their positions. Such persuasion ideally takes the form of *educating citizens* about public problems, alternative policies, and preferable solutions. The parties thereby engage in adult education, teaching voters about attitudes, ideas, and programs. Unlike the media, most interest groups, and political organizations, parties address a broad range of issues. In doing so, they force citizens to think about their particular concerns in the context of a broader agenda. Parties also conduct drives designed particularly to register those voters most likely to support their cause. In seeking to bring them to the polls, parties educate these citizens on the value of voting and other forms of political participation. While limited in their effectiveness, such party efforts are, nonetheless, particularly important in educating socially and economically disadvantaged groups, since so few groups reach out to them.[16]

While few U.S. party leaders advocate full-fledged ideologies, the parties do differentiate themselves in two reasonably consistent belief systems. While not as formal as the rigorous ideology of a Marxist or a nineteenth-century Liberal, these belief systems do provide a more or less institutionalized set of ideas. The parties thus provide their followers with a set of guiding principles. Although U.S. voters share many of these principles, they disagree on some, and on which should receive a higher priority. The logical arguments of liberal Democrats and conservative Republicans differ on the principles that should underlie candidate selection, priorities among economic and social values, and the limitations and promise of government. Each of these belief systems is sufficiently logical so that it implies an empirical theory of cause and effect and a theory of the nature of man.[17] These assumptions are not, however, considered in such theoretical terms. Rather, these latent assumptions manifest themselves through debating such issues as how welfare mothers or prisoners should be treated, the military's appropriate size, and which citizens are deserving of federal entitlements.

The parties' competing liberal and conservative belief systems are valuable even for reasonably well-informed citizens because few of us have the time to examine the numerous issues debated in the public arena. Our belief systems inevitably are based on those issues we know—and which party is closer to our views on those issues. Having identified the more congenial party, the citizen can then use the party as a philosophical frame of reference on less familiar issues. The party thereby distinguishes "right" from "wrong" and brings order out of a frequently confusing world.

Since the parties have operated for many decades, they must strive to maintain some consistency in their liberal or conservative belief systems over time, while even successful candidates come and go in a relatively brief period of time. The party thus becomes a symbol of identification and loyalty for its supporters as a result of the ideas, the outstanding standard-bearers, and groups with which it is most closely associated over time. Hence, ironically, even many of the independent voters who no longer hold partisan positions or see much point to political parties often have a better sense of Democrat and Republican Party beliefs than the views of their candidate—even though they like to boast that they make their own independent decision based on "the candidate rather than the party."

The party's significance as a belief system and symbol means little if voters cannot hold the political system accountable for its actions. Only the party can create the necessary incentives for its leaders—located in its own organization, the Congress, and alternately the presidency and executive branch or "shadow government" organizations like think tanks. Only the party can persuade followers and supporters to think and act in collective terms. Thus only the party can perform the function of generating collective responsibility for the adoption of public policies and programs. The party theoretically does so by bestowing or withholding its traditional means of influence—power, patronage, money, and ideology. Unfortunately, as Morris Fiorina wryly notes, "the importance of responsibility in a democracy is matched by the difficulty of attaining it." In the current era of candidate-centered politics and weak parties, individual responsibility is difficult to assess on most national issues. A Democratic or Republican officeholder confronted by constituents angry about a government decision is likely to respond, in effect, "Don't blame me. If 'they' had done what I suggested, things would be fine."[18] Such game playing is all too easy unless voters can fix collective responsibility for what went wrong. The assignment of credit or blame can occur only when these individual politicians are sufficiently aligned with their parties that they cannot wiggle out of collective responsibility for their actions.

Political parties, though, seek those issues likely to appeal to their voters and the independents whom they want to attract. In the 1990s, therefore, they sought to avoid discussing several potentially divisive issues that cut across their group coalitions—usually at the expense of the disengaged. Some of these issues, such as the impact of globalization of the economy and collective bargaining, to some extent pit the job losses and uncertainties many working-class and some middle-class workers feel against the interests of stockholders, managers, and workers in the export-driven sunrise goods and service industries. Nor did either party address who would be hurt by holes in the safety net.[19] Political parties, though, must articulate these complex issues, since it is difficult otherwise for disengaged citizens to move much beyond feeling a need that is not being met.

Balancing Contradictory Party Functions

Inevitably, political parties expected to perform so many tasks will encounter contradictions among them. Every organization other than a political party, for example, has control over recruitment of its leadership, but in politics such control conflicts with the public's expectation that it will vote for candidates in primaries. Yet these same voters hold the party accountable for the actions of presidents and members of Congress elected through this candidate-centered, "direct" primary. The great dilemma among these functions is between the expectation that the parties will stand for something—and not merely signify Tweedledum and Tweedledee—while they also mediate between the people and their government and find a basis among conflicting groups for compromise. This dilemma is not easy to reconcile, but neither unyielding principle nor eternal compromise provide the congressional, presidential, or party leader with an easy way out. Unyielding principle can result in the label of a "do nothing" Congress, while intemperate compromise can undermine the credibility of a candidate who invited voters to "read my lips." The ability to bargain and the capacity for compromise are unlikely to capture voter imagination unless a politician can combine them with the image of a wheeler-dealer. Nonetheless, the importance of bargaining can be seen through examples of those political (and party) leaders who have come to symbolize the fate of those who knew how—and those who did not know how—to compromise. President Lyndon Johnson is credited with parlaying his willingness to bargain into the passage of the Great Society programs in the 1960s. House Speaker Sam Rayburn possessed a similar reputation. More recently, the inability to compromise was put on display with Speaker Newt Gingrich's rapid demise, even though he was reputed to be the most powerful Speaker since Rayburn.

Perhaps nothing more sharply distinguishes the great political leader from his or her peers than the ability to identify the balance point between preserving principle and striking the mutually acceptable bargain. It is no accident that the classic successful bargaining examples are from earlier times. Hardened partisan positions in Congress, heavily seasoned with lack of political trust between the parties, have now created a political environment that only on rare occasions can assemble a citizen majority. Political scientists have debated how to obviate this dilemma. On the one hand, popular control of government requires that "responsible parties" give the public a choice between competing, unified parties capable of assuming collective responsibility to the public for the actions of government.[20] On the other hand, such a "politics of advocacy" undercuts a pragmatic policy process that possesses "a capacity to deliberate, weigh competing demands, and compromise so that a variety of differing interests each gain a little."[21]

The sad truth, however, is that the parties, far from having solved this critical dilemma, in our candidate-centered political era are neither delivering responsible government nor mounting the quantity and quality of dialogue necessary for successful compromise. One reason for this double failure is that the parties have largely lost control over a number of the functions they performed historically.

Institutional Encroachment on Party Functions

There is nothing necessarily wrong with having more than one institution engaged in performing these functions. The extent of the incursion is underscored, however, by the almost parallel descriptions of some of the basic functions now performed by interest groups and the media. Jeffrey Berry thus describes the functions of interest groups as representing constituents before government, enabling people to participate in the political process, educating the population about political issues, bringing an issue to light in the first place (agenda setting), and program monitoring.[22] Doris Graber sees the media performing the functions of throwing the spotlight of publicity on selected people, organizations, and events, determining who and what is "news," providing cues to the public about an issue's importance, conferring status and legitimacy on individuals and organizations through the sheer weight of coverage, setting the civic agenda, informing the public, and interpreting the meaning of events. By putting events into context and speculating about their consequences, the media teach basic political values and orientations to citizens and manipulate the political process through what used to be termed "muckraking"—what is known today under the more dignified title of investigative journalism.[23]

Both of the writers cited above, while primarily focusing on interest groups and the media, respectively, are well aware of the implications of these institutional incursions for political parties. Berry thus concludes his study with the plaintive observation that "more needs to be done to strengthen our parties so that the votes of the many are more influential than the voices of interest groups."[24] For her part, Graber writes that a major consequence of the "media politics" era is a decline in party influence, particularly at the national level dominated by candidates who "televise well" and made-for-media campaigns. In the electronic age, "the candidate as a personality has become the primary consideration at the presidential level. Second are issues associated with the candidate, followed by party affiliation and group membership." When voters can see and hear candidates in their own living rooms, party importance diminishes.[25] In the face of this severe damage inflicted on basic party functions in recent decades, the differences between political scientists debating the relative merits of responsible parties and political compromise are relatively minor compared with the common ground that many share in their concern over the implications of such party decline. There is thus a growing realization that "we must either acknowledge the mutual reliance of our parties and our democracy—or lose both."[26]

The Competitive Marketplace of Ideas

Politics entails a competition of ideas. The media are important partly as a conduit for those ideas. Where the political market does not function effectively, it is often because the production and consumption of political information through the media are dominated by the consumer power of those with the most money and other resources. Benjamin Page and Robert Shapiro thus contend that economic "market forces lead available political information to reflect the needs of the wealthier individuals and organizations. Economic inequality tends to overcome political equality in the information sphere, just as unequal resources to make campaign contributions may offset equal rights to vote."[27] It is this danger, perhaps more than any other, that is posed by the more powerful interest groups and the media to the extent that they often supplant political parties in carrying out their functions.

The danger that economic market forces will come to control the marketplace of ideas has increased with the historical shift from party-based organizations tied to partisan newspapers to candidate-based membership enterprises heavily dependent on purchasing TV and radio time. Presidential and congressional candidates are both now largely on their own. The congressional candidates' fortunes no longer rest on the approval of party leaders. Candidates now send themselves to Washington. These self-recruited entrepreneurs have won "through a combination of ambition, talent, and the willingness to devote whatever time was necessary to seek and hold office."[28]

While the candidate's own organization and local party overlap, the key vehicle is the individual's "membership enterprise." Where the local party once supplied candidates with fund-raising assistance, office space, campaign literature, and volunteers to answer the phone and knock on doors in order to turn out supporters on election day, these entrepreneurs now to some extent build their own enterprises and become beholden to their own donors. Furthermore, once elected, candidates have no reason to disband this successful campaign apparatus and every reason to maintain it.[29]

So congressional candidates are obligated primarily to those who comprise their membership enterprise—not to the party. In the case of the presidential-nomination process, the direct primary ushered in similar changes.

Where the state-party leaders historically selected their presidential nominees, now citizens in most states are able to cast ballots for their party nominee. Like the congressional entrepreneurs, presidential candidates, too, must build their own organization. These entrepreneurs will reach out for support from state party and interest-group leaders, but it is not the same. Now, explains political scientist Nelson Polsby, selected state leaders may be invited to participate in a candidate's campaign; no longer is the candidate merely a recruit and representative of the state party.[30] Presidential and congressional candidates thus must each strike their own political bargains de novo on each issue, and are less likely to represent a broad party position. This fragmentation of the competition of ideas has left elected officials without the protection of the party organization that in earlier times might have permitted them to vote their conscience on controversial issues.

Interest Groups as Political Intermediaries

The weakening of the parties is reflected also both in the success enjoyed by interest groups in partially or wholly preempting voter mobilization and other party functions and in the growth of the number and scope of interest-group activities. These groups (and social movements too) are important for the nation, but political interest groups and social movements have a single motivation as organizations—to achieve the goals of their exclusive membership by exercising influence on government. They achieve those goals through dispensing information, money, and, where possible, grassroots support. Their organization may frequently act in the public interest, but their membership feels under no such obligation, as it single-mindedly pursues its self-interest. The hope of pluralists is that the public interest will emerge from the clash of self-interested groups in the marketplace of ideas as a byproduct of the competition for public support. Sometimes the public interest does emerge in this fashion, but the distinction between public-interest and self-interest is easily blurred. Most people would endorse the view that GM contributes significantly to the U.S. economy, but few would endorse former GM president Engine Charlie Wilson's recollection in 1952 congressional testimony that "for years I thought what was good for our country was good for General Motors, and vice versa. The difference did not exist."[31]

Business and Professional Interest-Group Power

Jack Walker estimates that 80 percent of the nation's interest groups emerged from preexisting business and other occupational or professional communities, while 20 percent developed "in the wake of broad social movements concerned with such problems as the level of environmental pollution, threats to civil rights, or changes in the status of women."[32] Many of these groups primarily exercise their influence in Washington, D.C., which frequently suffices on those issues relatively invisible to the electorate—particularly since incumbent lawmakers and presidents from both parties can gain campaign contributions from these groups at the bargain political price of simply not bringing issues to the attention of an unaware electorate. Interest groups working politically at the grassroots level have the most profound impact on voters and, thereby, on parties, as they perform tasks traditionally performed by political parties.

Sometimes interest groups simply utilize a wide range of strategies to push their issues at the grassroots level and thereby impact Congress and the president. For example, journalist William Greider describes the boiler operation of Bonner & Associates, a public-relations firm that included a "boiler room" with three hundred telephones and a sophisticated computer system. As Jack Bonner sees it, "We sit down with the lobbyists and ask: How much heat do you want on these guys? Do you want ten local groups or 200 groups? Do you want 100 phone calls from constituents or a thousand phone calls?" Young people sit in little booths dialing across the country looking for "white hat" citizens who can be persuaded to endorse the political objectives of Dow Chemical, the Pharmaceutical Manufacturers Association, or Bonner's other numerous corporate clients. Some of these local opinion leaders are presumably flattered to be asked, since even they rarely have an opportunity to take a stand on any of the grander issues. So, Greider explains, "in a twisted sense, Jack Bonner does what political parties used to do for citizens—he educates and agitates, and mobilizes." But these contacted citizens are being manipulated rather than engaging in democratic expression. They are fed "facts" that are debatable, through a one-sided phone conversation designed to serve narrow corporate lobbying strategies, not free debate.[33]

More often, though, the large, wealthy interest groups know that Congress and the president are most likely to get the message when they hear it on the hustings rather than through the mail, telephone, or the Internet. The National Education Association Political Action Committee (NEA-PAC) employs numerous strategies on behalf of its 2.1 million NEA members. In addition to contributing more than $2 million to congressional candidates in 1992, it put another $2 million into state and national political parties and also developed its own TV ads and public-opinion polls, distributed political training manuals, and participated in get-out-the-vote efforts and member-contact programs. NEA-PAC believes, according to its PAC director, that its strongest asset is its ability to conduct campaign activity, and it has a large number of members willing to participate in person-to-person campaigning and perform other labor-intensive campaign tasks.[34]

The dramatic impact of grassroots interest groups on presidential and congressional electoral politics was captured by a major 1996 *Time* article that trumpeted the "new party bosses." Not a single one of these bosses had ever toiled for a party. Rather, they included the leaders of such mass-based organizations as the AFL-CIO, NRA, and the National Federation of Independent Business; social movements such as pro-choice and right-to-life; and funding networks backed by Hollywood moguls, the Association of Trial Lawyers of America, EMILY's List, and the cigarette industry.[35]

The power of these national pressure groups with grassroots organizations lies in their command of the human, financial, organizational, and technical resources to project their political power into congressional districts. In doing so, they are on a par with the national parties. Republican campaign consultant Mary Matalin thus describes how Rich Bond turned the Republican National Committee (RNC) into a campaign machine by using computers and building and segmenting voter lists in order to "individualize our message. What the labor unions do for the Democratic Party—get mail in people's hands, get people to the polls—Bond, an expert technician, made the RNC and the state parties do for the Republicans."[36] Substituting computers for volunteers may be more scientific, but the price of such efficiency is high, both for democracy and for three-fifths of the country. "It used to be," remarked Lee Ann Elliott, a former chairperson of the Federal Election Commission (FEC), "that a campaign would send information to every voter, and later on they would send it to every person registered in the party of that candidate. All gone. There's no one who sends to everyone. Now it's all targeted because you have to raise the money. Information going to voters is usually linked to a fund-raising effort. So fewer and fewer voters hear from the campaigns of their choice. If they're not givers, they're not on the list."[37]

The meaning of being a local party activist has now somewhat changed. It now often means that local party activists must compete, or join, with the Hessian foot soldiers dispatched to the district or state by *national* interest groups with headquarters often in different states. The politicization of these large-scale interest groups confronts the parties— even where party organizations have remained healthy and have grown— with sophisticated competitors also seeking to control the primary or general election. In these days of candidate-centered elections, the challenge confronting the candidate is to build a coalition including the party and as many of these interest groups as possible. The National Federation of Independent Business, for example, can target small businesses in numerous congressional districts.

Interest-Group Incursions in House and Senate Races

Sometimes the candidates and local parties lose electoral control as the interest groups and national parties wage war in several dozen congressional districts with vulnerable incumbents or two insurgent candidates to determine who will win the House. Similar gymnastics occur in key senate races. In a tight 1992 congressional race in Erie, Pennsylvania, money sluiced in "from all points of the political compass: from national political parties, from state parties, from business, from labor, from liberals, from conservatives, from the candidates themselves." The candidates, as one local media observer said, "didn't know where the next bullet was coming from, and they didn't know if they were firing the gun or it was being shot at them." Observing this outside onslaught, one local TV station owner complained that they "have no interest after the election in how the economy and business of our community will be affected." As if to corroborate the point, interest groups and both national parties relied on "cookie-cutter" television ads that used a similar text and montage across the country, but substituted different faces and subtitles to fit different districts.[38]

Single-issue groups have certainly existed historically. The difference is that in the old days, they were under greater pressure to reach some accommodation with the political party. The parties nominated candidates, financed candidates, worked for candidates, and, through party voting, protected candidates. Today, however, none of those conditions hold. Candidates seek primary nominations and election through contests that the parties no longer control. Interest groups and wealthy individuals provide most of their funds, and workers are assembled by candidates largely through their own ad hoc social, political, and professional networks. As Morris Fiorina explains, "when a contemporary single-issue group threatens to 'get' an officeholder, the threat must be taken seriously. The group can go into his district, recruit a primary or general election challenger, or both, and bankroll that candidate."[39] The threat is credible, because interest groups are no longer reluctant to oppose a candidate openly. Far from attempting to maintain friendly relations with incumbents, these grassroots interest groups are often willing to "use pressure tactics, including explicit threats of electoral revenge against members who oppose their views."[40] The growing ability of these single-purpose, organized groups to inflict electoral pain on those members of Congress who oppose them makes it harder to engage in the time-honored party politics of accommodation and compromise. Under these circumstances, the rise of single-issue groups becomes the flip side of party decline.

The extensiveness of these electoral interest-group incursions is evident from the actions in recent years of the AFL-CIO and the Christian Coalition. Both organizations encountered heavy criticism for their full-court grassroots political press in the mid-1990s, but neither backed off. The Christian Coalition, despite an IRS decision denying it tax-exempt status and staff defections, moved ahead with plans to distribute 75 million voter guides, raised $21 million, and used churches and the Internet to distribute its scorecards for the 2000 presidential campaign.[41]

The Media Is the (Discouraging) Message

The media also increasingly teaches voters about the candidates and issues—hence about the nature of the political system—and performs other political functions. Like interest groups, the media have never deliberately sought to assume such tasks. Teaching voters, for example, is a byproduct of the media's attempt to sell advertising; meet congressional public-service requirements; fulfill their professional obligations as reporters through describing, investigating, and interpreting the news; and, above all, attract an audience.

Conspicuous differences in how the parties and the media have chosen to convey their message to the voters, however, help to explain people's disillusionment with their political system. The parties for their part—at least to the extent that they operate through their local political workers and social networks—have tried to galvanize voters into action. Such mobilization requires that leaders supply activists with a positive message about their candidates and some discussion of issue content as well as strategy. Activists must themselves feel sufficiently comfortable with the content of such a message to convey it to their friends and neighbors. When R. Kenneth Godwin analyzed samples of Republican and Democratic Party direct mailings, he found that they both accentuated loyalty, belonging, and traditional party issues. Both parties stayed away from focusing on a single issue. The reasons were pragmatic. Republican leaders had found that their regular contributors did not respond well to single-issue pitches, while the Democratic leadership too felt that the direct mailing led to extremism and reduced the likelihood of compromise.[42] The media, however, are not engaged in the task of political persuasion, and, thanks to what sells, its message to the voters is inevitably more negative in tone and content. Television has learned that "bad news" is sometimes more effective than "good news" in competing for the attention of the mass audience.[43] Coverage thus will "continue to emphasize the controversial, negative, and unseemly side of politics and the mistakes and failures of politicians."[44]

Just as the media have an economic incentive to stick with a profitable news format, so the individual candidates have a political incentive to use TV to appeal over the heads of the political parties directly to the public. Too often, their winning formula centers around outspending their opposition and running negative ads on television. Neither strategy guarantees election, but more resources win political battles, and negative ads can alter a likely outcome unless they elicit backlash. In the long run these actions create a greater sense of distance between politicians and the public, but in the short run they often can win elections.[45]

Media Ads

The problem is akin to Garrett Hardin's "tragedy of the commons," which has come to symbolize the environment's degradation when many individuals use a scarce resource in common. Hardin uses the example of a pasture "open to all": the individual sheepherder benefits from using the pasture immediately and thereby gains a direct benefit for his own animals; the herder will only later suffer from the delayed costs of allowing the sheep to overgraze. The deterioration of the commons occurs because each herder is motivated to add more and more animals, since that person will receive the direct benefit for his own animals and pay only part of the costs resulting from overgrazing. "Therein is the tragedy. Each man is locked into a system that compels him to increase his herd without limit—in a world that is limited."[46]

Presidential and congressional candidates face a similar choice in deciding whether to "go negative" with their ads. Negative advertisements do not work with all voters. The messages that resonate with Democratic and Republican Party members are those consistent with their partisan belief systems, and such messages stimulate them to vote for their party. The electoral battle, however, is also waged to win the hearts and minds, and votes, of the one-third of the electorate who now are Independent (nonpartisan) voters. Negative advertisements appeal to these voters because they resonate with the already negative view that Independents have of U.S. politicians, government, and political parties.[47] Although the ads ring true to these voters and work in the short run, in the long run, negative advertising breeds not only dissatisfaction with the candidates but also distrust of the electoral process and pessimism about the value of an individual's voice in the political process. Political scientists disagree as to whether negative ads reduce turnout.[48] And on occasion voters have been able to distinguish between useful negative information presented in an appropriate manner and irrelevant and harsh mudslinging.[49] Through positive TV campaigns, candidates can promote their own ideas, successes, and abilities and can rejuvenate nonpartisan voters as well. Such exposure energizes people to vote and raises their confidence in representative government.[50]

Few journalists or political consultants, however, seem concerned about the long-term impact of their actions on the political system.

Professors James A. Thurber and Lewis Wolfson invited a number of these participants to spend a day discussing the provocative question, "Can democracy survive elections?" The result was an exercise in finger-pointing. The press blamed the consultants for sanitizing and almost robotizing their candidate-clients, walling them off from real scrutiny and avoiding unscripted situations. The political consultants described the reporters as "shallow opportunists, totally uninterested in policy ideas, prone to exaggerate conflict or create it where it doesn't exist, and distrustful of everyone's motives but their own." The journalists supported their assertions with a survey of two hundred consultants that found that while they blamed the news media for voter cynicism, they were nearly unanimous in finding nothing wrong in the negative campaigns they devise.[51]

The result of these pressures is that the main participants are engaged in a campaign of long-term mutual destruction. Marshall Ganz thus has argued that there is a direct connection between, on the one hand, the domination of politics by special-interest money, paid attack ads, and strategies driven by polling and focus groups and, on the other hand, the disillusionment of citizens: "The cumulative message of the negative advertising is that *all* the candidates are scoundrels."[52] In a "candidate-centered" age, candidate popularity is nose-diving. Whereas 65 percent of voters' comments about Kennedy and Nixon in 1960 were favorable—when candidates were more closely associated with their parties—in 1988 only 50 percent of the comments about George Bush and Michael Dukakis were positive.[53]

Protecting the Citizens from Journalism

While these circumstances seem to explain the television world of the thirty-second spot and the attack commercial, the problems posed by print journalism and the more serious type of TV reporting are somewhat different. To better understand this problem, it is necessary once again to return to a series of disillusioning events that have occurred since the early 1970s. The Watergate scandal profoundly affected the press's conduct. Two young reporters, Bob Woodward and Carl Bernstein, deeply embarrassed many in the media by uncovering the story that established reporters had missed. Watergate thus shifted the orientation of journalism away from mere description—away from providing an accurate account of happenings—and toward prescription—toward helping to set the campaign's (and society's) agendas by focusing attention on candidate shortcomings and related social problems.[54] Never again would journalists refrain from digging for the facts because they trusted political leaders who ultimately proved unworthy of such trust. Furthermore, the media succeeded in organizing the citizenry against these Watergate abuses (as they have in the case of other abuses). President Nixon, members of the House Judiciary Committee, and interest groups who were seeking the president's impeachment all tried to mobilize the public, but most of the Watergate mail that flooded in has been traced to the impact of television coverage.[55] Civics is thus increasingly taught to the voters by a new, tough-minded brand of investigators writing in the larger newspapers and reporting in a host of *60 Minutes* clones.

While much attention understandably has focused on negative campaign ads, the negativism conveyed by journalists also is destructive, since it comes from a seemingly impartial source. There are more rewards for finding dirt than writing puff pieces, but what is more significant is that these investigative journalists feel professionally obligated to protect the integrity of the political system. They have contempt for politics as usual.[56] In their view, the public can hardly trust political figures who have participated in so many cover-ups or a government that so often lies. Above all, one cannot trust the political parties and the other political and governmental institutions in which these politicians operate. President Johnson even marshaled the national-security apparatus in faking the Gulf of Tonkin incident that precipitated the Vietnam War. The deep-rooted suspicion of our leaders dates back to the late 1960s, when the character, rather than the platform, took center stage. As Larry Sabato explains, the failures of Edward Kennedy, Lyndon Johnson, and Richard Nixon were "not those of intellect but of ethos."[57] By 1998 and the impeachment of President William Clinton, public debate on even that centered around character: perjury and obstruction of justice were the constitutional questions, but character became the issue.

The heavy emphasis on disillusioning events and character flaws has distracted public attention from sustained examination of the issues. The journalistic message implied in disdaining such issue content is that these opportunistic political leaders will say anything to win. So, in the limited time set aside to consider what politicians or other governmental leaders have said, emphasis is placed, instead, on the strategies that lie behind such statements. Why is the politician or government official *really* taking a particular stand?

The news media's emphasis on strategizing is understandable, since politicians and governmental institutions now draw on highly perfected "news management techniques." To counter such managed news, the media must report what the facts really are or, at least, who benefits and who loses from a particular version. Investigative journalism is thus an extreme example of a more fundamental problem confronting all reporters; namely, the need to maintain eternal vigilance.[58] Candidates seeking to win election and reelection despair of conveying their authentic concerns in this strategy-saturated political environment and feel compelled to delegate more of their decisions on issue emphasis and even issue stands to their political consultants. The result is like a "Greek tragedy in which the three main actors—the media, the politicians, and the public—are locked in a vicious circle that none is willing to break."[59] Such strategic issue analysis, therefore, not only conveys a cynical message but also often serves as a substitute for consideration of issue content. The public is provided with an opinion on why a stand was taken without ever learning much about what was actually said or what it meant in a broader context. With few exceptions, journalists no longer believe that, as Jeff Greenfield argued following the 1980 election, "the flow of ideas and the underlying political terrain" had far more to do with Ronald Reagan's victories than all the twists and turns of campaign strategy.[60]

Although journalists justify their strategic emphasis by the need to protect the public from the incursions of the spin doctors, underplaying the importance of ideas and the underreporting of issue content trivializes our politics and denigrates the quality of our democracy. Public debate on such issues should consist of a genuine exchange of views and information. Such dialogue must enable us "to enter imaginatively into our opponents' arguments, if only for the purpose of refuting them, and we may end up being persuaded by those we sought to persuade. Argument is risky and unpredictable and therefore educational."[61] Such political discussions pay more attention to whether a given policy would actually solve the problem it addresses.[62] Studies show, furthermore, that the public is concerned with the moral impact of such problems and issues on people.[63] This moral dimension—and its meaning for the citizen personally—is largely ignored thanks to the underemphasis on issue content and ideas. We need more investigative reporting of the several dimensions of the candidate's *ideas* as well as strategies. It is not that the media is wrong in digging for the truth, but, rather, that its version of the truth is too limited.

Given the nature and spirit of the message conveyed by the media, the public, not surprisingly, has chosen to shoot the messenger along with the targets of such reporting. Perhaps it is poetic justice that in the public's perception, the news media now are scorned along with politicians. Since 1996, public confidence in Congress, the press, and television has trended downward.[64] More significantly, however, the motivations, goals, and incentives propelling these journalists prevent them from effectively mobilizing the electorate and performing most of the other political tasks formerly handled by parties (see Figure 2.1).

The Grassroots Challenge for Local Parties

While the dangers of allowing the interest groups and media to perform the electoral tasks of the political parties are patent, few would argue that the political parties, particularly in the modern era, have themselves performed

Figure 2.1   Overlapping Functions Performed by Political Parties, Interest Groups, and the Media in the U.S. Political System

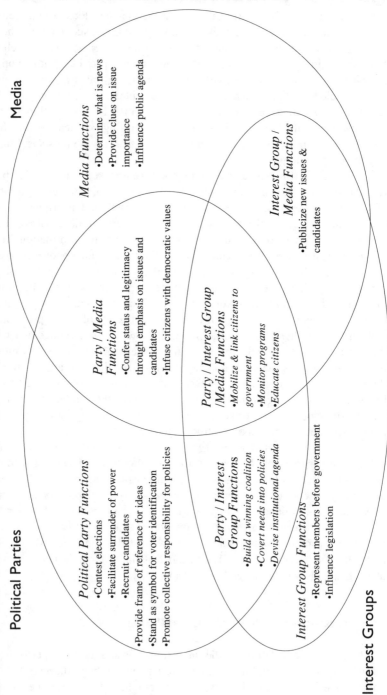

Political Parties

Media

Interest Groups

Media Functions
•Determine what is news
•Provide clues on issue importance
•Influence public agenda

Political Party Functions
•Contest elections
•Facilitate surrender of power
•Recruit candidates
•Provide frame of reference for ideas
•Stand as symbol for voter identification
•Promote collective responsibility for policies

Party / Media Functions
•Confer status and legitimacy through emphasis on issues and candidates
•Infuse citizens with democratic values

Party / Interest Group /Media Functions
•Mobilize & link citizens to government
•Monitor programs
•Educate citizens

Interest Group / Media Functions
•Publicize new issues & candidates

Party / Interest Group Functions
•Build a winning coalition
•Covert needs into policies
•Devise institutional agenda

Interest Group Functions
•Represent members before government
•Influence legislation

these functions well. Indeed, the parties' diminution may be seen both in terms of their inability to dominate nominations and elections and their reduced inclination and capacity to mobilize voters. The strategic choices that political parties, candidates, and grassroots interest groups and other interest groups make in deciding whom to mobilize—and whom not to mobilize—influence turnout. Such mobilization choices have an important impact not only on the decision to vote but also on the decision to participate in other forms of political behavior such as trying to influence how other people vote and contributing money to a political party or candidate. These strategic choices are manifested through *direct* mobilization, "when leaders contact citizens personally and encourage them to take action," and through *indirect* mobilization, "when leaders contact citizens through mutual associates, whether family, neighbors, or colleagues."[65] Given the electorate's size, indirect mobilization is particularly important.

Whether such mobilization is direct or indirect, the personal contact achieved through these social networks provides the information that saves time the voter would otherwise need to spend becoming informed on the issues and overcomes the citizen's feeling of ignorance on political and economic matters. Such mobilization also can supply the incentive to overcome the nagging feeling that the election will turn out the same whether or not a solitary citizen casts a ballot and to revive that fading sense of a citizen's duty to vote. Voters came to appreciate what their votes can mean as a result of the cliffhanger 2000 election results in several states, though this realization unfortunately came only during the prolonged vote count after the polls had closed.

When friends, family, neighbors, or colleagues contact the citizen, they convey a social expectation of desirable behavior—an expectation that people want to meet in order to continue enjoying the respect of their friends and colleagues. Voting thereby becomes a small price to pay for such social rewards. In short, "citizens feel an obligation to help people they like, people they identify with, people like them, and people who have helped them in the past."[66]

Party Mobilization

Parties mobilize voters to win elections, but, when functioning effectively, they differ from all other political organizations in having something to gain from mobilizing in every state and locality on a sustained basis to build a majority citizen coalition around important electoral issues. The parties seek through such *mobilization* to convey a partisan message to as many of their own partisans and as many undecided voters as possible. This partisan mobilization involves broad appeals often conveyed through personal conversation with local party workers. The result of such mobilization from the party's viewpoint is a heavy turnout of eligible voters across the board who are unambiguously casting a ballot for their political party.

Whatever the motives of the mass-based parties for seeking out the voters in election after election, such mobilization offers an opportunity for citizens of all political persuasions to discuss the issues and candidates. Furthermore, when such dialogue occurs in *their* neighborhoods, citizens do so with people of similar backgrounds in whom they are more likely to place some degree of trust. Supplying political support may help them, too, since they are similarly positioned in the society.

Mobilization and Citizen Participation

Political parties were more involved with such mobilization in earlier years; in recent decades, such personal contact and mobilization through social networks has declined. This decline has evoked little concern among citizens or journalists. Steven J. Rosenstone and John Mark Hansen, however, found that "the changing pattern of mobilization by parties, campaigns, and social movements *accounts for at least half of the decline in electoral participation since the 1960s.*"[67] The very nature of voter contact by these mediating institutions, particularly at the national level, has changed. This has been especially true of political parties that contacted proportionally fewer citizens, as campaigns abandoned the labor-intensive canvassing methods of the 1960s for the money-intensive media strategies of the 1980s.[68]

This connection between mobilization and political participation provides a powerful explanation of the decline in U.S. electoral turnout. To understand why, it is necessary to spend a moment exploring the types of rewards and reasons why some people are more likely to participate politically than others. Two kinds of rewards motivate citizens to participate. Collective rewards benefit every resident of a particular place or member of a group: a clean-air bill, for example, may benefit every resident of New York or Denver, but individuals will receive such collective rewards regardless of whether they personally participate politically. Selective rewards, in contrast, benefit only the political participant. Selective rewards may take a material form (such as a government job), a social form, (such as recognition for being a neighborhood leader), or that sense of purpose that comes from helping in a worthy cause or doing one's civic duty. Given the decline in material rewards to voters, selective social rewards are of increased importance. Mobilization by friends and colleagues is especially important for citizens who vote sporadically. Mobilizing citizens to vote is of particular interest because voting links citizens to other forms of political participation and because citizen turnout has declined so precipitously.

The linkage between participation and mobilization of voters individually is important for several reasons. First, in a media age especially, it underscores the importance of person-to-person contact with voters by active, local political elites. Second, personal contact can obviate the voter's feeling of not benefiting individually from the rewards that government provides to society collectively; contact between the voter and an opinion leader in a social network provides social and intrinsic rewards to friends and neighbors. Third, in mobilizing friends, neighbors, and colleagues, opinion leaders take the initiative in providing valuable information about the election to citizens who often pay little attention to politics. These political activists thereby remove from the citizen's shoulders the need to gather such information themselves and thus make voting a less painful and more likely act.[69] Fourth, the focus on mobilization as a social act emphasizes the critical role of political elites in stimulating mass participation. No longer is the onus for reduced citizen participation attributed solely to diffident citizens. In numerous cases, it stems from the failure of political elites either to canvass people directly or, by building the local organizations and creating the opportunities for popular electoral participation, to encourage them indirectly to vote. Finally, the emphasis on mobilization both pinpoints the problem of low turnout and, within its analysis, hints at a possible *political* solution for dealing with a significant amount of that low turnout—namely, by increasing the amount of party mobilization activity.

It must be noted, however, that the electoral turnout of those not mobilized varies on an election-by-election basis. Postelection surveys indicate that there is a link between contact by a political party (or another mediating institution) and the decision to vote, but lack of contact cannot be identified as the sole reason for declining voter turnout. Personally contacted citizens indeed are more likely to vote, but turnout rates for other citizens also fluctuate from election to election. In 1992, for example, only 20 percent claimed that they were contacted, but turnout was higher than in 1980. Four years later, more citizens—29 percent—were contacted, but overall turnout still fell some 6 percent from 1992.[70] Unlike the 1960s, however, in 1996 social movements and interest groups were no longer reaching out to as many unaffiliated citizens. Turnout fell from 62 percent of the voting age population in 1964 to literally half of the electorate in 1996 and 2000. Much was made of the small number of voters whose choices did not count in 2000, while little was made of the substantial number of citizens who did not choose to vote.

Expansion of the Conflict

The classic antidote to a large, disengaged public—and hence a weakened party in power—should be heightened competition in a general election or primary. The party out of power identifies appealing candidates and issues and reaches out to those disengaged from the political system. After all, that party is the hungry one, and it is its candidates who have the greatest incentive to mobilize uninvolved voters. Expansion of the conflict potentially could provide the support necessary to tilt the balance against the favored party.[71] Parties thus logically should seek to expand citizen participation not out of a sense of institutional citizen duty but through their competitive drive to win elections. To some extent such mobilization occurs, but the parties and candidates both, even while seeking issues to appeal to more predominantly disengaged voters, must take care that such stands do not jeopardize the goodwill of their contributors or alienate those grassroots interest groups that are now such an integral part of a candidate's nomination, as well as election efforts, and of a party's power. Donna Brazile, Al Gore's campaign manager during the 1999–2000 struggle for the Democratic Party nomination, unintentionally captured the weakened state of her party while imploring the Teamster's president, James P. Hoffa, to endorse her candidate, not Bill Bradley. Up for grabs, she said, "is the heart and soul of the Democratic Party and its foot soldiers."[72]

Interest groups do try to expand the electorate, but only to the extent that it will promote their more limited group goals. Furthermore, interest groups normally engage people who are better-off. The parties have an incentive to involve *anyone* who might support them and, as such, remain the only political institution whose self-interest at least potentially can be aligned with the needs of the disengaged. The reduced capacity of the political parties to mobilize the disengaged today perhaps can be seen best by examining how mobilization has changed in recent years and why the power of grassroots interest groups has grown in national political campaigns.

The Changing Nature of Party Mobilization

The changes in citizen contact with mediating political institutions are neatly defined by Steven Schier in his distinction between *mobilization* and *actualization*. *Mobilization* signifies the partisan method of stimulating high turnout in elections. This partisanship reached its zenith during the period of peak political-party power that lasted from 1876 to 1892. Schier then uses the term *activation* to describe "the more contemporary methods that parties, interest groups and candidates employ to induce particular, finely targeted portions of the public to become active in elections, demonstrations, and lobbying."[73]

Mobilization vs. Activation

Partisan mobilization is inclusive in its focus, seeking to arouse all possible voters through its direct partisan message. Conversely, candidates, interests, and consultants engaged in activation focus only on those carefully identified segments of the public most likely to become active on their behalf and then employ a variety of inducements to activate those segments. The 1998 election exemplifies this limited focus.

Anticipating that most voters would stay home, "turnout experts" from both parties looked past the uninvolved majority and focused instead on computer printouts of those most likely to vote. They were then divided into microtargets with labels such as "100-percent Democrats" and "Couch-potato Dems." "You're trying to sort out the grass from the weeds," explained a Democratic consultant engaged in the campaign, "collect the most data and figure out how many voters you can get out of these little clusters." Computer software programs with names like Turnout Advantage, Smart Select, and Vote Predictor accurately gauge the probability that a citizen will vote. At the beginning of the twentieth century, mobilization was a heavily partisan process dominated by strong political parties and even a partisan press. Now, literally thousands of different interest groups, candidate organizations, and consultants working on behalf of such groups and candidates are involved in activation. The parties continue to send a message during elections, but too often it is lost in the numerous activation appeals coming from the dizzying array of other agents competing for the citizen's attention.

The mobilization and activation processes also differ in their methods. Partisan mobilization involved broad appeals often conveyed through personal conversation with local party workers. By contrast, activation is research-driven by polling and focus groups.[74] With citizens less committed to the parties, already in the 1980s Thomas Edsell could write that a fluid and more malleable electorate placed a premium on such campaign technologies as polling and the precise application of demographic information and precinct voting histories to television commercials, issue selection, and more targeted mailings.[75] In focusing too exclusively on those most likely to vote, activation strategies today are the antithesis of the inclusive partisan mobilization practiced by the parties in their heydey. Furthermore, the term *mobilization* must be reserved for a richer form of two-way dialogue in which not only are the views of elites conveyed to the citizens, but also, through the medium of the local, state, and national party mechanism, citizen opinions are conveyed to the elites.

Public Talk

Just what constitutes such public dialogue today is a nice question. Such views, though, are not the product of a random sample of voters consulted on a one-time basis in a focus group or a supermarket survey; rather, they are the result of periodic dialogue, between as well as during elections—dialogues in which citizens test their ideas in informal conversations with others at work, around the kitchen table, and in civic groupings as well as in political organizations. When testing their ideas in this fashion, citizens are engaged in what David Mathews calls "public talk"—citizens conversing together. These discussions can take place on buses and in coffee shops, over the kitchen table, and in public forums. People being curious about how others interpret events and think about policy questions, the public dialogues drawing the most positive reactions would be those in which people could hold strong opinions without "everyone always contesting what someone else said."[76]

Neither the elites nor the public seem to be living up to their part of this democratic challenge. In the absence of a sufficient number of such public forums and sufficient media attention, though, even the attempts of responsible politicians from both parties to convey important information seemingly fall on deaf ears. Representative John Spratt, for example, during his 1996 election campaign tried to inform everyone in his district over age sixty-five about the Medicare debate. He had his office mail a brochure that he wrote on the subject but later recalled that no more than "a dozen people mentioned it to me." "Maybe it had an impact that I didn't know, but my campaign consultants keep telling me that people just don't read much of that stuff anymore. It comes in the mail, and they get a lot of junk mail."[77] Bill Bradley sounded a similar note of frustration in bemoaning the surrender of the role previously played by party organizations with their face-to-face associations to the media. The rule of thumb for local TV news is, "If it bleeds, it leads, and if it thinks, it stinks," and politicians now run campaigns that "short-circuit deliberative judgment. People sit at home as spectators, wait to be entertained by candidates in 30-second pre-polled, pre-tested emotional appeals, and then render a thumbs up or a thumbs down almost on a whim. . . . Public opinion does not result from reasoned dialogue, but from polls that solicit knee-jerk responses from individuals who have seldom had the opportunity to reflect on Bosnia, GATT, property taxes, or public education in the company of their fellow citizens."[78]

Ignoring the Politically Passive Citizens

Reliance on activation strategies also explains why—even allowing for the normal tendency of better-educated voters to cast their ballots—a disproportionate number of the voters come from the higher educational and income strata. Consumer products and services have become more differentiated in response to more sophisticated consumer demands, and so in politics, too, entrepreneurial candidates heed the special pleadings of attentive publics.[79] The better-off may be just as cynical about politics as their less fortunate brethren, but they are accustomed to participating in government in exchange for material benefits. So organizations employing activation strategies are more likely to focus on identifying niche markets to turn out their often predominantly upper–middle and upper-class members even while they ignore the majority of passive citizens. Rather than politics providing a forum for greater citizen equality, that 40 percent of the population that is better-off economically also is encouraged through activation strategies to become more engaged politically.

One would think that elections would become cheaper as the number of voters declines and as more political interest groups rush to fill the vacuum created by the shrinking electoral power of political parties. However, labor-intensive politics was largely voluntary. Capital-intensive politics involves strenuous activity among well-paid professional political elites competing through their organizations for favorable decisions on specific issues, for influence in the various issue arenas, and—in the case of larger interest groups—for a voice at the highest levels of the executive branch and the Congress. Furthermore, thanks to the frantic activity created by so many political interest groups and candidate organizations busily carving up issues and fragmenting the electorate, it costs more to be heard. To the extent that candidates and organizations play the new political game of big money, niche markets, television images, and activation strategies, the costs go up as voter turnout goes down.

The Impact of Grassroots Interest Groups

All candidates, parties, and interest groups find themselves compelled to mix-and-match mobilization and activation strategies. It is instructive, however, to note who the biggest political winners are today, and how they do it. Large, well-organized grassroots interest groups historically have often allied themselves with political parties. Today, however, they loom even larger because they possess the competitive advantage that comes from combining the financial clout and professional expertise of the new politics with the organizational capability to provide precious campaign foot soldiers. These grassroots interest groups mobilize their memberships—people who derive material and sometimes social, psychological, or ideological benefits from their organizations and stand ready and willing to work for leaders they trust and organizational goals they share. The good news is that these groups can beef up local and state parties with the resources to directly and indirectly mobilize voters. The bad news is that while some of these organizational recruits also identify with the party, most presumably identify with those who brought them to the dance.

Today such interest groups sometimes set the tone for party activity at the local and occasionally even the state level and are able to influence parties to accept their position even when the party would be better advised, when considering the general electorate's views, to take a different stance. There are, however, limits even to the influence of grassroots interest groups.

The Christian Right sparked fears in the early 1990s among some traditional Republican constituencies that it would dominate the Republican Party. However, in 1994 it was unable to extend much beyond those eighteen states where a large and geographically concentrated Evangelical Protestant constituency provided a base for it to capture the state-party organizations.[80] Nonetheless, in 1996 it funded contacts with an estimated three million voters and distributed about 46 million voter guides, typically at churches on the Sunday before the election.[81]

The AFL-CIO, under its militant president John Sweeney, has played a similarly visible role in the Democratic Party. It caused a stir in 1996 when it committed $25 million to highly confrontational ads attacking Republican congressional candidates and $10 million to political organization resources.[82] It derived these funds from a monthly assessment on each of the labor federation's seventy-eight unions of 15 cents per capita.[83] The result was that union households accounted for almost one-quarter of the total House vote in 1996 (up from 14 percent in 1994). According to exit polls, 63 percent of those voters cast Democratic ballots in the House races.[84] Republicans outspent Democrats and their union allies seven to one in voter-education programs, but these business organizations could not match the AFL-CIO grassroots effort.[85]

Like the Christian Coalition's grassroots effort, the AFL-CIO also concentrated on registering, educating, and mobilizing its own members on those issues of particular concern to its own organization. It, too, attracted suspicion not only from Republicans but also from the many "new" Democrats who are placed some distance from the party's left wing. For their part, some labor leaders expressed concern that labor was financially overextended.[86] The AFL-CIO thus reduced its congressional campaign spending in 1998 to about $20 million but retained its grassroots thrust and even increased the number of its labor coordinators in the field from 130 to 300, with teams of two or three committed to districts with hot races. Sweeney thus emphasized that the prospect for success lay in having thousands of labor volunteers talk with other union members in the workplace or at home. "Our strongest suit is going to be how many members we can mobilize, how many activists we can involve in the political campaign."[87]

These alliances give pause to those disengaged voters who are dubious about labor unions or the Christian Coalition, thereby pushing them further from the parties and the political process. The labor unions, the Christian Coalition, and other such grassroots electoral groups thereby come to occupy, particularly at the primary stage, a more powerful position on a shrunken political playing field. The balance of power has shifted, as parties have failed to match the growth in number, size, and power particularly of their large allies in our "interest group society." In order to take advantage of their grassroots clout, the candidates thus must reach some accommodation with these interest-group allies who supply a number of activists and amount of money greater than their electoral size.

In addition, primaries attract those voters who feel more strongly about the issues—a disproportionate number of card-carrying Democratic liberals and card-carrying Republican conservatives. Small wonder that in 1996 the candidates were faced with the imperative "to win some interest-group constituencies or increase the risk of being an also-ran." Just as the liberal Democratic candidates thus courted big labor, virtually all conservative Republican presidential candidates in the 1996 election "made a very public effort to associate themselves with the concerns of the Christian Coalition."[88]

The Promise and Limitations of Political Grassroots Interest Groups

The unintended consequence of the direct primary then is to select through a popular vote candidates who are less representative of the party and electorate even than in the days of the much-vilified party bosses. The bosses at least often sought to maintain local political control by dressing up the top of the ticket with candidates possessing widespread appeal. The direct primary ushered in candidate-centered politics, which forces those running for office to assume more extreme ideological positions in order to appeal to grassroots interest groups, thereby distancing themselves from the majority of voters who are more moderate but less likely to vote. Rightly or wrongly, these particular groups lack legitimacy in the eyes of many people. The net result of these alliances between single-purpose interest groups and candidates is to increase suspicion of politics.

Furthermore, thanks to their power within the parties today, these grassroots interest groups are often less willing to temper their demands to facilitate building a winning coalition. The parties thus become more collections of interests than partnerships with mutual goals. Such an interest-group coalition may seemingly broaden the party but can actually undermine its agenda. Interest-group activity within the Democratic Party coalition during the Carter administration, for example, was so much in conflict with so many cross-pressures that the result was ideologically incoherent and invisible and ultimately offered "little or nothing positive to the lower half of the American population."[89]

Grassroots interest groups, nonetheless, perform several important societal functions. First, they serve as a training ground for members to acquire political skills, representing their views in the democratic competition of ideas and raising ideas sometimes in opposition to the prevailing views of those in power. Second, such mass-based and other interest groups also serve as organizational bulwarks for democracy in preventing the state or any single source of private power from dominating all political resources.[90] Third, interest groups allow for the expression of new ideas and concern about large, politically unattended matters, such as the menace of air pollution or the rising aspirations of blacks for political equality. In the case of black equality, it was interest groups (and the courts)—not the parties—that, one hundred years after the Civil War, aired these grievances. Fourth, public-interest groups and social movements reveal a generous spirit in pushing concerns about safety, the environment, social regulation, or social welfare that provide no specific benefits to them personally.[91] For these professionals, worshipers, and others, the primary motivation is service, not self-interest. Fifth, interest groups sometimes are formed around those issues that do not conform well with the ideological fault lines within the polity created by the party system. Politicians seek to avoid issues that divide their followers, so party leaders cannot be relied upon to deal with problems sometimes important to a growing number of people. When interest groups begin to attract resources and attention to their causes, the parties are forced to alter their programs and reformulate their supporting coalitions to accommodate to shifts in the public's principal concerns. In this sense the parties are complementary and together constitute a more responsive and adaptive system than either interest groups or the parties could provide alone.[92]

Even when grassroots interest groups have muscled their way into a disproportionally strong party position, they cannot always exercise enough power to get what they want. Organized labor has sought to pass national health insurance for two decades without success, and some of the Christian coalition leaders were so frustrated over their failure to gain passage for their social agenda that, in 1999, they considered abandoning the political arena. Win, lose, or draw, however, interest-group issues tend to dominate the public agenda.

Conclusion

Historically, interest groups have served as the vehicles—or factions—of the better-off in areas where their single-minded focus on their own goals leaves other people ambivalent. "On the one hand," observes John Hansen, "we sympathize with interest groups because they *represent* popular demands, in many cases better than parties or unassisted public officials. On the other hand, we distrust interest groups because they represent only *some* demands, and by no means the most popular. Interest groups are both democratic and elitist institutions."[93] It therefore is not surprising that interest groups ultimately retain much of the stigma of factions in relation to the general interest, while parties are distinguished from factions by the broader purposes and roles that they are supposed to fulfill. The party is a part of a whole attempting to serve the purposes of the whole, whereas a faction is a part of a whole out only for itself.[94]

3

The Once-and-Future Party

Multipurpose political parties, like single-purpose interest groups, as they seek to gain acceptance for their principles, are on the make: so is there really much difference? Furthermore, parties, like grassroots interest groups, are essentially voluntary organizations: so they, too, must cater to the personal motivations of their active workers.

When it comes to principles, various critics have accused parties and their stalwarts alternatively of not caring enough about principles or of caring too much. Citizens often claim not to see a dime's worth of a difference between the parties on the issues. For their part, some political scientists argue that in the old days the "professionals" working in the parties indeed would compromise in exchange for patronage and other forms of material gain. Not so the "amateurs," who with such rewards largely gone now often dominate the party at the local level. Motivated by a strong concern about the issues, it is said, these zealots, too, often place their own principles ahead of the voters' policy preferences, thereby undercutting the likelihood of victory.[1] The parties cannot win. In their detractors' eyes the local, state, and national party leadership ranks are filled either with unprincipled louts or workers obsessed with their principles. Meanwhile, from the political wilderness, a few faint voices can be heard protesting that party leaders often seek to balance principle and victory. Which is the true story?

In Pursuit of Principle and Victory

In a 1960 study, Herbert McClosky and his colleagues raised two questions as important for parties today as then: Is there any difference between the parties? Where the parties possess strongly held views, are they willing to compromise in order to "broker" the necessary combination of interest groups and individual supporters to win elections? Thanks to this study and several others done since, it is possible to answer both questions with confidence.

Tweedledum and Tweedledee

In the nationwide survey of party leaders and supporters that McClosky launched, party leaders were defined as those attending the Democratic and Republican National Conventions. This sampling ranged from governors, senators, and national-committee persons to precinct workers and local activists. Rank-and-file party members were drawn from a special Gallup poll of voters. The opinions of these party leaders and members were sought on a wide range of issues, including government regulation of the economy, tax policy, and social welfare. With only a few exceptions, the polls consistently showed Democratic and Republican followers far less divided than their leaders. As for the leaders, it is remarkable how many of the issues separating the two parties' leaders in 1960 continue to separate them today. Republican leaders then were most united on issues stemming from the party's connection with business—government regulation, corporate taxes, regulation of trade unions, and minimum wage legislation. The Democratic leaders in 1960 were most united on those issues bearing on lower- and middle-income groups—taxes on small and middle incomes, antimonopoly, Social Security, and minimum wages.[2] There were occasional issues where party members supported or opposed a particular issue in larger proportions, but the pattern was clear: Republican and Democratic leaders were more united in their views on those issues that distinguished the parties, and these differences fell roughly along a conservative–liberal spectrum.

Subsequent surveys of Republican and Democratic leaders and followers in the 1970s and 1980s identified a similar pattern of responses.[3] Jeane Kirkpatrick, in a 1972 study of convention delegates, placed the Democratic and Republican Party members relatively close together in the center ideologically; the party leaders took stronger liberal and conservative positions.[4] After surveying 1988 convention delegates, Michael Kagay concluded that party activists were more polarized on the issues than either the public as a whole or party members.[5]

A series of polls done in 1988 (see Table 3.1) provides a more recent example of how the views of Republican and Democratic convention delegates and party members related on a series of domestic and foreign issues. Again there are a few cases where party members are for or against a particular issue more often than the delegates, but the overall pattern of responses here is consistent with the earlier studies. Furthermore, while a number of questions have changed over the many years since the McClosky study, certain themes persist. Just as the 1956 Democratic delegates most frequently saw the need for enforcement of integration, so too in 1988 it is the Democratic delegates who in larger numbers than the Democratic Party

Table 3.1   Republicans and Democrats in 1988: The Differences on Issues Between Delegates and the Rank and File

Question: I am going to read a few statements. After each, please tell me if you agree with the statement or disagree with it, or if, perhaps, you have no opinion about that statement. (The figures below show the percentage who agreed with the statement.)

	Rep. Delegates	Dem. Delegates	Republicans	Democrats	All Voters
A. The Equal Rights Amendment should be ratified.	29%	90%	56%	74%	64%
B. Black people in the U.S. are still a long way from having the same chance in life that white people have.	45%	83%	60%	48%	53%
C. The government should raise taxes now as one means of dealing with the federal budget deficit.	8%	44%	26%	36%	31%
D. There is nothing wrong with using the CIA to support governments that are friendly to the U.S. and to undermine hostile foreign governments.	65%	21%	56%	38%	46%
E. Large corporations have too much power for the good of the country.	14%	67%	66%	79%	73%
F. We should stop building nuclear power plants because of safety and waste problems.	10%	61%	48%	63%	55%
G. The military draft should be reinstituted.	26%	22%	37%	37%	37%
H. There should be a constitutional amendment outlawing abortion.	36%	6%	36%	35%	35%
I. The government should institute and operate a national health care program.	15%	82%	61%	83%	72%

Note: Figures are from a *Washington Post* telephone poll of 501 Republican delegates from July 26 to August 6, 504 Democratic delegates from June 21 to July 10, and a *Washington Post*/ABC News telephone poll of 1,147 registered voters from July 6–11, including 560 self-identified Democrats and independents leaning toward the Democratic Party and 501 Republicans and Republican leaners. Margin of sampling error is plus or minus 5 percentage points for figures based on delegates, and 3 points for figures based on all voters.

members or the Republican delegates or party members feel that "black people in the United States are still a long way from having the same chance in life that white people have." Just as the 1956 Republican delegates more strongly opposed increasing taxes on upper-income people than the other three groups, so today they more often disagree with the statement that "the government should raise taxes now as one means of dealing with the federal budget deficit."

The Party Will to Win

Unlike the general public, thanks to such strong partisan leader opinions, the parties do not merely represent Tweedledum and Tweedledee. The studies show that party workers and leaders in both parties possess more consistent belief systems than party members or independents. Does that mean that, like their counterparts in more ideological parties, these leaders will insist on stubbornly hewing the party line through thick and thin—or, where necessary, are these party elites prepared to moderate their belief systems and move toward the center in order to win elections?

The answer depends on whether they are willing to alter such views after the electorate has voiced its displeasure with their issue stands. Here the evidence suggests that U.S. party leaders are, with some notorious exceptions, generally less ideological. Party leaders certainly have taken positions at odds with the popular view when they thought that a new leader, congenial to their viewpoint, could sway the electorate. The ill-fated campaigns of Republican conservative presidential candidate Barry Goldwater in 1964 and of liberal Democratic presidential candidate George McGovern in 1972 come to mind. Goldwater echoed the sirens' call in his presidential nomination acceptance speech: "Extremism in the defense of liberty is no vice. And . . . moderation in the pursuit of justice is no virtue." In each case, however, after the party suffered resounding electoral defeat, subsequent polls of party leaders showed that they did shift their views in a more moderate direction.

Party Activist Responsiveness to Voter Concerns

Examination of the same party leaders over more than one election reveals that they proved responsive to voter demands and did not cling stubbornly to their belief systems or refuse to participate in electoral campaigns unless the candidates closely reflected their views. One such survey of the issue stands of county and state chairs, national committee members, and convention delegates in the 1980 and 1984 elections found that on several issues (e.g., defense spending) the parties continued to perform as mediating institutions in a two-party system. There was substantial evidence that elites from both parties moderated their views and moved toward the shifting center of gravity.[6] Nonetheless, there were a few issues (e.g., the advisability of detente) where leaders in both parties moved in the same direction even while there was little change in public opinion. Eventually the public might be persuaded by government actions in such areas, but in the meantime, the leaders were clearly acting as an elite at variance with public attitudes.

Both Democratic and Republican Party activists in Los Angeles during the 1960s and 1970s consistently differed in their views. They thereby offered meaningful alternatives to the voters and were able and willing to shift their own issue stances in response to shifting voter preferences. These activists, wanting to affect policy, have a voice in party affairs, and win elections, did not indulge themselves in voicing uncritically expressed hopes or wishes. Rather, their expectations were linked to what voters want, and their preferences were tempered by those expectations.[7] But not only did these party organization leaders differ in their views—more significantly, they shared a desire to win elections. A large survey of delegates who attended party conventions in eleven states during the 1980 Democratic and Republican presidential nominating campaigns concluded that "winning may not be everything, but it's more than we thought." When asked questions to determine whether electability or ideology weighed more heavily in their selection of a nominee, leaders in both parties opted consistently for electability. They realized that compromising some of their ideological interests in order to have a better chance of winning is preferable to maintaining strict ideological purity and suffering defeat.

Nor must compromise inevitably mean abandonment of party principle. After all, giving the voters a choice, rather than an echo or a "me too" candidate, is sometimes a pragmatic strategy.[8] These activists are in any event willing to strike a bargain. The importance of issue concerns to these activists did not undermine their attachment to their party.[9]

Choices that Distance Parties and Elected Officials from Voters

Candidates and state- and national-party leaders must, however, also make three choices that often temper their issue stances to satisfy other groups who are strategically located to make demands on the party in exchange for their support—wealthy individuals, professional and business campaign supporters, and interest groups. First, some wealthy contributors give for ideological reasons. One survey thus found that a number of well-informed donors felt strongly about the issues and sought candidates who supported their ideological positions. These Republican donors often appear well to the right of less involved Republican Party members and independent voters; the ideological Democratic Party donors for their part are well to the left.[10] Prior to the 1994 election and in the following year, when the Gingrich revolution was at its height, a new breed of these ideological Republican donors streamed into the party. The relative positions of party members, leaders, and activists are shown in figure 3.1.

Such Republican donors were at odds not only with the party membership but with the party establishment that had bankrolled past elections. Journalists Jill Abramson and David Rogers described these zealous supporters of less government, less taxation, and less regulation, as "younger, less establishment, more ideological, and more willing to attempt a revolutionary change in government than the denizens of the Business Roundtable." These supporters are far smaller in number than the numerous small-business donors who contribute $200 or less to the party, the traditional Republican establishment givers, and the business executives who pragmatically contribute to both parties. These more radical donors, though, sometimes supply big bucks. For example, they dominated one 1995 gala dinner honoring Newt Gingrich and Robert Dole where close to $10 million was collected—the largest amount at that point ever collected at such an event.[11]

In following the money in the 1994 election, Theodore Eismeier and Philip Pollock found that "the positions of both parties were hardened not only by ideology but also by cash. Their sharply different visions—one of malevolent government and one of munificent government—resonate well with different financial constituencies. The problem is that neither resonates with 'the great anxious middle of the U.S. electorate.'"[12] These ideologues thus represent something of a mixed blessing for the parties and candidates. The recipients crave the money, but in order to attract it they must move further toward the two ends of the political spectrum and away from that vote-rich "anxious middle." It seems likely that the radical donors' growing numbers and ideological bent have contributed to the trend toward greater partisanship and growing polarization across the board between the parties that, according to roll call analyses undertaken by veteran observers, increasingly have separated the two parties since President Ronald Reagan's second term.[13]

Numerous other donors expect tangible support from the federal government—through their political connections—in the form of contracts, tax concessions, or regulatory changes. For these high rollers, party victory is relevant primarily where it increases the likelihood of material gain. The existence of such a moneyed crowd is hardly new—its power has ebbed and flowed through historical periods of rapacity and reform. But donor power has increased both with the growing size of campaign war chests and with the increased opportunities that come with a federal budget that now represents more than one-quarter of the nation's gross domestic product.

Figure 3.1 The Liberal-Conservative Political Spectrum

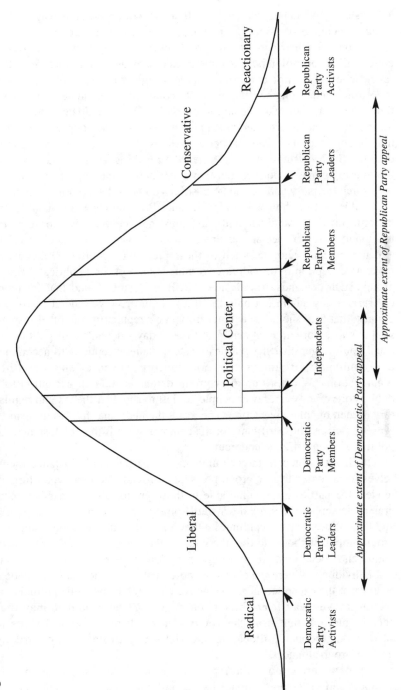

The visibility of such ideological and financial donor power also appears to distance members of Congress and the president from the public.

Second, for their part, the grassroots interest groups have the power to commit their foot soldiers, and sometimes money as well, in local and state races whether or not candidates have sought or even welcome their involvement. In doing so, they virtually compel the candidate—and some-times the party—to take a position on *their* issue. Candidates and parties must then calculate whether to support or repudiate a group whose views may be some distance from the belief systems of the party leaders or public opinion. Such calculations—and often the resulting visible alliances—are familiar dilemmas in politics, but they contribute to the impression on such issues that the party and candidate positions do not reflect public opinion.

A third set of choices has also distanced federal elected officials from the citizenry. The candidate and party must now continually choose either to support or reject special pleadings that favor one group or another at the expense of the electorate. Each of these pleadings requires politicians to make an exception in providing government support for a politically active group. Such demands are not new, but Eric Uslaner found that far more enterprises now claim not only that they should receive federal assistance but also that they should be exempt from one's regulatory and other responsibilities as a corporate citizen.[14] In the old days, defenders of politics-as-usual could argue that the political system made exceptions to accommo-date unusual circumstances confronting corporations or other organizations. When group after group demands such an exception to a public policy, however, fewer people are left to shoulder the tax and regulatory burden of collective action. The result then becomes hyperpluralism. A sense of purpose in sacrificing for the common good is thereby lost, and the politics of cooperation is undercut.

If citizens voted in larger numbers, the parties could distance them-selves from some of these group pressures. Instead, declining voter turnout renders the parties more vulnerable to those groups able to marshal vocal grassroots support, and the downward spiral in voter confidence in parties and the political system continues. Often the candidate can choose interest-group support without alerting the voters—the ones who must pay the eco-nomic and social costs of granting exceptions to particular organizations and individuals. Where the choice is more visible and the candidate choos-es to grant the exception in exchange for electoral support, the politician is seen to move away from the citizen majority. The candidate may thus become more distant from the voters as a result of ideological shifts to accommodate donors, allocating material support to donors, or striking interest-group alliances.

By now, furthermore, the rapid expansion of interest groups in size, number, and grassroots impact has complicated matters. Such interest groups always were represented in national party conventions, but in the old days, elected officials and activists who worked year-round for the party dominated the ranks of convention delegates. Now, David Broder finds that convention seats are "filled with people more loyal to interest groups—labor unions, teachers, the Christian Coalition, antiabortion movements—than to the parties."[15] Party activists thus find themselves sharing the most prominent symbol of their partisan activity—their national conventions—with fickle, strongly ideological allies whose ultimate loyalty lies elsewhere. For such an ally, party victory earned at the expense of their single-issue preference is tantamount to defeat.

The distinguished political scientist V. O. Key wrote in the middle of the twentieth century that a major party function is "the articulation of interests and aspirations of a substantial segment of the citizenry, usually in ways contended to be promotive of the national weal [or public interest]."[16] For Key, use of the word *segmentation* meant that the political party would seek to integrate a substantial portion of the electorate. Not so today for political consultants whose candidate strategy revolves largely around *segmenting the electorate*. Political-campaign consultant Richie Ross explains why and how, thanks to modern technology, it is done:

> Once a consultant goes to work for a candidate, he or she will cross-reference the district's population over and over, until the desired geo-demographic groups have been isolated. These groups are always exceedingly narrow. The number of demographic groups targeted in a specific campaign ranges from 60 to 1,200 with the precise figure depending on the level of office being contested and the amount of money a candidate has to spend. . . . A typical congressional campaign might have around 300 groups targeted.[17]

Information on each of these subgroups is then matched with polling data, and a campaign message is designed for each group. Instead of a single campaign with a single theme that unifies a candidate's supporters, concludes Marshall Ganz, parallel campaigns emerge, each articulating a theme narrow enough to appeal to a different segment of the electorate.[18]

The Party Drift Toward a Citizen Minority

The three sets of candidate choices described above and substantial voter segmentation distance both parties from the majority of voters and undercut the parties' ability to represent the majority of voters. The result is to push each party into taking positions that are *more partisan* than the views of its party members. One might argue that party members and independent voters are unaware of these circumstances. Focus-group participants, however, felt that public disaffection with institutions is largely the result of frustration with the way democracy is practiced in those institutions; the focus groups believed that Congress should pay more attention to majority concerns. Their complaints with Congress lay not so much in particular decisions as in a feeling that the government should conduct its business in a manner more sensitive to the public interest.[19] Their disappointment with the Congress thus lay not so much with *what* Congress did as in *how* Congress did it. The parties then are part of the electoral problem today. Can they become part of the solution?

Party Organization

The Founding Fathers and Political Parties

Just as few citizens or leaders have much good to say about parties today, so the founding fathers underestimated their importance. Parties are not mentioned in the U.S. Constitution. Leading Federalists and Jeffersonians criticized the very idea of partisan divisions in government, emphasizing the need for unity. Both parties were essentially collections of such local notables who sought to institutionalize a "consensus among enlightened leaders" and a "politics of deference." Success would depend on the ability of the exceptional man to instill personal loyalty in others and appoint men of high integrity to office.[20] As early as 1793, when elements of the Republican Party began to organize their supporters locally, rather than simply to leave it to local notables informally to rally support in their states, these efforts were viewed with suspicion.[21] The Federalists denied the legitimacy of such a nationwide party. Nor did they view themselves as a party, since the words *Federalists* and *patriots* were synonymous. President George Washington disparaged such local Republican organizations as "self-constituted democratic societies."[22] Jefferson, too, frequently showed at least a trace of condescension in his attitude toward them, even though he shared their republican philosophy.[23]

By the early 1800s, however, differences in an expanding nation had grown beyond the control of such a consensual elite. The Federalists had failed to attract congressional support for building government around executive branch initiatives, and even a patrician as esteemed as Jefferson could not, through his personal efforts, mediate executive/congressional relations in an increasingly democratic society. The national government was left without the capacity for concerted action.[24]

The election of Andrew Jackson as president in 1828 most dramatically signaled a new era of expanded democracy. Southern hunters, backwoods farmers, and Northern city dwellers—whose views had hitherto received short shrift—elected Jackson by an overwhelming majority. Patrician candidate John Quincy Adams received only 44 percent of the vote. On inaugural day, the White House was invaded by a mob of men, women, and boys who stood on chairs with their muddy boots. While Jackson escaped through a window, the unruly mob was finally lured outside by the promise of punch.[25] Adding insult to injury, legend has it that they even spilled the punch bowl on the White House lawn.

The problem of linking national party leadership to local party organizations and mobilizing the citizenry is thus not new. The Republicans began organizing around national officials seeking to exercise governmental power and provide national leadership and coordination. At the local level, there were two organizations—first, party structures (consisting of local leaders and activists), and second, the party's followers (including the mass party base and interest groupings). There were strong lines of direct, often face-to-face contact between the local party structures and the followers, as well as between the local and national party structures. Followers expected to influence national leaders through their local party structure and through their interest groups.

Popular choice would now govern, and the political parties would be the fulcrum for U.S. democracy in a large complex society.[26] The parties would take feedback from the electorate as a whole and, based on that feedback and the public interest as gleaned from Washington, would process these national and local ideas and present the electorate with alternatives concerning policies and leaders. After the election the losing party would go back to the drawing boards. There were no focus groups or polls with sentiments distilled and interpreted by experts; instead, it was a two-way democratic dialogue. But it was a limited dialogue. First, the triumph of Jacksonian democracy did lead to the elimination in most states of the property-owning qualification and of the taxpaying requirement that in many states had replaced it in yet a second attempt to limit the male franchise.[27] However, the triumph of the common man did nothing to alter the exclusion of slaves and women. Second, these politicians were anxious to restrict national power severely, in deference to more provincial local and particularly sectional divisions. Finally, while the electorate may have furthered the cause of democracy, the professional politicians, like Martin Van Buren of New York and James Buchanan of Pennsylvania were more interested in patronage and power than leadership and policy. The military hero dressed up the ticket, while the party pros pursued the Jackson administration doctrine that "to the victor go the spoils."

The Limitations of Party Organization Today

It is easy to dismiss the early party system—not only because it ignored so many citizens but also because it applied to only thirteen colonies. But ironically, this Jeffersonian Republican party structure—as modified by the Jacksonians and nationalized later in the century—in some ways resembled more closely successful large organizations today than the so-called modern parties. The national party leaders in those days *decentralized* authority and responsibility to the states and localities. Unlike devolution, this decentralization reserved some decisions at the organization's apex as well as the option to reclaim at least some of the delegated authority from the state and local parties. Like the global corporations, they thus gained the twin advantages of obtaining feedback on their activities and of adapting the organization to local conditions and concerns. In return, the parties surrendered the power to make decisions in some issue areas. The parties, like the political system, were more an amalgam of local, state, and federal governance.

Conversely, modern national party leaders have largely *devolved* the power to make critical policy decisions to political entrepreneurs, grassroots interest groups, and other constituency interests with access to valuable campaign resources. Devolved power is spun off, and hence irretrievable at least for some time. Party survival depends largely on a contest for party control among these several autonomous interests. It has been a long time since the national party chair was valued as a coalition builder or policy influential who, in conjunction with other state and regional party leaders, could cobble together a winning alliance on the party's behalf.

The national parties' weakness is reflected in their efforts to centralize as much control as possible over campaign fund-raising and technical support for the media activities of presidential candidates and members of Congress. Such expertise has strengthened the Republican and Democratic National Committees' staff capability, but tacitly acknowledges that the RNC and DNC continue to have little public-policy relevance for state and local parties. Increasingly, the national political parties are "centralized, fund-raising bureaucracies, not federations of precincts and wards."[28]

The role then, particularly of the national party organizations, has certainly changed. In the period prior to the advent of "big government" during the New Deal and World War II, power resided largely in the state and local parties and was brought to bear on the national committees. "Party bosses" like Richard J. Daley of Chicago, Thomas Bailey of Connecticut, and Tammany Hall's colorful George Washington Plunkitt in the Democratic Party and Philadelphia's William S. Vare, New York State's Tom Platt, and Pennsylvania's Matt Quay in the Republican Party wielded strong influence on the national parties, and the task of the national party leaders was to translate, or broker, the relative influence of these party eminences into a cohesive strategy and coherent program. In some areas the president or powerful Senate or House members could assume the leadership on issues that were national in scope, such as the Louisiana Purchase or our participation in World War I. Similarly, state leaders had to share power with local party leaders. D. W. Brogan relates, for example, how even in the state of Pennsylvania, when all of the big cities as well as the state government were "safely, impregnably Republican," Philadelphia, Pittsburgh, and Harrisburg were not mere wards or districts. Each had its own interests and its own resources. A state leader, Boise Penrose, thus had to persuade as well as order. And so it was with Cleveland and Cincinnati in Ohio, with Saint Louis and Kansas City in Missouri, and with other states.[29] This sharing of power across organizational boundaries may have limited the leaders' authority, but it also expanded the party's power by harnessing the energy of more party activists.

The DNC's and RNC's centralized power today underscores the limited national reach of the parties. The roles of partial financier and media-support technician are little more than staff appendages perched atop the overall party structures. Such *centralization* in this day and age, in the political as well as the corporate world, is usually an expression of organizational weakness.

Contrary to popular stereotype, the highly paid executives in global corporations (and other successful public and nonprofit organizations) understand their dependence on decisionmaking as well as on information residing elsewhere in their organizations. Once strategic goals are set in motion, the necessary organizational technologies and core competencies in place, and resources allocated, those "in the trenches" must have the power to make it work—and provide honest feedback on what worked and what did not.

Party veterans might well protest that they cannot remember when the national parties have played the role of decentralized organizations operating in close synchronization with their state and local party counterparts. But in their heyday they did. Some founding fathers and political theorists of the time recognized the need to develop political parties on a foundation of representative local party officials and a mass base of support. Edmund Burke, even before the revolution, in 1770, had described the party as a body of men united to promote the public interest concerning a principle on which they are all agreed. In pursuing that goal, public life is characterized by "power and energy," while the party becomes the medium for "a just connection" with its constituents. His alternative was ominous for readers today: the party would not "suffer that last of evils to predominate in the country: men [leaders] without popular confidence, public opinion, natural connection, or mutual trust, invested with all the powers of government."[30]

The Republican Party of the 1790s was in some ways more modern in its outlook than its Republican (or Democratic) counterpart more than two hundred years later. Its leaders realized that citizens must actually be engaged in national as well as local issues. And these party founders recognized the implications of failing to establish such a democratic dialogue.

Continental Congress member Melancton Smith warned that the superior opportunities "of the great" to join together for political purposes would give them preponderant power over men of "the poor and middling class," while Amos Singletary feared "lawyers, and men of learning, and moneyed men" who might "get all the power and swallow up all us little folks, like the great *Leviathan*."[31] But can political parties today prevent 60 percent of the population from remaining politically and economically subservient to the other 40 percent? The answer may lie in whether parties can function as organizations that enable the many unaffiliated citizens to participate in making collective decisions.

Learning from the Private Sector

Perhaps the ultimate puzzle confronting large organizations today is how in effect to get bigger and smaller at the same time. Global corporations—particularly those whose survival depends on staying close to consumer preferences—have solved this puzzle, while political parties have not. Large companies now simultaneously expand by CEO initiative in order to take advantage of growing markets and opportunities and decentralize to encourage innovation locally where the customer and organization meet. A number of global corporations have met the challenge of thinking globally and operating locally through a combination of granting autonomy for those working in flattened hierarchies with fewer organizational levels from top to bottom, downsizing and shifting work to suppliers, and rigorous, sophisticated computer-driven command-and-control systems. The hardware and software computer revolution has enabled upper-echelon executives to achieve economies of scale and take advantage of large-scale opportunities as well as clamp down locally when the ill-advised decisions either by their own employees or their suppliers become visible and threaten organizational goals. Heavy reliance is placed both on utilizing media technology and on enabling their employees to work more closely and personally with the customer. Sometimes such contact is achieved through interactive television or the Internet; more often, it occurs through face-to-face contact.

Sam Hill and Glenn Rifkin argue that global corporations using this integrative, grassroots marketing approach share three characteristics: "a visceral connection to the customer, a long-term commitment to the cause, and a willingness to work with and make the best of what's at hand."[32] The authors were struck by the warmth and respect for customers that they found among "radical marketers." The zealous CEOs of these corporate successes sought to imbue the same vision and values in their marketing departments that they were bringing through strategic management to their corporate cultures. Hill and Rifkin emphasize that one could dismiss vision, warmth, and respect as just so much "warm and fuzzy new-age folderol" were it not for the subsequent reactions inside and outside the companies. The close relation to their workers and customers enabled them to gain far more accurate information than if they simply relied on focus groups or polls. Furthermore, they acquired the information without relying on large marketing departments and multimillion-dollar market research budgets.[33]

Political Consultants as Antiquated Marketers

While global corporate executives moved with impressive speed in the 1980s and 1990s to reconstitute themselves and their organizations in order to reach out to a variety of peoples and cultures, the U.S. political parties have undergone no such transformation. Instead, as members of Congress have come to operate as "membership enterprises," these individual entrepreneurs have undercut the power of congressional leaders to engage in collective decisionmaking through their party caucuses. Similarly the "imperial presidency" lost much of its punch when the president could no longer as readily use the bully pulpit to appeal to his partisan majority. The president can, as Bill Clinton skillfully demonstrated on numerous occasions, use the media to temporarily outmaneuver congressional opposition strategically. No longer, however, does sustained popular partisan support—support derived from the people supporting their political parties—bolster our congressional and presidential leaders in making public policy. Instead, their support is derived from increasingly polarized congressional and presidential parties comprised of elites and political activists whose policy preferences are removed from those of most voters. And so, ironically, while the more astute U.S. corporations strive to move closer to their customers and their preferences in order to instill brand loyalty, political staffers advising presidents and members of Congress apply an ill-advised mix of public-relations techniques and often opportunistic strategies that have the desired effect of attracting temporary support even while creating more jaded citizens with less loyalty to the parties and our political institutions.

Organizations can adapt in order to grow as well as survive. Indeed, U.S. global corporations have come to view growth and survival as synonymous. Political parties would, of course, like to take the steps necessary for long-term growth, but even their well-intentioned candidates are pushed into short-term survival strategies. The 1993 New Jersey gubernatorial race between incumbent Democrat James Florio and Christine Todd Whitman exemplifies how urgent campaign needs take priority over grassroots politics. More significantly, the campaign also pitted Clinton advisers James Carville and Paul Begala against Ronald Reagan political consultant Ed Rollins, and so represented state-of-the-art political campaigning.

It was relatively late in the race when Whitman sacked her initial campaign adviser—who had focused on grassroots politics—and hired Rollins. He later reminisced about his campaign strategies and priorities in a world of weakened parties and mass communication. Reliance on parties is wishful thinking, he explained. "There are always hangers-on in campaigns, people with undefined roles who play a small part in the effort. They may be the precinct chairman, ward boss, or block captain. They always want to convince you nothing happens in their turf without their say so. In some cases that may be true. Most of the time, it's pure bullshit."[34] So grassroots strategies won't cut it. "I've never been in a campaign where any of that street crap really mattered, and when you're twenty-one points behind, street money is a real low priority. . . . My priorities were getting our television commercials on the air with a sharper message, getting ready for debates, and turning the spotlight off our missteps and back on Florio and his pitiful record."[35] To win the election, though, while Begala and Carville relied almost exclusively on TV, Rollins in effect built a quasi-party organization with one-way communication that served as a one-night stand for the voters: "I think the thing that a lot of people didn't see is that we mailed out two and a half million pieces of mail. They mailed no mail. We made one million *paid* phone calls to identify our voters. They made, to the best of my knowledge, no calls. We had 400,000 get-out-the-vote phone calls. We had about 15,000 coordinators."[36]

The candidates thus fund—and put themselves in the hands of— political consultants who largely control candidate elections and opt for the best negative ads, image-creation, voter-segmentation strategies, and quasi-party organizations that money can buy. These short-run strategies contribute to a long-term decline in political credibility, party membership, and democratic support. Rollins, however, is not paid to promote democracy; his job is to win a particular election for a particular candidate. Nonetheless, while the parties have lost the capacity to rally and sustain an authentic partisan majority and thereby control elections, they continue to exhibit signs of life despite an excess of self-defeating behavior.

The Organizational Vigor of the Parties

Unfortunately, this party vigor has received little attention except from a handful of political scientists who have noted two surprising trends. First, the Democratic and Republican National Committees have enhanced their influence somewhat on state and local parties thanks to their increased access to campaign funds and valuable technical campaign assistance. Second, and perhaps more importantly in the long run, local party organizational strength has persisted longer than the parties' many detractors predicted.

The weakness of the national political parties predates the electronic age. A 1960 study found that the results of the multilayered local, state, and national elections were "determined in large part by the effectiveness of the ephemeral relationships which are built up by hundreds of thousands of separate and discrete campaign organizations."[37] In 1984, however, researchers were more upbeat both about the national parties and about the organizational activities of state and local party. To be sure, the parties—as creatures of state law and various state and local political cultures, including thirty-six hundred county and equivalent jurisdictions— remained markedly different. But this extensive national survey measuring organizational strength, published in 1984, revealed that local and state parties were at least stronger at the close of the 1970s than in the early 1960s. Even though the tie of party identification for millions of voters to the Republican and Democratic Parties was weakening or disappearing during this period, the level of party organizational strength increased. The study carefully distinguished such growing party strength from other trends that were adversely affecting the party system—such as the declining partisanship of the electorate and the separation of candidate campaign organizations from the party. Furthermore, it acknowledged that the interest-group and media competitors for performing party functions might have increased in strength more than the party organizations themselves, thereby bringing about a decline in the *relative* influence of party organizations over the political process. The study concluded that party organizations were reasonably strong and not weakening."[38]

For their part, the national parties by the 1980s had solidified their position with their candidates and with state and local parties. The needs of presidential, Senate, and House candidates varied, but candidates were provided with the necessary gear and people for mass mailings, telephone boiler-room operations, and provision to the media of press releases, TV ads, and videotapes for use in the evening news. By centralizing these campaign activities, the national parties had become stronger political players, and they were now more closely integrated with state and local parties than in recent decades. The strength of party organizations would continue to depend, though, on what state and local workers (or activists) were willing to do. While party presence and power appear to vary by state and particularly by locality, some leaders at these levels could point to a respectable activity level—particularly for a voluntary organization in this day and age. Furthermore, in the 1990s a research team documented that, at least in the South, leaders and activists of both parties remained strongly inclined to work for their parties and to do it the old-fashioned way—by building their organizations from the bottom up.[39]

The perpetuation of this bottoms-up organizational characteristic is important for two reasons. First, it means that parties continue to represent and reflect the 57+ varieties of U.S. political life and society. This distinctive imprint of local and state political cultures, leaders, traditions, and interests continues to manifest itself in varying degrees through the practices that state and local parties follow, the candidates they recruit, the campaign money they raise, the auxiliary groups they form, the innovations they increase, the organized interests to which they respond, the campaign strategies and issues they create, and, most important, the policy orientations of the candidates who run under their label.[40]

Second, these state and local party efforts seem to compare reasonably well in vigor with earlier decades when the parties were more prominent. It is difficult to tell, though, since no national baseline exists against which to compare such party activity over time. Furthermore, party activist efforts to contact voters, at least since World War II, may never have been too high. Peter Rossi and Phillips Cutright thus estimated in 1956—when television was still in its infancy—that the campaign efforts of the best party workers added no more than 5 percent to a candidate's campaign margin.[41] While there is some variation in the proportion of voters contacted between 1952 and 1990, it seems to fluctuate between roughly one-fifth and one-quarter of the electorate.[42]

Conclusion

While viable party organizations are now in place, parties influence actual voting decisions only marginally. Even studies demonstrating an increase in party *organizational* strength make no such claims for either party's *electoral* strength. As early as the 1950s, when empirical political party studies came to the fore, the demise of most political machines had already weakened the parties. As one member of Congress bluntly declared in a 1958 Brookings roundtable discussion, "If we depended on the party organization to get elected, none of us would be here."[43] There also is little evidence that these rejuvenated organizations have succeeded in reversing the decline of partisan identification in the electorate. While a loyal core of party workers is in place, it remains too small to compensate in dedication for its lack of size. As one study put it, local leaders are "often glad to find even a few people who will help out, regardless of their feelings toward the party."[44]

There is a certain irony in the state of affairs now confronting the parties. The weakening of the parties at the local level (where their contact with the voters makes them most valuable) has occurred partly as a result of the disappearance of paid precinct captains.[45] While such compensation was not illegal, the public came to regard it as illegitimate, even while we pay much higher fees to a new class of political consultants who shun the grassroots strategies that give sustenance to democracy and refine the mass-media, direct-mail, and public-relations strategies that undercut it. Paying precinct workers from lower-income, middle-income white-collar, and working-class economic and educational levels—who are seeking to involve their peers in the political process—smacks too much of the old-time machines, but compensating upper-middle-income professionals—who are devising strategies that turn voters off in the long run—is socially acceptable. This reduces the electoral participation of that 60 percent of the electorate already least likely to vote, who would more likely trust precinct workers closer to their social and educational status.

In canvassing and other activities, though, the party pros remain hampered by defeats they suffered at the hands of the Progressive movement, loss of control over nominations as a result of the direct primary, and other political changes mentioned in the last chapter. Furthermore, political scientists have tended to compare state and local party activities now and in earlier decades. But the challenge to the parties then came from far fewer interest groups and a smaller media corps—exclusively of print journalists—that was far less intrusive and closer in partisan terms to one party or the other. In addition, parties in the earlier decades were dealing with more partisan, less jaded voters who were likely to hear their message.

These daunting problems notwithstanding, viable and adaptive state and local party organizations operating close to citizens remain in place. To be sure, this organizational renaissance has occurred even while the parties have failed to stem either the tidal wave of voters drifting away from party identification or the downward trend in turnout. Nonetheless, the existence of these nationwide grassroots political organizations signifies an opportunity.

PART 2

THE ESCALATION OF COZY POLITICS

4

Uncontrollable Campaign Costs and Their Consequences

A lthough voters normally return a high proportion of members of Congress to office, these members, nevertheless, must live with great uncertainty. Politicians run scared, observes British political scientist Anthony King, because they are exposed to a high "vulnerability equation," consisting of "frequent general elections *plus* primaries *plus* lack of party cover *plus* the need to raise large amounts in campaign funds [which] *equals* an unusually high degree of electoral exposure for American politicians compared with those in other countries."[1] Furthermore, there is always the danger that an apparently underfunded opponent will pull an October surprise through a TV attack ad blitz or that a powerful grassroots-based interest group, such as the AFL-CIO or the Christian Coalition, will throw its money and volunteers behind a sustained, targeted effort to teach a lesson to an arrogant incumbent who voted the wrong way.

The Campaign-Finance Superstructure

The price of incumbency is eternal vigilance, which requires political entrepreneurship and a lot of money. Washington is run "by one president, 100 senators, and 435 members of the House—each of whom got here essentially on his own. Each chooses the office he seeks, raises his own money, hires his own pollster and ad maker and recruits his own volunteers. Each of them is scrambling to remain in office, no matter what."[2] The incumbent alone cannot control the nature of the electoral or party system but can increase the flow of campaign funds by using the visibility that incumbency bestows. Thanks to the substantial government largesse controlled by these politicians, campaign contributions are, more often than not, available for the asking.

Few U.S. businesses can boast the growth rate since the 1970s of those professions associated with federal reelection. The number of lawyers practicing in the capital, according to the Washington, D.C. Bar Association, rose from about eleven thousand in 1972 to about sixty-three thousand in

1994.[3] Business and labor lobbyists have also increased in number to the point where an estimated $1.2 billion was spent on the costs of their salaries, office expenses, research, travel for policymakers and their staffs, and meals and other favors they were permitted to lavish on members of Congress even under the somewhat tightened gift rules.[4] These figures do not include part-time lobbying, the selling of "strategic advice" and public relations, the lobbying of six hundred professionals or firms on behalf of foreign interests, or "grassroots" lobbying, which by itself is estimated to generate $400 million in salaries and expenses.[5] Many interest groups work through the thirty-two hundred trade associations that magnify the voices of individual groups, and they, as of 1995, employed 100,000 people, or 187 for each member of Congress.[6] This expansion is hardly surprising in light of the roughly $250 billion awarded by the federal government in federal grants and contracts, in addition to tax preferences and regulations that can significantly impact corporate earnings, labor conditions, or interest-group goals. Decisions on approximately one-quarter of the sum of all goods and services produced in the United States (the gross domestic product) are made inside the D.C. beltway.

The best measure of the high economic stakes for interest groups engaged in political influence has been their willingness to increase the size of their political contributions substantially so that total expenditures for the congressional and presidential races rose for the first time above $2 billion in 1992 and then to $2.7 billion in the 1996 election.[7] Only two decades ago, the presidential and congressional races totaled less than one-quarter of that amount. Today, during *every week* of a six-year term, the average senator must raise $10,000 for reelection campaign expenses.[8] Far from reflecting the rate of inflation, campaign-finance expenditures are now more likely raising it, as candidates vie for choice TV and radio spots or the latest consultant guru.

The pressure to spend more stems in part from the knowledge that a large, early war chest can discourage a serious primary or general-election challenge, but there are other reasons. Strategies, and consequently costs, differ depending on whether the race is districtwide, statewide, or national in scope, but certain trends dictate that it will be more expensive than previously. The acquisition of votes through political technology, rather than volunteer power, is a capital-intensive enterprise.[9] And every race involves technology, whether it be computerized direct mailing on a targeted basis to likely congressional supporters or television ads in a senatorial or presidential campaign. Lee Ann Elliott, a former FEC chair, explains that "computers are essential to a campaign because they do campaign chores faster and more accurately than volunteers sitting around a table."[10] The professionalization of politics has also ushered in the era of the consultant, as experts have replaced less efficient and often less available volunteers. There are now advertising and strategy consultants, management consultants, press and research aides, pollsters, experts at organizing volunteers, consultants who put voters' names on computer tapes for direct mail appeals, and consultants who prepare commercials. The rule of thumb, according to Herbert Alexander, is that radio and TV production costs range between 10 percent and 33 percent of the air-time charges.[11]

Perhaps no group has demonstrated the potency of campaign money more dramatically than the Class of 1994 House members. Committed to changing the political system, and elected with that mandate, an unusually large bloc of seventy-three newly elected members of Congress came to the capital having defeated enough Democrats to end forty years of Democratic hegemony in the House. The group maintained its identity in supporting adoption of the conservative Contract with America bills introduced by the Republican leadership within one hundred days of the new session. However, some of the House leaders (if not their Senate counterparts) acknowledged that something also had to be done about money in politics. An opportunity seemed at hand to deal with campaign excesses. These seventy-three insurgents had benefited comparatively little from Political Action Committee (PAC) support and had few contacts within the Washington establishment. Incoming House Majority Leader Dick Armey told CNN, "We are very willing to have—anxious to have—campaign finance reform," while Representative Bill Thomas promised to reintroduce a proposal that, among other things, would reduce the level of PAC donations per election cycle and collect a major portion of funds from individuals within their own districts.[12]

Meanwhile, however, other party elements were already focusing these political newcomers on the requirements of reelection. The National Republican Congressional Committee stressed that first-term incumbents are vulnerable, thanks to the lack of the requisite years of constituency service to solidify their position in their districts. Fund-raising efforts would be critical, and, with few exceptions, they began even before 1994 was over. The neophytes were advised to return to their contributors with the message: "We're trying to change Washington. I need your help." Contributions in the House are supplied largely by PACs. Republican House Whip Tom DeLay wrote to numerous PACs on behalf of one such freshman and laid it on the line. The Republicans were now in control, and a shift from the old pattern of giving to Democratic incumbents to one of giving to these Republican freshmen was key to a "positive future relationship" with House leaders.[13] The National Republican Congressional Committee (NRCC) told the newcomers that it would be prudent to have $200,000 in the bank early if they had won with less than 55 percent of the vote. In addition, the Republican House leadership placed twenty-five of the freshmen on such key committees as Appropriations, Ways and Means, Budget, and the Rules Committee, which also aided their fund-raising.

By May 1996, before the general-election race had even begun, those seeking reelection already averaged $384,376 in the kitty, including $139,800 from PACs. The electoral success rate was unusually high for freshmen; fifty-seven of the seventy-three were reelected (and several of the others ran for other offices). Ann McBride, president of Common Cause, a public-interest group, viewed the outcome wryly: the freshmen had "come to shake Washington up; they stayed to shake it down."[14]

The Emergence of the Second Constituency

Following Watergate, Congress took some steps to reform campaign finance in the 1974 FECA Amendments, as it placed limits on the amounts of money that individuals, PACs, and party committees could contribute to candidates even in the case of "independent expenditures" made without the cooperation or knowledge of the candidate, and ushered in public funding for presidential elections. But even this celebrated reform, like so much of the history of money and politics, is shrouded in some ambiguity. Fred Wertheimer and Susan Manes emphasize that this legislation for the first time authorized the establishment and operation of PACs by corporations and labor unions with government contracts.[15] Thanks to subsequent events, it also ushered in a sizable second constituency, consisting of wealthy individuals, corporate, and interest-group campaign contributors to whom a candidate must, at a minimum, provide access.

Multiple Sources of Money and Power

Already in the 1970s, two trends were in any event working against the success of a comprehensive regulatory system of campaign-finance reform. First, in 1976 the Supreme Court in *Buckley v. Valeo* (1976) ruled that it was a violation of free speech to limit campaign spending by candidates on their own behalf or to limit "independent expenditures" by individuals or groups in support or opposition to a candidate, provided that such spending was made without the knowledge or cooperation of the candidate. Individual or group expenditures served to express why they favored or opposed a candidate, and such expression could not be limited unless Congress were seeking to prevent "corruption or the appearance of corruption." The court argued: "The concept that government may restrict the speech of some elements of our society in order to enhance the relative voice of others is wholly foreign to the First Amendment."[16] Only party expenditures could be limited. Sorauf dryly observed that the court had now elevated "money talks" from a popular saying to a constitutional principle.[17]

The second trend involved the growth in the number and importance of interest groups. As public membership and identification with political parties continued to decline, an "interest-group society" filled the vacuum.[18] The people of the United States increasingly sought representation in Washington, D.C., through business, labor, professional, ideological, and public-interest groups. PACs were a natural extension of these groups, particularly in the case of large companies and unions with the financial muscle to capture attention through contributions.

By 1996, individuals, groups, and parties could all contribute heavily to the candidates of their choice, thanks to the increased supply of funds, the pressure of greater competition for office, and a campaign-finance system protected by a Supreme Court concerned about freedom of speech and incumbent members of Congress concerned about survival. The vote in the 1996 House races reflected this competitive pressure, as the nationwide total for Republican candidates exceeded that for Democrats by less than 300,000 out of nearly 90 million ballots cast—a margin of roughly one-third of one percentage point.[19] The campaign regulatory system—riddled with loopholes—finally collapsed.[20] The lines demarcating the system's boundaries became blurred, as candidates fiddled with existing rules, expanded old loopholes, and developed new ones. Figure 4.1 depicts the porous superstructure of donors and financial conduits that, Scotch-taped together, comprise prevailing campaign-contribution practices.

Reformers designed the 1971 and 1974 Federal Election Commission Act (FECA) to reduce the importance of large individual donor contributions, subject all funds raised and spent on presidential and congressional elections to the requirements and restrictions of federal law (so-called "hard money"), and bring "sunshine" to the process through full disclosure of contributions by political committees, parties, individuals, and candidates. Because the candidates (particularly incumbents), wealthy donors, and parties have succeeded in undermining so many of these statutory provisions, it is worth examining how these mechanisms were supposed to function, and what actually happened.

The Subtle World of Campaign Finance

There are two types of political committees: "nonconnected," or independent, committees and PACs affiliated with ongoing organizations such as corporations, professional groups, or unions. The "nonconnected" committees include any club, association, or other group that is not affiliated with a parent organization. Such committees, if they receive contributions totaling

Figure 4.1 Campaign Funding Flow Chart

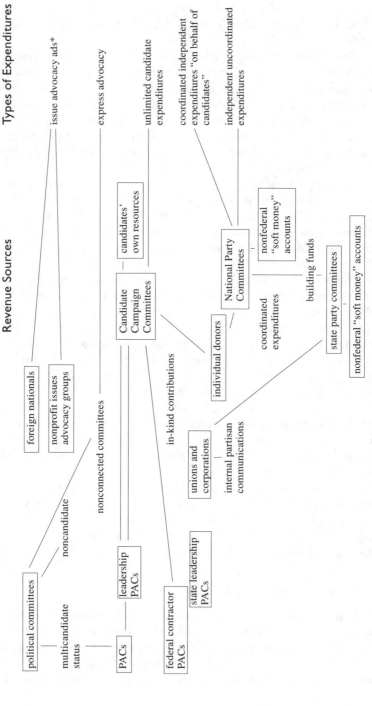

*Unions and corporations, PACs, Political Committees, and Individuals can also finance issues and advocacy ads.

more than $1,000, are subject to FECA regulations only in the event that they engage in "express advocacy" by specifically naming a candidate whom they support or oppose in their literature or political advertisements. Otherwise, given the centrality of policy substance for many of these groups, the Supreme Court has remained reluctant to curtail their freedom of speech. Because a committee such as the American Israel Public Affairs Committee is separate and distinct from the parties and candidates, it is entitled to engage in "issue advocacy," unburdened by FEC regulation.[21] About 25 percent of the political committees are unconnected.[22]

In 1996, political committees (and parties) exploited the potential of such issue advocacy for political mischief more fully than in the past. The U.S. Chamber of Commerce and the Democratic and Republican National Committees financed media advertisements that, while taking care to avoid express advocacy, tied the merits of candidates to particular issue positions. The unions and the Christian Coalition published "nonpartisan" voter guides that, nonetheless, managed to cast Republican and Democratic candidates respectively in an unfavorable light. Funding for such advertisements and publications could be collected from any source, used in any amount, and required no FEC disclosure.[23]

It was tax-exempt nonprofit organizations, however, that by 1996 offered donors all the trimmings, as they engaged in more, and sometimes more questionable, issue advocacy than in the past. Supporters could give unlimited amounts, without whatever embarrassment disclosure might bring, and the organization could spend unlimited amounts on its advocacy commercials. Furthermore, these organizations could favor a candidate so long as they did not expressly urge people to vote for or against a named candidate or coordinate their activity with a campaign. In response to a television campaign sponsored by the unions, "a handful of tax-exempt groups backed by an even smaller number of conservative multimillionaires, poured hundreds of millions of dollars into last-minute advertising blitzes that sent Democrats scrambling and stunned even some of their intended GOP beneficiaries."[24]

For its part, the Democratic National Committee, according to the *Los Angeles Times*, regularly referred donors to the tax-exempt group Vote Now '96, which spent $3 million nationally, registering voters among groups traditionally loyal to Democratic candidates.[25] The Republican National Committee also claimed tax-exempt status for its National Policy Forum (NPF) when the party chairman, Haley Barbour, founded it as a place where Republicans could exchange ideas, debate policy, and publish a conservative magazine. Joseph Sandler, general counsel to the Democratic National Committee, claimed that the forum was purely partisan in nature: "They took core functions of the party and spun it off into the National Policy Forum and then called it a 501(c)(4)."[26] Defending their actions, Republicans pointed to the Democratic Leadership Council, which received tax-exempt status in 1985. Tax-exempt status is granted with the understanding that these organizations can engage in political activity so long as it is not their primary activity; they can lobby for a particular cause but not push a particular candidate or party. The notion that national committees and party leaders will head such organizations and act in an essentially nonpolitical fashion strains credulity. Small wonder that PACs view tax-exempts as "the emerging problem. They dwarf soft money because no one has any idea how much is being raised and how much is being spent."[27]

Political Action Committees

Some labor and other PACs already existed, and it was anticipated that, under FECA, more issue groups and business, labor, professional, agrarian, and grassroots membership organizations would organize and collect funds from their members, stockholders, or employees. Most PACs could contribute up to $5,000 per candidate per primary and $5,000 per election.[28] Just how many PACs did emerge, though, proved something of a surprise, as the number rapidly grew from 608 in 1974 to 4,009 in 1984, after which the rate of growth leveled off. Most PACs contribute to members of Congress, and it is the large, wealthy PACs that give disproportionately.[29] Of 4,700 PACs in 1992, about 6 percent accounted for $265 million, or two-thirds of all contributions. Even more tellingly, 74 committees each spent more than $1 million, disbursing $161 million.[30] The total amount contributed by PACs grew from $12 million in 1974 to $201 million in 1996—a 400 percent increase, accounting for inflation.[31]

In recent years, Leadership PACs have also drawn criticism as a vehicle designed to skirt PAC contribution limits. These PACs enable House and Senate leaders or would-be leaders to curry favor with potential congressional supporters by steering money to their campaign funds. By flying around the country and hosting candidate forums to assist colleagues, these leaders are, in addition, increasing their own visibility—and living well in the process. Critics of what in some cases are largely "slush funds" under the leader's control point to thousands of dollars in catering, telephone calls, limousines, hotels, and air fare reported to the FEC. Furthermore, where corporations, unions, and trade associations can give only $1,000 to an individual candidate, they can give $5,000 to another PAC, even if it is run by a lawmaker.[32] The amounts are comparatively large for "hard money" contributions that can be used directly for candidate and party activities. For example, in 1994, Senator Robert Dole raised $6.5 million for his Campaign America, and that same year Richard Gephardt raised more than $1 million for his Effective Government Committee.[33] Congressional leaders from both parties have drawn considerable criticism for mounting such large Leadership PACs. It may say something about how much members of Congress think that money influences their colleagues' actions that they have continued to expand such activities in the face of such criticism.

Another emerging loophole concerns "state-based PACs." These PACs operate at the state level and are ostensibly designed to aid state and local candidates. As such, they are not subject to FEC disclosure and other requirements, even though they often are controlled by House and Senate members. Instead, they are under the aegis of state laws that vary from state to state but often lack the disclosure requirements or rules comparable to the federal ones that prevent companies, unions, and trade associations from contributing directly to candidates. Some states have no restrictions on the size of political contributions; at the very least, these state-based PACs allow donors to "double up," or contribute at the state as well as the federal level to a member of Congress. Such contributions are sometimes defended as state "party building" activities (and thus immune from federal regulation even if they were reported), but there are few controls to prevent members of Congress from drawing funds from these "back-door PACs" to cover personal campaign finances.[34] It is also difficult in any event to differentiate the proportion of time and money that should be allocated to joint federal and state political activities.

Several loopholes enable political committees to expand the amount of their political activity on behalf of candidates and parties. Larry Sabato and Glenn Simpson describe the extensive in-kind contributions, for example, that labor unions made to the Democratic Party in 1996, including phone banks, voter registration and get-out-the-vote drives, publicity, and even the services of paid union staff provided to the candidate free of charge. All such activities are termed "nonpartisan" and thus need not be disclosed to the FEC. Such activity may not directly support or attack a candidate, but can be couched in a "thinly veiled, partisan manner."[35] The delicate dance performed around partisan internal communications is reflected in the advice to trade-association members given by an FEC lawyer on writing an appropriate internal communication:

> In a letter to your members outlining Jones's legislative record and support for the industry, you can suggest that members support his reelection and even recommend that members become active in or contribute to his campaign. But you may not "facilitate" contributions to the campaign. The association can provide the address of the Committee to Reelect Jones but cannot provide an envelope addressed to the campaign committee to send in contributions.[36]

The amounts can be substantial. In 1996, the AFL-CIO reported partisan expenses of $35 million and estimated that it spent another $20 million on issue ads that, technically, were nonpartisan.[37]

PACs can also multiply the amount of their donations to a particular candidate by "bundling" contributions from their members and others. The PAC takes these checks, made out to the candidate, and delivers them in a bundle to the candidate, thereby leaving no question as to who is responsible for facilitating the contributions. The advantage of such donations is that they do not count against the limit on PAC contributions to a single candidate. They enable the PAC to supply amounts far in excess of FECA's statutory intent.

The Triumphal Return of Soft Money

Political parties use some of the same loopholes as political committees and, with an assist from the Supreme Court, exploit more fully some financial flexibility of their own. In 1979, Congress amended FECA to encourage party "soft money" contributions that would support party building at the state and local levels. There are no contribution or expenditure limits because the funds were not intended primarily to benefit federal campaigns. David Broder captures well what happened: "originally intended as a modest kitty to support grassroots party activities, such as opening local volunteer offices and registering voters, soft money was converted by greedy politicians of both parties—President Clinton notable among them—into a limitless source of cash for their relentless TV ads."[38] The parties collected a record $263 million in such soft money during the 1996 election cycle. This is three times as much as they collected in 1992 and more than thirteen times what they raised in 1980, the first election to allow soft money.[39]

Whatever its intent, soft money has evolved into a loophole that allows parties to collect funds from corporations and unions in amounts that would be prohibited in federal elections. Wealthy individuals, also limited to a total of $25,000 per year in contributions to federal candidates, can nevertheless also contribute as much as a particular state's law permits. In state elections, forty-one states allow contributions from union treasuries, and thirty allow them from corporations. These state regulations govern the flow of these contributions. The funds technically are kept in "nonfederal" bank accounts by the parties—in contrast to "federal" hard money accounts collected in legal amounts from federally permissible sources. Funds in the nonfederal accounts are then transferred to those states that allow such contributions.[40]

In theory these funds are used at the state level only for state and local candidates, while other money from "federal" party accounts is transferred to assist presidential and congressional elections. Where election activities are joint, careful bookkeeping is required to insure that such "mixed activities" are accounted for in accord with formulas supplied by the Federal Election Commission; only hard money should be used for federal candidates. Under the best of circumstances it would be difficult to calculate what is state and what is federal participation, but neither party is striving for precision in its calculations.

In practice, while some money goes to party-building activities, the national parties have played fast and loose with such funds. In 1980, the first election involving soft money, two California farming corporations and the Marriott Corporation of Bethesda, Maryland, gave contributions to the Illinois Republican Party. Robert Perkins, a Republican National Committee executive, admitted that he had directed these contributions as part of a multimillion soft-money Victory Fund '80: "We picked out the states that needed the money, identified money from major contributors, and funneled it into those states." Similarly, in 1984, the executive director of the Florida GOP, candidly admitted using a *state* charter to form a group designed to mobilize Hispanic votes for President Reagan, since we then "can take a check for $1 million (and) we can take corporate checks."[41] H. Susan Estrich, presidential candidate Michael Dukakis's campaign manager in 1988, observed: "There were a lot of (state) chairmen who didn't understand that money in their state party was not necessarily within their control."[42] Nor is the FEC likely to control this soft-money flow. Party campaign records in many states are difficult to unearth and interpret. Huge sums surface under vague entries such as "administrative/voter drive." The result is substantial amounts of unregulated, unexamined money.

The largest party soft-money expenditures in 1996 were for issue ads. Distinguishing these ads from campaign ads previously funded by the national party committees with hard "federal" money is a stretch. The Supreme Court, however, has rejected efforts to restrict such spending on the ground that for parties, as well as political committees, issue advocacy is a form of constitutionally protected free speech so long as the advertisement does not expressly advocate for or against a candidate and is not coordinated with the candidate. Whatever their constitutional virtues, issue ads enabled the Clinton campaign to make an end run around the candidate campaign-spending limits to which presidential candidates allegedly agree in exchange for public funds. The president wanted to maintain a successful media blitz early in 1996 but did not want to exhaust precious and dwindling authorized campaign expenditures, so he decided to utilize Democratic National Committee (DNC) and other party organization resources. The DNC, which had never before engaged in such advertising in a significant manner to promote a presidential candidate in an election year, now spent an estimated $18 million. To remain within FEC regulations, much of the money was transferred to those state parties that allowed such expenditures, and these states made the actual media purchases. For its part, the Republican National Committee was pleased to run $20 million of its own issue ads since the Dole campaign was "financially topped out" after the long and expensive primary season.

But the Democrats did not observe even these minimal rules of the game. Bob Woodward, in his book *The Choice*, divulged that the DNC ad campaign was directed by staffers on Clinton's personal campaign team and that the president was "intimately involved" in some of the ad decisions.[43] While this revelation loomed as something of a smoking gun for political junkies and FEC staffers, perhaps not surprisingly, it caused little stir in a U.S. public far removed from the arcane world of express advocacy, coordinated expenditures, and candidate spending limits.

The Reemergence of Fat Cats

Individual contributions remain the largest single source of campaign funds (see Table 4.1). In 1996, $1.3 billion of the total of $2.4 billion in campaign funds came from individuals—$734 million from small donors and $597 million from large donors. Small donations, those less than $200, are particularly important in Congress where they represent 20 percent of a member's campaign funds. While the phrase "small donors" may evoke an image of grassroots contributions, these donations come from only 4 percent of the people.[44] The citizenry as a whole does have another way to contribute: the public funds in presidential elections are collected through a voluntary $3.00 checkoff on tax returns. This contribution literally does not cost the taxpayer a penny since the amount is drawn from the person's tax obligation; yet the proportion of citizens contributing in this fashion declined from 29 percent in 1980 to 13 percent in 1997.

For senators, presidential candidates, and political parties, large con-

Table 4.1　Sources of Federal Campaign Contributions in 1996

Public money	$211 million	9%
Small donations	$734 million	30
Large individual donors	$597 million	25
Pol. action committees (PACs)	$243 million	10
Soft money	$262 million	11
Candidates	$161 million	7
Other[a]	$200 million	8
Total	$2.4 billion	100

Source: Federal Election Commission.
Note: a. Includes interest from candidate loans and interest on accumulated contributions.

tributors continue to grow in importance. Substantial contributions are not new. Joan Kroc, widow of the founder of McDonald's, in 1984 gave $1 million in soft money to the DNC. And already by 1988, the RNC's $100,000 donor club, dubbed Team 100, consisted of 249 members.[45] By 1996, the pressure to collect even more soft money could be seen in the growth of sometimes curious innovations used by party committees and financial solicitors to collect funds, the brazenness of some donors and solicitors, and the drive to reach higher campaign-funding goals that resulted in the solicitation of sleazy and sometimes illegal domestic and foreign campaign sources.

The DNC and RNC by 1996 had developed new events for corporations to sponsor and donors to attend. The DNC guaranteed Philadelphia philanthropist Peter L. Buttenwieser a seat at the president's table at a 1996 lunch in exchange for a $50,000 contribution. When the head of a Kansas metal-casting company wanted to invest in a foundry in Romania, he wrote the Clinton administration to urge that a friend be named director of the European Bank for Reconstruction and Development. A fund-raiser then contacted him, saying, "If you want to talk to the president, make a donation of $25,000, and you'll get invited to the White House." He added that DNC officials had told him not to offer anything in return, that would be against the law, just a chance to meet with the president.[46] The price in Michigan for nineteen donors was $50,000 for such a presidential meeting, but it included what one called a chance to eat "stale cookies" and get "on the radar screen"—a phrase that surfaced in many such donor and lobbyist explanations as to why they gave.[47] The price of being an RNC Team 100 donor had risen, too. Speaker Newt Gingrich hawked this designation in exchange for those who, giving $100,000 in 1996, now also contributed $25,000 for each of the following three years.[48] In this auction, Democratic fund-raisers held the trump card—the Lincoln bedroom in the White House, where appropriately generous donors could stay overnight.

Changes in the election law also allowed corporations for the first time to become official party-convention sponsors. The DNC told donors that the convention now offered an "unparalleled opportunity" to help the party raise money for the fall campaign. It circulated a list of $2.5 million worth of "sponsorship opportunities," including $15,000 for baseball tickets, $50,000 for a DNC "After-Hours Club," and $150,000 for a formal donor dinner party.[49] The Democratic and Republican Congressional Committees have also run expensive soft-money events. The NRCC in 1997 ran an opera gala where a donation of $100,000 made the House Commerce Committee chair, Thomas J. Bliley, available at a "targeted" session for donors who had issues pending in the legislative or executive branch. Surveying this aggressive posture, political scientist Larry Sabato speculated that "where others have seen scandal, fundraisers at the congressional committees may have seen golden opportunities."[50]

Some wealthy contributors skipped the sponsorships and cut to the chase. A few were shady even by 1996 standards. The Cone family, for example, made a controversial contribution of $1.8 million through a "Republican-oriented consulting firm" and through two tax-exempt organizations.[51] Other contributors at best stretched the rules. While the purpose of soft-money contributions allegedly was to build the party, both parties adopted the practice of "tallying," whereby large donors could discreetly "earmark" which candidate should benefit. For example, the Association of Trial Lawyers of America (ATLA), which gave more than $3 million to the Democrats in 1996, ran a phone bank urging members to give to selected candidates—and identify themselves on their checks as ATLA members.[52] Political scientist Thomas Ferguson captured just how creative wealthy individual contributors now can be in making direct, indirect, and in-kind campaign contributions (see Figure 4.2).[53]

All Fat Cats Welcome

It is illegal for foreign companies and individuals to donate to U.S. candidates or parties, but numerous contributions surfaced in 1996, particularly for the Democratic Party, where John Huang was appointed to head a $5 million fund-raising effort in the Asian American community. Huang appeared unconcerned about the illegal nature of these contributions, which resulted in congressional hearings. The DNC eventually refused a number of contributions, sometimes after newspapers disclosed specific transactions. The party returned $300,000 to an Indonesian couple who had illegally served as a financial conduit for the Lippo Group, a foreign corporation; $250,000 to a South Korean corporation after it was determined that it did not have a U.S. subsidiary; and $5,000 to a foreign national who had tried to contribute through a Buddhist nun at a $140,000 fund-raiser held at a California Buddhist temple.[54] The temple fund-raiser was attended by Vice President Al Gore, who thanks to his energetic fund-raising efforts, was named "solicitor-in-chief." Presidential candidate Robert Dole proclaimed that "foreign aid has finally reached America, but it's all going to the Democratic National Committee."

Not quite all. The Republican National Committee was compelled to return $15,000 to a Canadian firm after the newspaper *Roll Call* questioned its legitimacy.[55] And the RNC chair, Haley Barbour, arranged for a Taiwan businessman to put up collateral for a $2-million bank loan to the tax-exempt National Policy Forum. Those funds shortly thereafter were transferred to the RNC, which in turn channeled the funds into congressional

Figure 4.2   The Many Pockets of a Politician's Coat

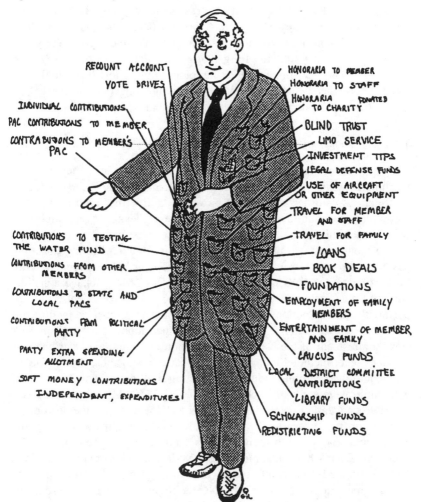

Source: Thomas Ferguson, *The Golden Rule,* Chicago University Press, 1995, p. 353. Used by permission of the publisher.

races. Months later, the NPF defaulted on the loan, thereby freeing more money for the RNC.[56] When, at congressional hearings, Barbour denied knowing that the money came from a foreign source, the committee chairman, Fred Thompson, asked how that was possible since "you were sitting on the deck of a yacht in Hong Kong harbor talking to a citizen of Taiwan."[57] The hearings on 1996 campaign abuses left little doubt that wealthy foreigners were largely succeeding in making contributions to both parties through residents and U.S.-based subsidiaries.

The Growing Need for Fat-Cat Donors

Such questionable contributions are one manifestation of a frantic money machine pleading "feed me." Another such manifestation is the emergence of solicitors who derive political power by delivering large numbers of soft-money contributions. Descriptions of these packagers vary slightly in different tellings of the story, but in both accounts quoted here there is a shared identity as Washington influentials for whom collecting donations has been one more arrow in the solicitor's lobbying quiver. Some describe these collectors as "Washington lawyer/lobbyists" who package donations and cut policy deals for their corporate and professional clients.[58] Others portray them as a "nationwide network of lobbyists" organized by directors of key trade associations. The head of one such lobbyist network in 1996 was the president of the National Association of Wholesale Distributors— his sales team included lobbyists from tobacco companies, drug manufacturers, and the gambling industry. Collecting multiple contributions would yield multiple rewards. In exchange for selling $250,000 worth of tickets to the 1996 convention gala fund-raiser, the RNC would give the head of the sales team two seats at the head table, six convention passes, four Republican Eagles club memberships, and access to the convention's exclusive Team 100 events, including breakfast with presidential candidate Dole.[59] But the largest contributors would often give on their own, presumably for maximum impact, as the RNC tacitly acknowledged in promising the same rewards to $250,000-plus individual donors.

While the donation apparatus increasingly is riddled with improprieties and illegalities, donors' motivations differ. A 1988 and 1992 survey of donors who contributed $200 or more to presidential campaigns differentiated among those giving for economic advantage, those seeking the opportunity to interact with candidates, and those who shared the candidate's values and policy goals. While many of these well-informed donors felt strongly about the issues, others responded out of a sense of civic duty or from fear of not giving to socially and economically prominent solicitors (much like donors pressured in philanthropic fund-raising campaigns).

A number of contributors to both parties were not shy about expressing such economic or ideological expectations. As money has assumed greater importance in elections, the demands of what some political scientists and journalists now call the second constituency—a telling phrase—resonate. The second constituency really delivers. While elections are often closer now, in 1996 House races, the candidate who raised the most money won 92 percent of the time; in Senate races, they won 88 percent of the time. Winners are more likely to attract donors, but even in races rated by independent analysts as toss-ups before election day, money overwhelmingly correlated with victory.[60] Money, however, is no guarantee of success, and collection of large campaign sums can sometimes signal that a candidate is in trouble. In the 1996 Senate races, seven of the top fifteen fund-raisers lost, and three of the top twenty-five House fund-raisers were defeated.[61] Furthermore, insurgents need not outspend incumbents; their task, rather, is to spend a considerable sum to gain the necessary voter recognition.[62]

The money race and dependence on large donors inevitably increased during the 2000 presidential race, and it will continue to do so. Jack Germond and Jules Witcover emphasized that in a Senate race without an incumbent, a serious candidate needs to raise $20 million.[63] The higher the amounts needed, the more likely that candidates will seek them from large donors. Direct mailing costs, too, are high, and the additional needed funds are unlikely to come from a jaded electorate. In addition, the organizational cost of soliciting small donations is high, and the proportion of donors has remained the same in recent years. The declining role of these donors is particularly disturbing, since these people would not expect to exercise political influence in exchange for a small contribution, while their removal from politics leaves a political vacuum to be filled by PACs and large individual donors with greater expectations. So the fat cats are back.

While the fat cats are the prima donnas in this political game, there are numerous other, often significant, role players in the second constituency. As in baseball, it takes a scorecard (see Table 4.2) to follow the players and see where they fit into the political lineup. Like any challenging game, this one has rules, and they must be carefully observed by the players—in this case the donors and politicians. We turn now to a discussion of the game's goal and those rules.

The Rules of the Game

What do the fat cats and other members of the second constituency get for their money? When questioned by journalists or political scientists, the invariable answer is "access," or, as it is frequently phrased, the right to see the member of Congress or "have your telephone calls answered." PACs and other donors are definitely purchasing the opportunity to be heard. As

Table 4.2 Scorecard for the Second Constituency: The Campaign-Contributor Lineup[a]

1. Lead-off hitter	Makes a point of getting into the action a lot so the heavy hitters will bring him or her home, too. Walks; is willing to be hit or whatever it takes to make good contacts.
2. Spray hitter	Hits the ball to all fields to gain access where it counts and to move along the other base runners. EMILY's List,[b] a spray-hit supporter of female congressional candidates, is one of the best.
3. Extra-base hitter	Has a high batting average and brings considerable clout to the plate, which attracts a lot of independent expenditures. While sometimes appearing "uncoordinated," s/he is a reliable hitter who comes through in the clutch when really needed by supporters.
4. Cleanup hitter	The individual fat-cat contributor who has the money to hit the ball out of the park financially, thereby bringing the politicians to their feet cheering. A master, like Dick Vos, of the million-dollar soft-money swing.
5. The chatterer	The sponsor does not have the fat cat's power but creates even more power by bundling together many contributions and bringing them home. A wheeler-dealer on the base paths. Defends the right to talk a lot while playing—called freedom of speech—to cover up stealing the bases.
6. Erratic power hitter	Leadership PACs are capable of hitting higher in the order but are less consistent. Dick Gephardt or Dick Armey may hit it into the seats or strike out ignominiously in the caucus. These congressional leaders and aspiring leaders collect a lot of money from wealthy organizations and distribute it to other members of the congressional team. Some team members resent the notion that the captain can buy his position, but they usually bat farther down in the pecking order and sometimes depend on the captain to get into the game.
7. Singles hitter	These players have lost some of the power in their PAC swing. As individual PACs they still are forced to play by the hard-money rules. They are starting to ignore the FEC umpire and may soon shuck the disgrace of having choked up to avoid being reported to the commissioner.
8. Pop-up hitter	The small donor viewed now with contempt for contributing only chump change to the game. They are an embarrassment to the team because they are just not worth the time and money that go into recruiting.
9. Designated hitter	The batter who hits for the pitcher—often a switch hitter willing to bat from either side of the plate. Switch hitters in the political game grease the palms of whichever team holds the upper hand, and, like Carl Linder and Dwayne Andreas, switch to whichever party is in power in order to keep playing. Doesn't care who wins.

Notes: a. People at the grassroots level are in charge of keeping the playing field mowed.

b. EMILY—early money is like yeast (it rises to the top).

one Washington lawyer put it, "A member's time is very limited. Who do you see? They'll certainly see the ones who gave the money. It's hard to say no to someone who gave you five grand."[64] Political scientists claim, however, that far from guaranteeing success on large, visible roll-call votes, donor concerns usually have less influence on the vote cast by a member of Congress than pressures from constituency, party leaders, or ideology or the position of the administration. Furthermore, the large number of interest groups increases the possibility that in the push for influence, they will simply cancel each other out.

So why do donors continue to pour money into politics and place so much emphasis on access if it really accomplishes so little? Richard Hall and Frank Wayman emphasize that contributions gravitate to the House-committee level not only because early votes are taken there but also because so much of the activity necessary for a bill to become a law takes place there. It is thus critical to give funds in a manner that mobilizes potential "coalition leaders" and demobilizes likely opponents by encouraging them to refrain from opposing the legislation. The key activity is not the final vote, but rather the numerous steps leading to that point—such as authoring or blocking a proposed amendment while in committee, negotiating compromises behind the scenes, and pushing the bill during and after committee action—and promoting the bill through its subsequent rite of passage. The member's time and intensity of support during the formative stages thus become more important than the formal roll-call vote. Access is the prerequisite to such participation.

The case of conservative Democratic congressman Bill Brewster bears out this argument. Low in seniority, Brewster nonetheless landed a seat on the powerful Ways and Means Committee and, over six years, parlayed it into $2 million in campaign contributions. Jean Mastres, of Occidental Petroleum, one of the oil-industry lobbyists who has organized fund-raising events for Brewster, is frank in explaining why. We meet "as concerned constituents, if you will, not just constituents of Oklahoma but constituents of the energy industry." You "always look for someone like Brewster to 'carry the water' on an issue." Brewster proved a skillful coalition builder, as he organized a bloc of 117 members of Congress to bring a "wish list" of oil-industry issues to the White House's attention.[65]

The transaction between campaign-finance donors and politicians does not involve the crass purchase of a vote. Considerations other than contributions come into play during the final vote. Rather, the essence of the transaction is an exchange of donor money for the politician's time and energy—important resources in the House (or the Senate and White House).[66] Access confers opportunity—often ongoing contact during deliberations—both to obtain the politician's involvement and sometimes also to assist in molding the nature of the legislation. Access, though, is not enough. Donors must also meet two other expectations. First, since legislation is also a contest of ideas, when face-to-face with the politician the donor must have persuasive information. Indeed, lobbyists spend more money on staff research in amassing reliable information than on contributions. But the two are often inseparably intertwined: access without information spells futility; information without access spells impotence. Second, certain rules of the game need to be observed.

It's the Little Things

Lobbyists' studies also address items less visible in a document the size of the Fiscal Year 2001 budget of $1.8 trillion. Important to donors (and district constituents), these items add up. Take, for example, the Tax Reform Act of 1986, a measure rightly hailed for closing $300 billion in loopholes over five years and for raising corporate taxes by $120 billion over five years.[67] That measure included numerous "transition rules" ostensibly intended to ease the transition between the existing and the new tax law. In actuality these rules provide the committee chair opportunities to allocate enough special favors for the first (geographical) and second (money) constituencies to pass the legislation. The official estimate for passing the Tax Reform Act was $10.6 billion in such "transition rule" favors, but Donald Bartlett and James Steele, in a series in the *Philadelphia Inquirer* that won a Pulitzer Prize, estimated the figure as considerably higher. They detailed a large number of these estimated 650 "giveaways" to the wealthy and politically well-connected with access that in most cases lacked even the semblance of a rationale. Presumably for this reason, the House Ways and Means Committee and the Senate Finance Committee have refused in such legislation to name either the individual lawmakers requesting tax immunity for their constituents or the beneficiaries of such provisions. A typical amendment thus reads:

> (C) SPECIAL AUTOMOBILE CARRIER VEHICLES.—The amendments made by section 201 shall not apply to two new automobile carrier vessels which will cost approximately $47,000,000 and will be constructed by a United States-flag carrier to operate, under the United States-flag with an American crew, to transport foreign automobiles to the United States, in a case where negotiations for such transportation arrangements commenced in April 1985, formal contract bids were submitted prior to the end of 1985, and definitive transportation contracts were awarded in May 1986.

The entire legislative process surrounding such tax indulgences is so dependent on secrecy that most members of Congress are themselves unaware of the provisions when they vote on tax legislation.[68]

But such fine print is hardly confined to tax legislation. Forty pages of extensions, exceptions, and qualifications were added to the Clean Air Act Amendments of 1990. Some could be justified on grounds of economic necessity, but others were far more questionable. One provision allowed the steel industry thirty years to alter twenty-six coke ovens that pose a cancer risk greater than one in a thousand, and six years for ovens where the risk is greater than one in a hundred.[69]

Many measures sought by donors do not require passage of legislation—some require simply maintaining a profitable status quo, dealing with a technicality, or assuring a road not taken. Lobbyists may be entrusted with watching a valuable mining subsidy or ozone tax exemption to insure that it remains in place. Or the favor may take a more subtle form. Former Senator William Proxmire provided illustrations of such payoffs to PACs and other donors: "It may not come to a vote. It may come in a speech not delivered . . . a colleague not influenced . . . calling off a meeting that otherwise would advance legislation . . . a minor change in one paragraph of a 240 page bill . . . (or) hiring a key staff member for a committee who is sympathetic to the PAC."[70]

Be a Friend

The jobs of lobbyists and politicians are similar in that both require a compelling personality, a reasonable amount of intelligence, street smarts, and the capacity to eat, drink, and be civil, if not merry, for extended periods of time. Consequently there is a natural inclination for these people—who also share an interest in politics, power, and the Washington scene—to like each other. That instinct easily becomes intertwined with self-interest. These friendships all too often are forged between lobbyists, their clients, and the members of Congress on the committees closest to their interests. For example, members of the House Agriculture Committee received an average of $76,000 from farmers, ranchers, pesticide manufacturers, and other agricultural interests during the 1991–1992 election period. And Hollywood film studios and TV broadcasters gave heavily to the Telecommunications and Finance Subcommittee of the Energy and Commerce Committee.

There is a consistent pattern of such giving by professional associations, companies, and unions to members of both parties across the congressional committee spectrum. The pattern in the House (where members are usually assigned to only one or two committees) is different from the one in the Senate (where members belong to three or four committees and giving is focused on those senators up for reelection).[71] The amounts also differ by congressional cycle depending on which issues are under consideration. For example, when the Senate considered legislation that sharply limited the financial liability of accounting and securities firms for fraud by corporate clients, campaign donations by financial-service PAC contributions to the five senior senators in charge of overhauling securities law and regulation nearly doubled from $420,786 in 1994 to $829,726 in 1995.[72] The political logic of cultivating long-term friendships in strategic locations remains a constant, however.

The resulting access is carefully orchestrated in friendly surroundings. One lobbyist captures nicely how this seductive process works, "We'd like to have an opportunity to talk to people. They have to listen and sift, and we just want to be part of the listen-and-sift process. . . . One sure way that people recognize you is that your name has been signed on the bottom of a check."[73] Senator Bob Packwood appreciated this aromatic blend of money and friendship: when his wife filed for divorce, he turned to "his" lobbyists for help in finding a part-time job for her and a "small, two-bedroom town house" for him. When questioned by the Ethics Committee about the propriety of "hitting up" such favor-seekers, he explained, "These were old friends. I've been in politics a quarter of a century, and there would be, I suppose, a thousand lobbyists you could get to and make this kind of request? . . . I didn't go to them. I went to people that I had known, that were friends of mine, in some cases drinking buddies of mine."[74] Small wonder that PAC contributions so heavily favor incumbents—not only do these members of Congress have the power, but donors already have a major investment in time and money in these relationships.

Remember to Say Thank You

When members of Congress or the president vote in a manner consistent with the interest of a particular company, large union, or professional trade association, they expect to be rewarded in turn. A notorious case in 1980 involved the Senate majority whip, Alan Cranston, who wanted to obtain a campaign donation from the California S&L industry. He therefore successfully pushed for legislation that would insure up to $100,000 in S&L deposits (a guarantee that eventually cost hundreds of billions when the S&Ls collapsed). Cranston subsequently met James Grogan, a lobbyist for the later-notorious S&L banker Charles Keating, at the 1984 Democratic convention. "I've worked hard for California savings and loans," Cranston said, whipping out a three-by-five index card to record Grogan's name. Within days, Grogan received a phone call from Cranston's fund-raiser.[75]

When Al Gore, as vice president, telephoned a telecommunications executive to acknowledge a $125,000 party contribution, the donor, according to journalist Bob Woodward, subsequently expressed some surprise. After all, the donation was the result of advice from a Gore fund-raising solicitor, who was also a telecommunications lobbyist. He had earlier

phoned the firm to say that it would be a good idea to "thank" the administration for an award to the firm of a $36 million contract. In a similar vein,
according to the *Boston Globe* Democratic fund-raisers approached large
corporate donors soon after the Commerce Department aggressively mar-
keted their operations abroad. Jonathan Cohn observes that if it could be
shown that the administration had made such promotions on the basis of
likely campaign donations, a scandal would have resulted.[76] Such connections can rarely be drawn definitively in the ambiguous world of campaign
finance, but the Democratic fund-raisers, nonetheless, thought that the
administration's efforts merited a thank-you.

Let Your Friends Help

Formal lobbying implies there is something of an adversarial situation in
which an organization is attempting to exercise influence. Where possible,
lobbyists prefer to not be the aggressor. "The best of all possible worlds is
to be in constant contact with policymakers, continually giving them information about the problems facing the group."[77] The Audubon Society has
described how in 1995 the process of amending the 1972 Clean Water Act
provided an example of how advocacy can evolve into such a trusting relationship. The story goes that what the society dubbed the 267 "Dirty Water
PACs," pursuing an antienvironmental agenda, between 1989 and 1994,
contributed $57 million to Republicans who were already ideologically
sympathetic to such deregulation. Thanks also to their know-how on getting what they wanted statutorily and on parrying the thrusts of the environmentalists, the relevant committees in 1995 allowed the key lobbyists for
these PACs to provide staff to the lawmakers, draft parts of the bills, and sit
on the dais with members of Congress during the hearings. In addition, the
lobbyists had an office to write amendments during the floor debate on legislation that provided regulatory relief to oil and gas companies, chemical
manufacturers, ranchers, and developers.[78]

Democratic and Republican members of Congress have drawn on this
ability of well-heeled companies, trade associations, and unions to marshal
expertise and money in support of their friends. While such practices have
existed in the past, they have increased with the growth in campaign spending. Charles Lewis has thus observed a similar pattern of representatives
sitting side-by-side with the lobbyists whose money helped to elect them as
they deliberated on workplace safety, information technology, and public
health.[79] Such cozy arrangements hardly guarantee victory or such legislation would never have been born in the first place. But it is difficult to galvanize public opinion or the media in seemingly undramatic cases where a
balance is being struck between important, but technical, environmental
issues and legitimate economic concerns over rulemaking excesses.

Cultivate Your Second Constituency

Tony Coelho, a former congressman and chair of the Democratic Congressional Campaign Committee, realized by the early 1980s that matching Republican Party power under the Reagan administration would require money. Money in turn would require the cultivation of the second (money) constituency. As Brooks Jackson put it, "Coelho interceded for a donor from another state just as naturally as he would have for a businessman from Modesto, in his own district. One was entitled to help by virtue of residence, the other by virtue of his currency."[80]

While big, visible roll-call votes are driven by other concerns, members of Congress or even the president must concentrate both on satisfying voters so they will continue to provide their votes and on satisfying donors so they will continue to write their checks. The stakes are certainly clear. Where investors do not receive a return on their money, they will go elsewhere. Former Senator John Culver explains the problem: "All other things being equal, [the members of Congress] hope that if you've got a problem, they can support your position, and they realize that if they can't, they're not going to get any money from you in the future."[81]

Many issues, though, attract little public attention, and here, members of Congress can devote more attention to the second constituency. In the 1980 campaign, automobile dealers spent $675,000 to overturn a Federal Trade Commission (FTC) regulation requiring them to list the major defects of each second-hand automobile for sale. Of the 286 House members who voted to kill the FTC regulation, 242 received money from the auto dealers. "Of course it was money," remarked one dealer; "Why else would they vote for used car dealers?"[82] Former congresswoman Patricia Schroeder calls this "coin-operated legislation."

Political scientists are beginning to find systematic evidence that, under certain conditions, members of Congress may lean toward the second constituency even when district voters are concerned about an issue. Thanks to the pressure to collect political money, members are sometimes more responsive to organized business interests within their districts than to unorganized voters even when those voters feel strongly about an issue.[83] Thomas Stratmann demonstrates that PACs contribute on the basis of highly rational strategies that pressure members of Congress to comply on the basis of their financial support. Under these circumstances the politician must sometimes trade-off positions favored by constituents for the sake of an adequate war chest. Indeed, close roll-call votes concerning budgetary, regulatory, and social policy issues have indicated that the further the politician moved from a position favored by constituents, the more money the politician received from the concerned PACs.[84]

Politicians historically have traded-off constituent votes on some issues in exchange for support from politically active supporters who help them mobilize voters and are ideologically committed to some positions. But while it is one thing to engage in such a vote calculus with members of the politician's district or state constituency, it is another thing to make such an exchange with members of the second constituency for campaign contributions on matters also important to their geographical constituents. Both President Bill Clinton and the Republican leadership made such trade-offs with high rollers who were close allies. Trial lawyers represented the largest single group of contributors to President Clinton's two presidential campaigns, and he reciprocated in 1996 by vetoing a popular product-liability reform bill. He also vetoed a securities reform opposed by virtually no one except a small collection of lawyers who viewed the suing of stock-brokers to be, as one of them put it, "a growth industry."[85] As expected, Congress immediately overrode the veto on the securities-reform bill, but it is significant that the president deemed it politically advantageous to undergo such legislative repudiation in order to signal loyalty to a powerful member of the second constituency. Similarly, in 1997 the Republican House leadership, who receive far more campaign contributions than the Democrats from the tobacco companies, attempted to slip into the balanced-budget negotiations a $50-billion tobacco tax credit against the sum the tobacco companies would have to pledge to settle antitobacco legislation. Such action was apparently viewed as politically advantageous in the long run, even though their primary constituency, the public, was insisting that members of Congress should take a strong stand against Big Tobacco.

Don't Be Shy

Just as donors have become less shy in making explicit their demands on politicians, so have members of Congress and the president become more brazen in expressing their wants. Hustling donors for money is certainly not new. Historians Samuel Eliot Morrison and Henry Steele Commager describe how Mark "Dollar" Hanna in 1896 "shook down" metropolitan banks, insurance companies, and railroad corporations for colossal campaign contributions.[86] George Cortelyou, while serving as secretary of commerce, founded a Bureau of Corporations designed to gather information on big corporations. When he later became Theodore Roosevelt's campaign manager in 1904, he vigorously pursued campaign contributions from these companies, and was accused of blackmailing those who refused to contribute—a ploy that came to be known as "Cortelyouism."[87]

Fred McChesney has described colorfully some of the more recent strategies. "Cash cow" legislation is introduced by "milkers" to threaten corporations unless contributions are forthcoming. Such legislation rarely passes but reappears every session to fill legislative coffers. McChesney cites the example of product-liability legislation that is likely to remain in legislative limbo but, just in case, attracts PAC money from both sides of the issue. Sometimes called "fetcher" bills, these quickly draw campaign funds from lobbyists.[88] When Representative Jim Leach introduced a bill to reduce speculation in financial futures, he learned within twenty-four hours that his bill was shaping up as a classic fetcher bill. One of the first to defend the traders thus was Illinois representative Cardiss Collins, who had just received $24,500 from futures-industry PACs.

In the case of tax policy, members of Congress almost seem to be running a protection racket, as wealthy individuals and PACs are pressured to contribute regularly in order both to "play defense, protecting yourself from being a victim of a drive-by tax increase" and offense, thereby gaining new tax advantages. In addition, the president wants a piece of the action, which adds another level to the game: "You pay with generous campaign contributions for a tax break only to find it knocked out at the White House. Better buy some protection there too. Gaming the tax code has gotten a lot more expensive."[89] Furthermore, Congress has raised the stakes in recent years by writing more provisions that expire annually into the tax law.

The Irrelevance of the "Smoking Gun"

Lawyers, social scientists, and politicians agree that there is one type of transaction where politicians and donors risk going to jail. When the politician offers support in exchange for a contribution, and the donor agrees to the deal and provides the check, either a bribe or extortion has occurred. Which it is depends on the circumstances. Extortion would result from a threat by the politician to eliminate something of value to the donor, while bribery would follow from a donor's request that the politician undertake an illegal act. In both cases there is explicit agreement over a specifically identified matter.

Just how difficult it is to prove such acts is demonstrated in the *McCormick v. U.S.* case. Here a West Virginia legislator had supported legislation favored by a particular group after telling its lobbyist that his campaign was expensive, that he had paid considerable sums out of his pocket, and that he had not heard anything from the group, even though he was supporting its legislation. The lobbyist raised some money from group members and gave McCormick an envelope containing $2,900 in cash. McCormick was convicted of extortion, but the ruling was overturned on appeal after McCormick contended that the money was a campaign contribution. The court ruled that such contributions do not violate the law unless "the payments are made in return for an explicit promise or undertaking by the official to perform or not to perform an official act."[90] Here it was not demonstrated that the legislator performed a specific act in exchange for the campaign contribution.

The Quid Pro Quo

Proving the buying of votes requires evidence of a particularly stringent nature. It must be more stringent than—to pick another venue in which evidence must be weighed—the demonstration of an "association," or statistical correlation, in social science. For example, data may demonstrate an association when more cases of lung cancer develop among those who smoke than among those who do not. The association suggests a connection between the "inputs" (cigarettes) and the "outcomes" (lung cancer).[91] Amitai Etzioni is able to report a number of associations between sizable campaign contributions by private interests and legislation favorable to them. But such associations, while persuasive to many citizens, do not suffice in a court of law and do not constitute what the media call "the smoking gun." Such evidence could be circumstantial. The evidence that would have sent McCormick to jail would have shown the process—the "mechanism"—by which an "input" causes an "outcome"—the process in our example by which smoking cigarettes causes lung cancer. Where a quid pro quo can be established, it takes on dramatic meaning, not only in a court of law but also in the political realm.

The line between legal campaign-fund solicitation and an illegal quid pro quo is a thin one. This delicate distinction is lost on a number of the less sophisticated donors. Former Democratic Congressman Pete Stark explains the potential danger: "I've got guys coming into my office who are felonies waiting to happen. I've got dipshits talking about tax amendments, and in the same breath talking about raising money. You could put them in jail for that." As a congressman, Tony Coelho acknowledged the danger and would tell donors: "I want you to help out the party and I want you to do something, but don't think you're buying anything. Don't think you're making a deal with me."[92]

Because the evidentiary rules are so stringent, examples of quid pro quos are rare. The Senate Ethics Committee, though, has examined campaign-contribution cases that led to censure. Senator Robert Packwood's diaries in 1995 recorded two such violations. While Packwood's several well-documented cases of sexual harassment attracted more attention, the funding references are of more relevance here: one referred to a discussion with Senator Phil Gramm, then chair of the National Republican Senatorial Committee, and some staffers. Gramm was said to have promised to skirt the law in order to pump $100,000 in soft money "for party-building activities" into Packwood's 1992 reelection campaign. "Now, of course, you know there can't be any legal connection between this money and Senator Packwood, but we know that it will be used for his benefit." Packwood later wrote about this exchange, "What was said in that room would be enough to convict us all of something."[93] The other violation related to solicitation of an independent expenditure contribution from Auto Dealers and Drivers for Fair Trade by a top Packwood aide—an illegal contact since such soft-money contributions cannot be coordinated with a candidate.[94] While no legal action was taken, Packwood stepped down from his powerful position as chairman of the Senate Finance Committee and later that year resigned from the Senate.

Although the 1996 election did not result in any legal proceedings, because of the more aggressive fund-raising pitches, the line between legal campaign-fund solicitation and an illegal quid pro quo had now become even thinner. Take, for example, the loan by Nationsbank (now BankAmerica) to cover a Democratic National Committee shortfall. President Clinton spoke personally with bank president Hugh McColl about providing a $3.5 million loan. McColl at the time was pursuing interstate banking legislation that would enable Nationsbank to do business even in those states where it did not maintain an office. McColl is alleged to have made such legislative passage a *condition* for the loan—a possibility that looked more like a probability when the loan was granted two weeks after the legislation passed. When pressed on whether this constituted a quid pro quo, a Nationsbank official reported laconically that "Hugh came to believe that President Clinton understood the issues." Upon seeing McColl and the president subsequently sitting together at a basketball game, a banking-industry commentator observed,

> Based on what the president has done for him lately, I would have expected to see Hugh sitting on his lap. . . . In days gone by, political *quid pro quos* were usually paid off with stuffed ballot boxes. Laws were passed to stop that sort of chicanery. Now it is done with money.[95]

The Irrelevance of Watergate

In reviewing the Watergate campaign-finance deals of the 1970s from the less innocent perspective of three decades later, the most striking impression is how relatively small, even allowing for inflation, the amounts collected by the Nixon White House were, and how many of the same goals, with only a few minor adjustments, donors and politicians can achieve legally today. A brief recital of these earlier deals underscores how much the political system has moved toward a Watergate mentality.

The Watergate saga revealed that numerous corporations during the 1972 election year maintained secret funds for the financing of federal campaigns. Richard Nixon's personal Committee for the Re-Election of the President (CREEP) had raised almost $17 million from only 124 contributors, who gave more than $50,000 each. The subsequent criminal investigations also revealed that 1,254 "fat cats" had contributed a total of $51.3 million. The biggest and most notorious donor was W. Clement Stone, who gave more than $2 million to CREEP. And $7 million had been received from people who were given ambassadorships.[96] Subsequent laws were drawn with the specific purpose of preventing large donors and corporations from dominating future elections.

The scandal drew its name from the failed attempt to bug the DNC offices in the Watergate complex in Washington, D.C. The Watergate scandal, however, also came to include numerous dirty tricks involving the collection and spending of illegal corporate and foreign campaign funds and a series of official lies that eventually became known as "the cover-up." These lies included the misuse of federal agencies with the capacity to gather and disseminate politically delicate information—the CIA and FBI—and potentially damaging financial information—the IRS—which took on a particularly sinister glow in light of "enemy lists" compiled in the White House. It also extended to what Larry Sabato and Glenn Simpson have termed "gross political and governmental improprieties, such as massive, hidden cash contributions to a presidential campaign."[97]

The volunteer executives working for CREEP caused quite a stir by suggesting to corporate executives that a "quota" of $100,000 was expected. For their part, the donors did their best to hide the fact that these monies came from their corporate treasuries, and in doing so, recounts Herbert Alexander, introduced the term *money laundering* into the U.S. political lexicon.[98] Some of this cash was transported in suitcases to pay the burglars who broke into the DNC's Watergate offices. Nonetheless, large corporations often were clearly maneuvering for future gain and were punished; 21 major corporations, including American Airlines, Goodyear Tire and Rubber, and Gulf Oil, pleaded guilty to making illegal campaign contributions totaling nearly $1 million to five Democratic presidential candidates as well as to the Nixon campaign.[99]

Conclusion

While some critics have blamed politicians for shaking down campaign contributors, others have put the onus on the contributors. With a few exceptions, though, both have readily agreed to enter into arrangements that enable them to profit financially or politically by making or accepting such contributions in situations where without such agreements they could not, or would be less likely to, achieve their goals. The idea is to purchase through campaign contributions what might not (or might) otherwise be achieved through the normal political process. It is precisely the failure of this political process to adapt to changing electoral realities that has led to the acceptance of what previously constituted illegal or unethical behavior.

Where corporations fail to adapt to changing conditions, management consultants often invoke the parable of the "boiled frog." Peter Senge describes what happens. When a frog is placed in a pot of boiling water, it will immediately try to scramble out. However, if the frog is placed in room-temperature water, it will stay put. If the pot sits on a heat source, and the temperature is gradually raised, the frog will do nothing. Indeed, it will show every sign of enjoying itself. As the temperature gradually increases, the frog will become groggier and groggier, until he is unable to climb out of the pot. Though nothing is restraining him, the frog will sit there and boil. Why? Because the frog's internal apparatus for sensing threats to survival is geared to sudden changes in his environment, not to slow, gradual changes.[100]

The temperature of campaign-finance activity has already risen to the point where it now includes numerous examples of misfeasance (the doing of a lawful act in an unlawful or improper manner), malfeasance (wrongdoing or misconduct, especially by a public official), and nonfeasance (failure to do what duty requires to be done). The historically unprecedented amounts in congressional and presidential contributions are incurring a disturbing number of obligations to contributors. If the frog does not scramble soon, it will be too late.

5

Pathways to Congressional Decisionmaking

M embers of Congress seeking to control their uncertain political destiny must first build a political base within their district or state and then raise the campaign funds to sustain that base. Within the Congress, Morris Fiorina observes, there are three ways that members can seek to strengthen their reelection chances: lawmaking, casework, and pork-barreling. While lawmaking is more central to the congressional task, going on record may well be controversial and alienate some voters. Furthermore, it is rarely possible to take much credit for large bills involving actions by numerous congressional leaders, committees, and other members. Casework and pork-barreling, by contrast, involve activities by the member that are both uncontroversial and visible to his or her constituents. Aided and abetted by the growth of an activist federal government, members of Congress accordingly have shifted the mix of their congressional activities so that less of their congressional effort is now going into programmatic activities and more into pork-barrel and casework activities.[1] Reelection supplied the motive and activist government the opportunity.

Porkophobes vs. Porkophiles

Considerable controversy has surrounded the prevalence and growing significance of pork-barreling. "Porkophobes" claim to see a little porker behind every tree and roundly condemn the practice as bereft of purpose and antithetical to the public interest. Their angry literature details a congressional politics where members focus on cutting deals with special interests and neglect vital public-policy concerns. Some porkophobes, such as the Washington-based Citizens Against Government Waste (CAGW), focus on cataloging specific cases of waste throughout the political system; others, such as numerous "public choice" economists, concentrate on the theory of "rent seeking"—the widespread and growing use of political or institutional power by influential predators to extract money illegitimately from others in the economy. These rents are in effect unavoidable costs provid-

139

ing no benefit to society. They must be paid to those possessing the public-
or private-sector power to collect them. For example, Washington lobbyists
are little more than parasitical public-sector rent seekers who are paid to
extract rents by influencing legislation on behalf of their corporate clients.[2]
"Porkophiles" include a number of political scientists who view pork as
limited in scope, valuable in the role it performs for geographical areas in
the political system, and necessary as a means of achieving agreement on
the bigger issues. Their analytical literature decries the danger that reformers might succeed in abolishing pork, believing it would reduce the ability
of the political system to make sound public policy.

Both porkophiles and porkophobes accept the fundamental principle
underlying cozy politics. Namely, those engaging in such activity are driv-
en primarily by their own needs rather than by the needs of particular categories of people, the public at large, or, arguably, society. Just what constitutes the public interest sometimes is difficult to say, but those engaged in
cozy political arrangements seldom feel obliged to resolve that thorny
issue. Members of Congress can, and sometimes do, claim that everyone
solicits pork projects for their district or state; therefore, they say, the sum
total of such activity is in the interest of the public as a whole. But that
claim depends on the pork's quality, which varies considerably. Members
of Congress who solicit friends and neighbors for campaign funds in
exchange for the possibility of political favors sometimes justify such
activity as, while not necessarily in the public interest, a normal part of the
political process. "Everybody does it" becomes the rallying cry, and members are surprisingly frank in delivering this rejection of any broader justification for spending the taxpayers' money.

The committee chair or member who engages in cozy politics by
squeezing money from special interests or the second constituency in
exchange for access that later translates into legislative favoritism can
make no such defense. Ladling pork to the second constituency is cloaked
by no such legitimacy. The concerns of wealthy individuals, powerful interest groups, and professional elites increasingly must be taken into account
when making public policy in which they have important interests at stake,
but these individuals or groups possess no real or implied right to pork.

The Nature of Congressional Decisionmaking

Who has it right—porkophiles or porkophobes? The answer lies in how
Congress makes decisions and involves understanding not only the decisions themselves but also the pathways leading to those decisions. Four
such pathways to decisionmaking are summarized in Table 5.1. They
demonstrate that both porkophiles and porkophobes have it partly right and

Table 5.1   Four Pathways to Congressional Decisionmaking

	District or State Support	Policy Subsystems	Second-Constituency Support	Public Programs and Regulations
Programs	Allocations distributed on geographical basis	Program subsidies sanctioned & distributed by committees	Tax preferences & program subsidies allocated by committees	Large entitlements, tax preferences, defense & regulatory decisions made by Congress & the president
Primary actor	Individual legislator	Cong. committees, interest groups, & executive bureaus	Committee member or other interested legislator	Policy entrepreneurs
Power source	Grassroots influentials	Information	Money	Popular ideas
Policy configuration	Logrolling	"Porous triangles"	Tacit exchange relationships	"Issue networks"
Type of pork	Geographical	Pet programs	Campaign-fund inducements	Piggy-back pork
Funding size	Small to medium	Medium	Small to medium	Large
Examples	Lighthouse	Cotton subsidy	Ethanol subsidy	Social Security
Who benefits	Members of first constituency	Groups active in the policy area	Individuals & groups from the second constituency	Majority of citizens

partly wrong. Each pathway contains an implicit or explicit public-interest version, but each also contains pork that now extends beyond its historical and legitimate boundaries both in size and in the number of public-policy areas where it is ladled.

Contrary to popular impression, though, decisions on the vital issues are driven primarily by voter sentiment and by competing personal and congressional party visions of what constitutes the public interest. The basic intent, however, frequently is lost in the pork deals and the increasingly shrill dialogue that precedes the key roll-call vote. Furthermore, these key decisions sometimes seem akin to needles buried in a haystack of decisions on less pivotal issues characterized by some waste and, at best, ambiguous intent. These decisions, if discovered, are labeled as "political" by the media, a word that has come to symbolize actions undertaken at the expense of citizens by members of Congress and the president. The decisions frequently benefit wealthy campaign contributors, powerful groups within the member's district or state, or special interests that are national in scope. Such cozy political arrangements, while not representative of Congress at its best, suffuse the political system. They are driven by the increasing expectations of geographically based individuals and national interest groups as to what government can and should do for them, and by the entrepreneurial zest of those members of Congress who seek out additional means of satisfying such great expectations. As election costs continue to expand rapidly, the financial and political costs of meeting those expectations rise, too. The pressure to maintain and expand the number of such cozy political arrangements thus experiences comparable growth.

The nature of this increasing cozy-politics problem can be seen by examining the four pathways to congressional decisionmaking. Each pathway contains a different type of decision making with its own public-interest version. These decisions pertain to district and state representation, policy subsystems, the second constituency, and the more important public programs and regulations. But also strewn along each pathway are cozy political arrangements characterized by a different type of pork.

District and State Support

Pork-barrel politics consists of annual, geographically distributed congressional allocations that, while having comparatively little impact on the overall budget, are viewed as important politically to members of Congress. This perceived importance is thanks to constituents' gratitude toward their legislators for "bringing home the bacon." As such, argue the porkophiles, these projects can sometimes bestow large political rewards on an individual member of Congress. Furthermore, since Congress "is chiefly a collection of local representatives attuned to local interests," *traditional pork* is an integral part of a member's job.[3] By bringing home to the district or state such trophies as a courthouse, a marina, or some other small local subsidy, the member of Congress is doing what district and state citizens expect.

The Advantages of Traditional Pork

If pork did not already exist, members of Congress would need to reinvent it today. For Congress to tackle controversial budgetary and other large issues, "pork, doled out strategically, can help to sweeten an otherwise unpalatable piece of legislation."[4] It can appease local-constituency concerns and thereby free members of Congress to do the right thing on the critical issues. Pork thereby becomes "the necessary glue that holds political coalitions together."[5] These coalitions enable members of Congress both to meet local needs that otherwise would be unpalatable to other districts or states and to build support on larger issues where strong differences on ideas throughout the country would otherwise undercut legislative agreement. Members of Congress in effect trade away their opportunity to support or oppose a major decision in exchange for the bestowal of small, visible, and popular projects that will attract more votes in their home district or state.

Such logrolling, though, can take different forms. One is indeed the addition of small pork projects to a major authorization or appropriations bill or to another bill in exchange for congressional support on the large measure. Another form is a so-called "Christmas tree" bill that consists of nothing but a laundry list of locally supported projects. Insertion of each member's proposed project then imposes the obligation to support the overall bill and not to question anyone else's project. Lumped together, these projects can total billions of dollars, and the problem arises as to how much pork is enough. Where is the line to be drawn?

Pork Allocations vs. Deliberative Decisionmaking

This problem is complicated by the difficulty in distinguishing between pork and the distribution of all other goods and services by the federal government. After all, the distribution pattern of any legislation ultimately reflects the values of those who passed the program or implemented it. Hence, all "distributive" programs, whether they deal with, for example, maintenance for national parks, the location of employment and training programs, or the use of federal funds to hire police in high crime areas, impose one set of policy preferences over others. They also constitute decisions on which localities and states win and lose. As former House Speaker Tip O'Neill liked to say, "all politics is local"; a national need from this vantage point consists of nothing more than the sum of local preferences expressed through the winning coalition. This argument is periodically made more briefly and pungently by some of the more zealous congressional porkmeisters.

While it is difficult to justify one set of values and winners over another, there are critical differences between pork and distributive decisions endorsed by society. First, a majority of legislators representing districts or states have voted explicitly on the distributive program. This majority has gone on record in endorsing the policy. These members may well have reflected strong local preferences, but often their constituents may not have an opinion or be unaware of the issue, thereby leaving the politician to vote on the basis of her or his perception of which programs that benefit his or her locality are also in the national interest. Or constituents may support a popular distributive policy, even where it will not particularly benefit the member's district or state, such as the Special Supplemental Food Program for Women, Infants and Children (WIC), on the grounds that all U.S. children should be fed properly. Second, while pork must be passed as well, it is often written in such oblique form that members of Congress frequently have no knowledge of what they have authorized. Third, even when the pork is more visible, most members of Congress are simply endorsing the project without any knowledge of its quality or any intention of overseeing it (though the agency charged with implementing the pork sometimes does such evaluations).

Finessing the System

The pork additions are the products of cozy political arrangements rather than of a deliberative democratic process. The project has thus not withstood the test of having its relative strengths and weaknesses scrutinized in comparison with competing policies. Open policies, endorsed after hearings and full debate, have a legitimacy that pork lacks. While ultimate values may be difficult to justify when pitted against one another, the *process* of reaching agreement—that is, the pathway to the decision—is clearly less democratic in the case of traditional pork than for those distributive programs that have to justify themselves through the normal legislative gauntlet. The conservative public-interest group CAGW captures a number of these distinctions in defining pork: "Pork (1) is requested by only one chamber of Congress, (2) is not specifically authorized, (3) is not competitively awarded, (4) is not required by the president, (5) greatly exceeds the president's budget request or the previous year's funding, (6) is not the subject of congressional hearings, or (7) serves only a local or special interest."[6]

Republican senator Peter Domenici's success in pushing through a performing arts center for Albuquerque in 1997 demonstrates just how much of the legislative process can be avoided for a traditional pork project. Although most Republicans oppose federal funding for the arts as a matter of principle, such philosophical instincts are stifled at the prospect of servicing the district or state. On July 31, 1997, Domenici announced on the Senate floor that federal assistance to build the center was "critical." Appropriations of $3 million and $2.5 million were inserted into the Interior Department and Veterans Affairs and HUD appropriations bills, respectively. Domenici introduced the bill authorizing the center on November 7, whereupon with no hearings and little floor debate, it passed and was introduced in the House on November 8. By November 13, it had passed the House, and it was on President Clinton's desk by November 19. Such traditional pork is sprinkled through virtually all of the appropriations bills to benefit particular districts or states. Members of Congress thus assign a high priority to programs and projects viewed positively through the lens of district or state support; "waste" and dubious "government programs" do not register on their radar screens when reelection looms.

"Earmarking"

When adopting traditional pork, Domenici and others sometimes play fast and loose with the normal legislative process by earmarking the funds. The term *earmarking* is derived from the old herdsman's practice of cutting a notch in the ears of, say, swine or cattle as a mark of ownership. Earmarks are usually attached to special projects or activities in committee reports (rather than in the actual appropriations bill), often as a footnote or a short paragraph demanding that "money be spent on a certain program in a particular place, usually somewhere in the author's home district (or state)."[7] When used more loosely, though, the term also can refer to a small "rider" attached to an appropriations bill concerned with a set of larger issues on a different subject.

While some of these projects would eventually be funded anyway, members of Congress want them in writing now, thereby conferring on themselves credit for passage. Other projects, though, would never be funded purely on their merits. Take the case of the Earth Conservancy earmark, designed by Representative Paul Kanjorski for a nonprofit agency that included on its board some of his former staff aides. The Defense Department (DOD) ruled originally that the environmental technology project required more expertise than the Earth Conservancy possessed and awarded the $20 million to Rice University. Back came the earmark the following year, requiring that the contract go to Earth Conservancy.[8] Where such an earmark is merely in the report language, it does not carry the weight of law. However, only a suicidal DOD official would risk jeopardizing more important issues in the department's budget of a quarter of a trillion dollars by incurring the wrath of members of the appropriations committee and its staff.

Inflated Pork

If pork cost relatively small sums, there would be little cause for public concern. A few too many lighthouses, lonely roads, or muddy water projects are a small price to pay for legislative harmony and progress. However, while it is difficult to measure the precise amount of such largesse, there is evidence that the total amount of traditional pork—after escalating during the Reagan military expansion and congressional Democratic social program expansion in the 1980s and then subsiding in the early 1990s—has risen again. This is partly because pork has found its way into more substantive areas and partly because of the growing cost of military construction, highways, and other distributive programs. CAGW thus estimated that in FY1998, $13.2 billion was allocated in what is termed here traditional pork. That represented a drop of $1.3 billion from 1997, but in each of the two prior years, such pork had increased by 16 percent. In its widely reported *Pig Book*, CAGW found 302 of the 2,100 pork-barrel items particularly objectionable.[9]

The increasing price of pork also is reflected in a study that analyzed the electoral margins and amount of pork going into member districts. It found that members of districts with more pork won reelection by higher margins. In an average district, an additional $100 of pork-barrel spending per capita earns an incumbent about 2 percent more of the vote. Such citizen support does not come cheap. Economists Steven Levitt and James M. Snyder estimated that one vote cost $14,000. They also explain that pork is hard to target specifically, so some benefits go to neighboring districts.[10] Thus, traditional pork pays off, but only up to a point.

While the price of pork items has risen in some cases, the trend in the total amount of traditional pork seems to fluctuate somewhat, depending on budgetary exigencies and the state of the economy. But when opportunity knocks, members of Congress are ready. While congressional leaders and the president engaged in a philosophical debate over how to spend the small budgetary surplus in 1998, members pushed through earmarks in virtually every appropriations bill. Indeed, the practice is so pervasive that the press regard it as newsworthy when an appropriations subcommittee chair reports out a "clean" bill.

Struggling to Counter Pork Inflation

The relationship between the Army Corps of Engineers and Congress demonstrates that some checks on such pork-barrel spending can indeed evolve. Because dam, jetty, and other local water projects provide such visible and important opportunities for credit taking, Congress historically has exercised an unusual degree of control over the activities of the corps. By the 1970s, the corps' professional reputation suffered as its name became associated with pork-barrel politics, and porkophobes clamored to limit its appropriations. In self-defense, the corps developed cost-benefit criteria, which enabled it to eliminate thousands of economically unjustifiable projects and improve others.

"Postindustrial Pork"

While pork may be abating in the Army Corps of Engineers, it has metastasized into additional policy areas that Paul Starobin has named "post-industrial pork." Environmentalists who initially fought against some dams and other historical pork forms are now the beneficiaries of sewer projects, waste-site cleanups, pollution-control research, and other "green pork." Innumerable projects have flowed from the Clean Water Act, the Superfund, and other environmental initiatives.[11] The scores of earmarks added to the 1997 Environmental Protection Agency budget came to several hundred millions of dollars.[12] Within the Department of Housing and Urban Development that year, $100 million was also set aside for economic development projects supported by lawmakers from both parties.

"Academic pork" represents an example of just how rapidly postindustrial pork can grow. Academic earmarks are funds that Congress allocates to research projects or facilities at specific higher-educational institutions, even though money has not been requested by the administration or by a congressional authorizing committee. The lucky institution usually is located in the district or state of members of the appropriation committees. When this practice peaked in FY1993, there were more than five hundred academic earmarks allocated at a cost of about $707 million.[13]

The appropriations chairs and members pushing such awards argued that peer-reviewed science tended to favor the largest universities—numbering two dozen—at the expense of other meritorious projects and institutions. The chancellor of the University of Maryland agreed with the critics, but observed that "absent a large-scale national competition, we have no choice but to participate in the game that Congress plays—earmarking."[14] An argument can be made for casting the research net somewhat more widely. A 1984 General Accounting Office report found that powerful schools such as Stanford University, Johns Hopkins, and MIT provided one-fourth of the scientists sitting on the NSF review panels, and their universities then received 46 percent of the foundation's grants. A similar pattern appeared at the National Institutes of Health.[15] The earmarked projects thus do spread the money more widely and have in the past yielded some respectable research.

But academic earmarking in its present form is an expensive solution to the problem. Two of the schools receiving the largest grants in 1992 were in the state of the then Senate Appropriations chair, Robert Byrd. Wheeling Jesuit College received $21 million to study technology transfer, even though it had no technology program or Ph.D. and even though the award was larger than the college's annual budget. Browning found that the five most consistent state winners of such earmarked funds from 1983 to 1991 boasted high-ranking members on the congressional appropriations committees.[16] Others obtained grants with the assistance of veteran Washington lobbying firms.

The Seesaw Battle Against Pork

Not all pork reaches the table. The world's largest, atom-smashing super-collider exceeded its projected billion-dollar budget by so much that even though construction has already begun, it was discontinued. The Omnibus Crime Bill of 1994 was initially defeated because opponents were persuasive in arguing that the bill contained too much pork.[17] In addition, some members refuse to engage in earmarking, bolstered by the awareness that their particular constituents are in less need of such assistance and look askance on such politics. But for every supercollider that is quashed, there is a $700 million Animas–La Plata water project in southwest Colorado. Though the Bureau of Reclamation estimated in 1995 that the project's economic benefits would be less than 40 percent of what it would cost taxpayers, the project passed Congress.

Subsystems

A second pathway to congressional decisionmaking is the normal political process for distributing large, annual, discretionary program subsidies such as housing support for lower-income families. Such subsidies are sanctioned by the congressional committee and subcommittee members, administrative agencies, and interest groups most immediately concerned and involved in these specialized policy areas. They are increasingly important as well to individual members of Congress who introduce their district and state concerns into these subsystems.

Thanks to their constituents' or memberships' concerns or their agency's mission, such allocations are of intense concern to policy-subsystem actors. Provided that in these sometimes conflict-ridden issue areas they can achieve consensus through the bargaining process, the issues are often of relatively less concern to other actors. The way to achieve consensus, however, has changed dramatically since the 1970s. The process remains decentralized, but more congressional and other subsystem players have become involved when they perceive program opportunities. Randall Ripley and Grace Franklin explain, "The essence of distributive policy is the decentralized award of federal largess to a seemingly unlimited number of recipients—individuals, groups, and corporations."[18]

These subsystems have evolved gradually from the iron triangles of the earlier period; they handle agriculture, veterans' affairs, highway construction, and numerous other discretionary programs that account for considerable congressional activity, even though entitlement programs and social and economic regulatory issues are in the limelight more often. These subsystems are an amalgam of parts of the old iron-triangle structure, new reforms, and new concerns that periodically confront the subsystem as a result of changing socioeconomic and political conditions. To understand the subsystem today, it is necessary first to understand its iron-triangle predecessor.

Deciding at the Subgovernment Level

Iron triangles were distinguished by their inclusion of informal actors, concerned interest groups, and the formal actors belonging to the congressional committees and agency bureaus. The iron triangle thus was defined by those who were organized, willing and able to participate, and had an ongoing—and hence normally legitimate—interest in the issue area. These actors were not, however, the ultimate decision makers in their formal or informal institutions. The Speaker of the House or the Senate majority leader, elected in each case by their peers, would set the issue priorities for the Congress, and those decisions could encroach on an iron triangle. Similarly, most large federal agencies often are compared to "holding companies," divided as they are into numerous bureaus, like the FBI, the Bureau of Highways, or Bureau of Employment and Training, that actually administer programs. While a few bureau chiefs, such as J. Edgar Hoover, could prevent it, normally the agency head or the president could preempt the chief who, after all, like his iron-triangle compatriots, operated on a "*sub*government" basis one level below those officials vested with responsibility and power for overall congressional or executive decisionmaking. Similarly the interest-group participants were subordinate to political parties—the vehicles through which the views of all *unorganized* as well as organized people could be expressed (see Figure 5.1).

Iron-Triangle Strengths

The political leverage of the long-established "iron triangles" lay largely in the detailed information accumulated by key congressional committee members from both parties. The committee's specialization and division of labor within a legislative body provided its members with invaluable experience over time, as they were mentored by senior members and, after patiently waiting their turn, rose through the seniority system to positions of power. Members were motivated by making good policy as well as gaining reelection, seeking power in the House or Senate, and higher office.[19]

Figure 5.1   Government and Subgovernments

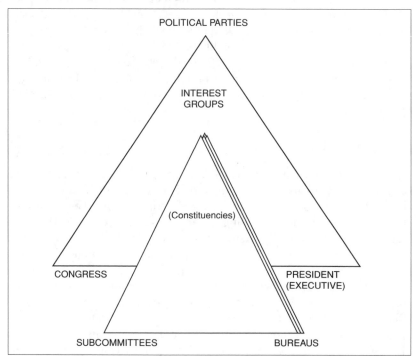

Mastering the information available through the iron triangles would contribute to more effective policymaking, which in turn could lead to more congressional power as well, and that was one of the alliance's strengths.

These committee members thus drew on the professional knowledge and experience of their federal-bureau allies who were vested with the responsibility for working with members of Congress in these issue areas. One can overestimate the vaunted "bureau autonomy" and power that these bureau chiefs brought to their iron triangles. At least by 1981, these bureau chiefs already operated within a constrained environment.[20] Nevertheless, some leaders at this level absorbed the major goals of their organizations and, where possible, pursued them.[21] Furthermore, normally these officials belonged to professions and were thus under pressure from fellow professionals inside and outside government to promote what Frederick Mosher called the *work substance* of such an elite.[22] Finally, they frequently possessed a public-service commitment that encouraged them to pursue a public-interest solution to iron-triangle problems.

The interest groups participating in these issue areas also possessed the information that comes from representing those who are participating or have participated on the firing line as, for example, a farmer, a road builder, or a veteran of a foreign war. As representatives frequently of individuals involved in the private or nonprofit sectors, these groups also legitimated the iron triangles by providing the information from sources outside of government.

The Demise of Iron Triangles

A number of iron-triangle advantages were altered in the 1970s by congressional reforms in the House—reforms aimed largely at the power of congressional committee chairs (the Senate experienced a number of these changes, but committee chairs already played a different institutional role there). The 435-member House relied heavily on its chairs, and the Democratic caucus—composed of all Democratic House members—found a number of independent-minded senior House chairs strongly at odds with its positions. These chairs gave every indication of continuing to run their fiefdoms in the same manner. The liberal Democrats were not so much attacking the committees or the seniority system, but rather looking for a way—as one of their leaders, Congressman Donald Fraser, put it—to "make the people who held positions of power . . . more responsible to rank and file Democrats."[23]

The bitter ensuing tug-of-war resulted in several rule changes that were particularly relevant for iron triangles. Within each committee, numerous subcommittees were created in a manner that made them more responsive to members collectively and individually. A "Subcommittee Bill of Rights" specified that committee members could now bid for subcommittee chairs in order of seniority, but the committee caucus, comprised of all Democratic committee members, could and did overturn a number of these choices by secret ballot. Committee chairs were eventually also selected by the majority-party committee caucus. Increased voting and amendment activity on the House floor bolstered yet another center of power separate from the committee's control.[24] Additional responsibilities for the agenda and other matters enabled the Speaker to become a stronger congressional-party leader. Last but not least, members of Congress emerged as more powerful individual power centers by gaining additional office resources, a somewhat larger voice in their own committee and subcommittee assignments, and access to participate informally in committees where they had an interest even though they were not members.

The weakening of committee-chair autonomy had great significance for the iron triangles. Its congressional allies could no longer consistently deliver the political support on which the bureaus and constituencies relied. Similarly, attacks on "permanent government" by Presidents Nixon, Carter, and Reagan curbed bureaucratic participation as well as power. Career executives were forbidden to participate in some forums, thereby reducing networking, and when they did participate, they were sometimes limited in their freedom to share expertise on issues, policies, and problems with either Congress or interest groups.[25] This erosion of bureau autonomy also weakened the iron triangle's mutual-support system.

Finally, the very success of interest groups in insinuating themselves alongside the quasi governmental partners in iron triangles opened them to political attack. Political scientist Theodore Lowi made the case most elegantly in his attack on the "interest-group society" as an illegitimate expropriation of public authority and money by well-organized private groups unable to control their fate in the marketplace. The classic examples are agriculture, labor, and commerce, where farmers, the trade-union movement, and small businesses historically sought help from the government and stayed to indulge themselves through self-regulation. The Soil Conservation Service, as of 1976, was thus a unit of local government, but each district office was in fact controlled by its own farmer-elected committee. Agreements involving approximately 90 percent of the farms were actually struck between the farmer and the service for acre-by-acre soil surveys or for increasing productivity.[26] Organized interests emerged in every sector of our lives, and for Lowi and other critics the role of government came to insure access to the most effectively organized. It was named "interest-group liberalism" because it defined the public interest as nothing more than the result of the amalgamation of various claims. The bargains struck by these groups in effect became the law.

The Rise of "Subsystem Politics"

Besieged committee chairs and weakened bureaucrats were coupled with grassroots interest groups whose legitimacy was now in question due to their quasi-governmental role and slowness to change. Small wonder that by the 1980s a number of scholars and politicians alike questioned whether iron triangles still existed at all. But institutions do adapt, and, if anything, the actors in the iron triangles needed each other more now in their weakened state than before. When political scientists Robert Stein and Kenneth Bickers studied these relationships in the 1990s, they found a somewhat different configuration of actors and relationships that they termed "subsystem politics." These policy systems were open to more actors and so now included, in addition to the usual cast of characters, attentive publics, a few program recipients, and journalists for specialized media. John Kingdon found a relatively hidden cluster of information specialists working within these larger and increasingly sophisticated alliances that now included not only congressional staffers but also academics and administration appointees below the top level.[27] Soon think tanks in growing numbers would join as well.

Cooperative subcommittees also stood ready to accommodate individual legislators who were now in a position to fix problems either by securing resources in existing programs or, if necessary, by introducing new programs. The operative word is *accommodate*. More and more actors concerned with an increasing number of regulatory or program elements cluster within the same broad issue area. Under these circumstances, conflict is sometimes inevitable. The subsystem's task then is no longer to avoid conflict but to absorb it—to find ways by bargaining to satisfy, at least for a time, the mutually antagonistic and competitive ideas and actors that reside uncomfortably within the same issue area.

The major thrust of the 1996 Freedom to Farm bill, for example, was to deregulate commodity programs, giving farmers fixed, declining payments over seven years. To attract the necessary political support, the bill made key concessions to, for example, certain commodity groups that contravened this objective. The contradictory provisions would coexist uncomfortably—testimony that the subsystem, unlike its iron-triangle predecessor, could agglomerate, but not fully coordinate, its program and regulatory package. The bill thus insured that farmers would not lose money in the early years, even while moving farm commodities closer to control by the market mechanism; allowed peanut subsidies to prevail; allowed sugar cane and beet planters to triumph against a coalition of manufacturers, consumer groups, and environmentalists seeking to end sugar subsidies; and extended dairy supports for another five years. Similarly, Senate Agriculture Committee chairman Frank Lugar's strategy was "to compromise early and often" with the committee's ranking Democrat, Patrick Leahy, and with other powerful subsystem actors.[28]

Establishing a "Policy Niche"

The new proactive role of the individual members of Congress in relation to these policy subsystems bears close scrutiny. From the day they arrive, all members now possess an impressive array of resources: in addition to larger personal staffs than in the past, new members can draw on those units that are in business to serve Congress; namely, the General Accounting Office, the Congressional Research Service, and the Office of Technology Assessment, and these units themselves have expanded. In short, each individual member has become an increasingly self-sufficient "member enterprise."[29] Spurred by a desire for visible acts that will promote reelection, the temptation is great to identify "policy-niche" opportunities that will enable them to milk these subcommittee opportunities for short-term electoral gain. There are certainly legitimate district or state needs deserving of such attention, but the line between such a policy niche and pork often appears indistinguishable.

Where the members of Congress choose not to screen district or state proposals in light of overall district needs, there is precious little standing in the way of helping those who are better-off and better able to provide other electoral assistance. As always, among the first to notice such opportunities are the members themselves. "I've been here only weeks and I've already (got) two pressing problems, saving my shipyard and helping local apple growers with some disaster assistance. My work here is about jobs, and both kinds count." From this premise, it is but a hop, skip, and a jump to pork-barrel logic. "My feedlot ranchers get no price-support payments and, by God, they pay a high price for corn growers who do. I use government policy to even that out."[30] Nor are Agriculture Committee members, invariably catering to similar interests themselves, in a position to take the high ground: "If I write dairy policy for those in central California, it's fair that [naming another member] push farm protection policy for New Jersey apple growers. How can I seriously tell him to protect the integrity of national policy?"[31]

Treating All Distributional Programs as Pork

Confronted with such program activities and logic, some political scientists have simply thrown up their hands and written off all distributional programs as pork. Several mechanisms similarly operate in Congress that guarantee the construction of inefficient public-works projects. The principal institutional features leading to overspending "constitute the very basis of representative government as it exists in the United States: geographical representation, majority rule, and the committee system." John Ferejohn saw this set of biases as pervading much of the policy made in Congress that is either "purely divisible" (such as public works, military construction, and urban housing policy) or policy with major divisible components (such as defense expenditures, agriculture, and veterans' affairs).[32]

In some cases critics have professed not to see much of a problem; after all, when compared with overall federal government expenditures, distributional programs are comparatively small, and getting smaller. Even though, in dollar terms, the amount of grant and project money earmarked to designated states or districts is probably at an all-time high, its budget share has declined relative to program expenditures.[33]

The Real and Symbolic Costs of Distributional Program Waste

Of course, when compared with entitlement programs that spend tens and hundreds of billions of dollars and a national debt in the trillions, even Bill

Gates plays merely a supporting role. Contrary to the way that it is sometimes treated by Congress and the president, however, even federal money dispensed through distributive programs is real. Its waste understandably offends people.

But these many cozy political arrangements have political and symbolic consequences, too. The symbolic damage in the form of citizen discontent manifests itself particularly when, because of the narrow focus of each policy subsystem, they periodically are caught operating at cross-purposes. For example, when a farm-focused tobacco subsystem persists in subsidizing tobacco growers even while the U.S. surgeon general is issuing warnings that smoking may be dangerous to your health, the public perceives yet another example of government hypocrisy or incompetence. Such contradictions are particularly damaging because they place in question the legitimacy of other, more defensible, policy-subsystem decisions, as in, for example, the employment and training subsystem. This loss of legitimacy, in turn, feeds public disillusionment with government.

Second-Constituency Support

Policy niches in numerous cases fill important needs for individuals and organizations and can play a legitimate role in accord with the public interest. In a decentralized, fragmented Congress characterized by porous policy subsystems eager to please individual members, however, such niches have the potential for mischief. There is little preventing the opportunistic legislator from creating a policy niche that fulfills political rather than program purposes. The United States certainly did not invent such cozy political arrangements: we just do it bigger and better than anyone else.[34] Policy subsystems provide a wealth of such opportunities.

The emergence of the second constituency, consisting of wealthy individual, corporate, and interest-group campaign contributors, provides additional opportunities. The entry of more high-rolling individuals and organizations has simply altered what is more and more often called the political marketplace. George Will captures the nature of contemporary district representation in those cases where such degradation occurs:

> Running for Congress is today an activity akin to pure entrepreneurship on the part of candidates who put themselves forward. They find a market (a district) and a market niche (a potential majority to be cobbled together from various factions); they merchandise themselves with advertising paid or by venture capitalists (contributors) who invest in candidates. The return on this investment is access to decision-makers and influence on legislation and other government actions.[35]

On an aggregate basis, relatively small allocations, much like traditional pork, have a comparatively limited public impact. These program and regulatory concessions are made to those in the second constituency seeking favors in exchange for money or in-kind financial assistance, accompanied sometimes by other forms of political support. Such actions may draw objections from similarly powerful competitors active in the same business or issue area. Other times, however, they benefit one actor without posing much of a threat to other wheeler dealers.

Inducements for Campaign Funds

The road to financial gain is then thrown open. Industry entitlements, such as tax preferences and regulatory concessions, decried by their detractors as "welfare for the rich," are more significant politically than economically. Such comparatively small, long-term tax preferences (such as oil-depletion allowances) and corporate subsidies (for example, timber subsidies) are justified on the basis that they serve as incentives for particular kinds of business or economic activity desirable for society; politically, they serve as congressional inducements for campaign funds from wealthy recipients.

In the case of such campaign-fund inducements, legislators do not benefit directly through program benefits accruing to their districts, but rather *indirectly* through the airtime and other campaign activities that the campaign contributions of interest groups and private individuals can buy. The contributions are, therefore, comparable to programmatic benefits in enhancing the electoral fortunes of legislators.[36]

The Direct Influence of Campaign Contributions on Distributive Politics

Inducements for campaign funds are allocated through the medium of distributive politics, and as such they are usually less visible and controversial. Largely for this reason, there is a strong statistical relationship between contributions and votes—a relationship that does not appear to exist in the case of larger redistributive and regulatory issues with their larger political stakes.[37]

Distributive political arrangements (such as tax-code loopholes) lend themselves to rewarding the political faithful. Such rewards, either in the form of benefits or the avoidance of costs, while concentrated in the hands of the few, are paid by the many, who, thanks to the comparatively small amount each time, are oblivious to being fleeced. Furthermore, it is in the interest of the politician and contributor to reach these agreements quietly; were there to be conflict, word of the illegitimate gains would surface and place the deal in jeopardy. Robert Stein and Kenneth Bickers thus looked at PAC influence and found it most clearly visible and statistically significant in consensual subsystems in which the specific issues at stake could be tied to the allocation of concentrated costs and benefits.[38] Those comprising the second constituency often want more than access, and such correlations suggest that they get it. "Political analysts have long agreed," writes Larry Sabato, "that access is the principal goal of most interest groups, and lobbyists have always recognized that access is the key to *persuasion*."[39] Where politics is distributive and the conditions are right, access can yield PAC private contributors a nice return on their investment.

Silent Spending

While business subsidies are also important second-constituency incentives, nowhere does access appear to translate into political influence as effortlessly as through tax expenditures. Such expenditures are tax-code provisions that allow particular individuals or organizations to receive preferential treatment. The tax preference is provided as an incentive to encourage an activity viewed as beneficial for society. It can take the form in the federal tax laws of a special exclusion, exemption, deduction, credit, deferral, or alteration in a tax rate.[40] By contrast, where such tax preferences are $10 billion or more, they generally favor middle- and upper-income people, and consist of such well-established items as charitable-contribution deductions, accelerated depreciation to stimulate business investment, and exclusion of employer pension contributions from taxation. Together, these tax incentives total hundreds of billions of dollars and are some of the most important ways that the federal government affects economic decisions and social welfare.

The Indefensibility of Tax Loopholes

But a number of the tax preferences that cost less are, ironically, among the most controversial. These breaks are created for wealthy people or corporations and cost between several million and a few billion dollars. The glaring inequities created by such loopholes are at issue and distinguish them from generally accepted tax expenditures. No public-interest vision exists that might conceivably justify these tax breaks. One may favor or oppose generally accepted tax expenditures, but at least a case can be made for them. For example, a Republican can argue that while tax-free bonds for state and local governments do, indeed, benefit investors in high-income tax brackets, they save those governments billions in interest payments. Or a Democrat can justify tax credits for low-income working people on the grounds that the credits encourage them to remain in the labor force and off welfare. By contrast, loopholes possess little in the way of socially redeeming importance and are gained through economic clout, rather than political persuasion. They provide campaign contributions to incumbents rather than service to society.

Some loopholes were justifiable historically but have outlived their usefulness. Such loopholes are particularly open to attack because items in the tax code, unlike appropriations, once adopted are not reviewed annually. In addition, while some of the larger loopholes are widely known and generally accepted—such as mortgage interest on owner-occupied homes— many smaller loopholes—such as corporate-owned life insurance—represent a form of *silent spending* whose survival depends somewhat on maintaining their political invisibility. They then normally remain in place for years thereafter, unless politicians choose to open them up as a tax reform or, more often, as a means of squeezing additional political contributions from loophole beneficiaries.[41]

Milton Friedman underscored this importance when he despaired of accomplishing fundamental tax reform since the present tax system enables "legislators (and presidents) to raise campaign funds by inserting or removing loopholes in our present obscenely complicated code."[42] For their part, PACs are as anxious to obtain those loopholes as most members of Congress are to dispense them. When researchers asked PAC executives to give an example of what their offices did, "about 90 percent described a tax loophole they had won. It reached the point where we started asking for an example of anything but taxes."[43]

Measuring the Growth in Tax Loopholes

It is difficult to measure individually the number of tax preferences inserted into the code for generous second-constituency supporters, but evidence suggests that the number of beneficiaries is well beyond the "small price to pay for democracy" stage and is growing. Indeed, the tenacity of politicians in clinging to particular tax breaks for their patrons itself is significant— often in the face of years of attacks by investigative reporters and reformers. Such willingness to take so much media heat underscores the source of much political money today.

While the aggregate amount in tax loopholes for the second constituency is unavailable, there is an indirect measure; namely, the escalation of words in the tax code. Even allowing for modifications in major provisions of the code and those tax preferences like the Earned Income Tax Credit or employer pension—inserted mainly to help lower- or middle-income taxpayers—the marked increase in the number of words suggests that members of Congress are taking good care of their financial benefactors. Arthur Hall, senior economist at the Tax Foundation, has measured the tax code's growth since passage of the Internal Revenue Act of 1954. As indicated in Figure 5.2, the number of words that define the body of both the federal income-

Figure 5.2 Growth of the Income Tax Code

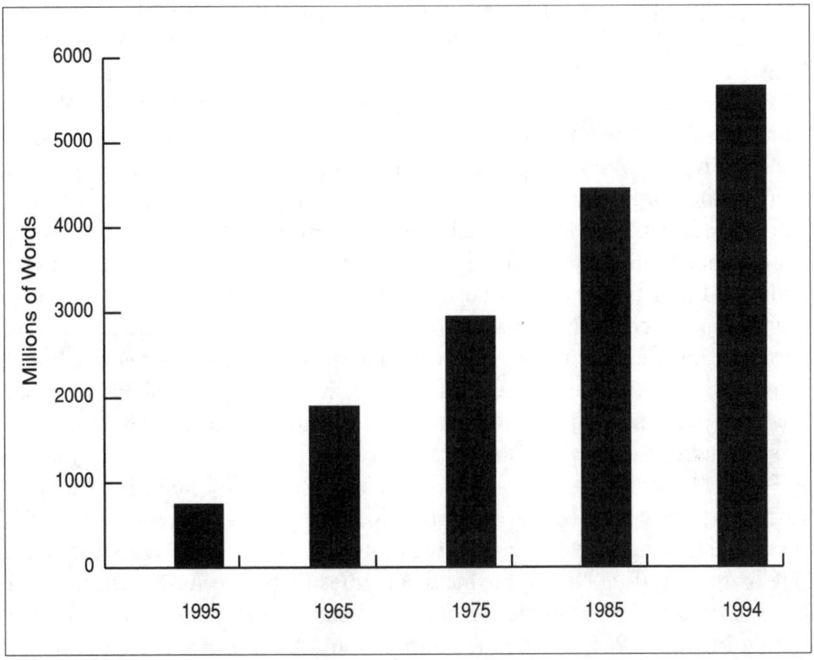

Source: Arthur Hall, "The Compliance Costs and Regulatory Burden Imposed the by Federal Tax Laws," Special Brief, Tax Foundation, January 1995, p. 3.

tax laws and their attendant regulations has grown from 744,000 in 1955 to 5,557,000 in 1994.[44] Most of that growth relates to tax-base questions and is due to massive tinkering with the tax code for broader purposes.[45]

The tax code, however, is also where tax favors are granted to the second constituency, and the growth has steadily increased during the last two decades, when pressure for more and larger campaign contributions increased. While not the only factor explaining this change, it presumably contributed to the finding that the tax code's instability was much more pronounced between 1974 and 1994 than during the prior twenty-year period.[46] Former Republican senator Nancy Kassebaum nailed the problem: "Tax loopholes, once enacted, tend to outlive Methuselah, regardless of their effect on the public good. The ease with which they are enacted into law must be reduced."[47]

Corporate Welfare

Examples of corporate welfare, or welfare for wealthy companies, abound. Take oil, for one. While the larger integrated oil companies have the intangible drilling-cost deduction (which allows them to write off fully 70 percent of their investment in the first year), the two biggest oil players in Alaska and on the Washington scene—Exxon-Mobil and BP Amoco—have bigger fish to fry. When Congress opened Alaska's North Slope to drilling in 1973, Congress placed a ban on exporting this oil. Then Senator Walter Mondale warned that the oil companies would eventually succeed in having the export ban overturned; such a move would simultaneously provide them with a large market and keep winter heating fuel prices higher in the Midwest. In 1996, the Clinton administration did, indeed, overturn the oil-export ban. Millions in campaign contributions, thereby, yielded billions in additional profits. Pressure is now building to allow drilling in the National Petroleum Reserve, an area roughly the size of Indiana.[48] Little debate has surfaced on the critical issue of whether to preserve these resources for future use. Political leaders have not pressured the oil companies to make the case in a public debate for using the oil now; instead, they appear to prefer stacks of campaign funds to stocks of oil.

Spurred by the excesses of the oil companies and a number of others, Robert Reich, when secretary of labor in 1994, gave a speech to the CATO Institute challenging the conservative think tank to criticize "corporate welfare"—to identify a "list of business subsidies that don't make sense."[49] He cited a 1995 estimate by the Democratic Leadership Council's Progressive Policy Institute (PPI) that $131.2 billion could be saved over five years by eliminating its detailed list of wasteful corporate subsidies.[50] The CATO Institute accepted this challenge and concurred on the need to eliminate all of the special tax breaks identified by the Progressive Policy Institute. It also recommended abolishing 125 separate programs providing subsidies to particular industries at a price tag of $85 billion.[51] As a result, such "aid to dependent corporations" now came under further attack from think tanks on the Right as well as the Left.

The battle proved tough going, but the corporate-welfare reformers persevered. The CATO Institute pressed its attack on such federal subsidies. It identified an annual total of $37.7 billion budgeted for fifty-five of the least-defensible programs. In 1995 it found that Congress did reduce such subsidies; in 1996, however, the amount spent on the subsidies actually increased by $500 million.[52] Presumably, in an election year Congress and the president were more interested in increasing second-constituency incentives than reducing corporate subsidies.

The Perseverance of the "Dirty Dozen"

After the 1996 election, Representative John Kasich and Sam Brownback joined with a bipartisan coalition of policy groups to push for the elimination of a "dirty dozen" corporate-welfare spending programs. A few examples show how rarely these particular corporate incentives serve any public interest. One of the "dirty dozen" provided subsidies for roads in national forests; most such roads are constructed by timber companies in order to pursue their lumbering activities, yet the Forest Service has paid for these roads. The Clean Coal Technology Program assists private industry in developing commercial technologies that would use coal in environmentally sound ways. With the passage of the 1990 Clean Air Act Amendments, though, electric utilities and larger coal producers, much like other companies affected by the act, now have a strong economic motive for selecting the lowest-cost option for reducing emissions. Finally, under another piece of corporate-welfare legislation, the Overseas Private Investment Corporation provides loans, guarantees, and political-risk insurance to U.S. companies that invest in unstable developing countries. The major beneficiaries from these programs are large corporations and politically connected individuals who receive high rewards when these investments work—whereas the financial risk for covering the bad loans falls on the taxpayer. After considerable lobbying and publicity, however, the reform coalition could persuade Congress only to cancel the Clean Coal Technology Program and to cut timber roads' assistance by $5.6 million.[53] As Stephen Moore put it, "we fought a war on corporate welfare, and corporate welfare won."[54]

This coalition did not disband but, falling back, focused on a fourfold, abbreviated hit list, including the Overseas Private Investment Corporation; the Agriculture Department's $90-million market-access program that finances advertising to sell crops, wines, and food products overseas; and the Energy Department's $365-million fossil-energy research-and-development program, which studies ways to develop reserves of coal, oil, and gas.

Reaping the Spoils

These campaign-fund inducements, when compared with the amounts allocated through policy subsystems, are comparatively small. While periodically the subjects of TV or press investigative stories, they rarely make a public impact as issues. The media stories do, however, appear to communicate a stench emanating from Washington, coupled with a vague but persistent sense of illegitimate gain by wealthy individuals and organizations in cahoots with Congress and the president at the expense of the little guy. Symbolically these stories of cozy political arrangements lengthen the distance between citizens and their government.

But such regulatory adjustments and program subsidies, devoid of any real benefit for society, do periodically become visible to the public when an investigative reporter uncovers a particularly egregious example in a nationally read newspaper, wire service, or TV news magazine. Table 5.2

Table 5.2   To the Big Soft-Money Donors Go the Spoils

Donations to President Clinton

Goldman Sachs and Robert Rubin	$375,000	$2 billion in Mexican government bond purchases made good by the United States
Gallo Family	$50,000	$2.5 million in federal market-promotion money retained in Department of Commerce for Gallo Corporation
Maurice Tempelsman	$169,000	Persuaded the U.S. Export-Import Bank to back a $54.5 million loan to a business partner in Russia

Donations to Candidate Dole

Glaxo Wellcome	$100,000	$2 billion in drug sales for Zantac thanks to extended protection from generic competition
Fanjul Family	$902,580	Maintenance of the sugar subsidy programs worth $65 million to this family thanks to its extensive holdings
Archer, Daniels Midland (ADM) Corporation	$217,800	Maintenance of an Ethanol subsidy of $500 million per year for ADM

Sources: Charles Lewis, *The Buying of the President* (New York: Avon Books, 1996); "The Mother Jones 400," *Mother Jones* 22, no. 3 (1997): 40–62; Marc Breslow, "Who Owns the Government?" *Dollars and Sense*, 1992, pp. 10–11 ff.

records some of the more prominent persons who have benefited from second-constituency rewards and the problems those gains pose for the political system: Goldman Sachs, the investment firm where former Treasury secretary Robert Rubin previously served as CEO, contributed $375,000 to President Bill Clinton's 1996 campaign. One might well justify the generous U.S. support engineered by Rubin for the Mexican government on public-policy grounds, but its benefit to bondholders in the United States (the customers of Goldman Sachs and other international investment houses) left a cloud over the transaction. Jose Fanjul and his three Cuban brothers, "the first family of sugar," continue to receive, in exchange for hundreds of thousands in contributions over the years, millions in subsidies resulting from strong import quotas.[55] The wine-rich Gallo family benefits from Department of Commerce subsidies to encourage large corporations to market their products abroad (another program that, while years ago it provided a valuable incentive to encourage companies to expand abroad, strains credulity in a global corporation era). Long-time contributor Maurice Tempelsman persuaded the Commerce Department to back a questionable $54.5-million loan after making his $169,000 contribution. These second-constituency regulars give frequently so one cannot connect any particular contribution with a particular reward. But all of their contributions together do not equal the amount that each benefits annually from federal favors. The dependable and sizeable returns on these investments underscore that politics pays for the second constituency.

The Glaxo Wellcome case is less subtle and suggests just how giddy lobby life in the political fast lane can become. In 1994, harried White House and congressional staffers made a technical error when drafting a bill to enact the fast-track General Agreement on Tariffs and Trade (GATT). They inadvertently gave 109 drugs extended protection from generic-drug competition. Glaxo Wellcome in particular stood to gain $2 billion by maintaining high prices for Zantac, its popular ulcer drug. After the error was detected, a group of mostly Democratic senators tried to insert the missing clause. The drug companies by then had learned about the error and moved to block the correction. Arguing facetiously that even a minor change in GATT would invite massive cheating by Third World countries, a group of largely Republican senators then led a successful fight to prevent the amendment. The day after the vote, Glaxo Wellcome gave $100,000 to the Republican National Committee, and during the subsequent election cycle gave $387,000 more.[56] Glaxo Wellcome thus did even better than the second constituency usually does by turning thousands in contributions into billions in revenues.

Ignoring Cozy Politics in the Voting Booth

Where some of these more infamous cases surface, citizen anger with such PAC and individual contributor excesses is genuine. That anger is fed periodically by the media with fresh horror stories. Why then are incumbent politicians punished so rarely for getting into bed with the second constituency?

Polling data indicate few cases where such anger becomes the basis of a voting decision. More often, bread-and-butter issues, general economic conditions, candidate personalities, and positive or negative TV ads in a particular House, Senate, or presidential election appear to capture the electorate's attention during those few weeks before an election when they pay attention at all. So politicians who need money to reach the electorate weigh the political cost of occasional criticism for engaging in cozy politics on the peripheral campaign-reform issue against the electoral benefit of investing additional funds gleaned from the second constituency to reach voters on gut reelection issues. By acting against the public interest, incumbents from both parties can often raise their reelection chances. They do, however, have to deliver the goods to the second constituency—particularly since the 1980s, when, as Brooks Jackson has shown, the power of cash constituents became "crisply focused, vigilantly exercised, and growing."[57]

Rewarding the Second Constituency Through Inaction

The studied indifference of Republican Senate majority leader Trent Lott in the 1990s to the campaign-reform issue underscores this same kind of political calculus. Lott liked to say that voters do not care about campaign reform; more precisely, he was calculating that campaign reform was not a cutting issue that would determine their vote. By contrast, a *Wall Street Journal* poll of the 144 contributors giving the $5,000 PAC maximum to the senator's New Republican Majority Fund showed that "four out of five donors had identifiable stakes in specific programs and policies pending before government."[58] An attentive public expecting a high return on its money and a general public more concerned with other issues hardly represent a promising recipe for political reform. Public-opinion polls do show, though, that the voters are increasingly condemning the political system for such waste. So a vicious circle ensues. Voters become increasingly jaded, even while incumbents individually enhance their reelection chances by engaging in behavior that encourages collective cynicism. The tragic result of these cozy and indefensible political arrangements is that they obscure what government continues to do well.

Public Programs and Regulations

The bulk of the federal budget still pertains to established public programs and regulations characterized by a large federal commitment, long time periods, and widespread acceptance and legitimacy throughout the society. It is here that one finds the best-known social-entitlement programs, the most widely held, expensive, and extensive tax preferences, and social and economic regulatory decisions. These programs and regulations are public in the sense that citizens are engaged in the dialogue over how to resolve these issues through their vote and through polls, focus groups, and other means by which political elites gauge public opinion.

High Politics

These issues turn into "high politics" as a result of what has become a political or economic crisis, such as the September 11, 2001, terrorist tragedy, the civil-rights movement, or the serious recession in the early 1980s, or as a result of public discussion during an election, as when President Ronald Reagan reduced taxes in 1981 shortly after coming into office. Such a major issue may surface as a presidential initiative, as in the case of President Bill Clinton's health care–reform package, or a congressional initiative, as with the 1994 Republican "Contract with America," sponsored by Speaker Newt Gingrich and Majority Leader Dick Armey.[59] Technological breakthroughs (such as the silicon chip), a shortage in oil or another basic resource, a change in a major "control event" (such as abolition of the military draft), or a change in belief patterns may also generate new activity.[60] A high-politics issue such as the events of September 11 absorbs the attention of the public and political elites alike and puts politics as usual on hold as the country closes ranks to take actions in the public interest.

When such large, sprawling issues extend across two or more policy subsystems and become visible, raising concern among competing major interest groups and the voting public, they create conflict. The higher political stakes then demand the attention of high-level government officials—congressional leaders and party leaders as well as the president and White House staffers. Such issues inevitably are controversial, volatile, unpredictable, and noisy (less strident issues can be settled by subsystems), thereby attracting the attention of the national media and numerous peak associations (coalitions of interest groups sharing a long-term interest). Often administrative agencies as well as corporations and interest groups find themselves competing against one another in these conflictual networks. The resulting programs and regulations are designed primarily to benefit the middle class or the public-at-large—although lower-income people benefit where they are eligible for a redistributive program, such as the Earned Income Tax Credit, and the wealthy qualify for such entitlements as Social Security and Medicare.

The "Visible Cluster"

High politics is dominated then by top-echelon organizations (rather than subsystem echelons). John Kingdon calls these participants, who receive a lot of media and public attention, the "visible cluster"; they include the president and high-level presidential appointees, prominent members of Congress, and party leaders. A supporting cast of "policy community" actors provides policy alternatives to these key actors once they have assigned a high priority to a particular issue. This hidden cluster of information analysts includes academics and think-tank members, congressional staffers, and administration appointees below the top level.[61] Corporations and interest groups move back and forth between the two clusters. As Thurber has written, the resulting "issue network" thus consists of "general policy decisions with major political effects involving broad public interests, visibility, divisiveness, extensive media coverage, and many participants."[62]

The Role of Policy Entrepreneurs

Persons in the visible cluster of power have historically played a leadership role in marshaling public opinion and moving issues through the Congress. In the more freewheeling Congress today, however, additional policy entrepreneurs have also emerged, not surprisingly. These entrepreneurs are lured by the siren song of issues with the potential for high politics. They realize that the road to congressional leadership and the presidency runs through the promotion of compelling issues that provide the opportunity to demonstrate their vision. These entrepreneurs also enjoy being close to the seat of power during the development and promotion of these issues; they are themselves excited by the power of ideas. Their task, as policy entrepreneurs, is to dramatize ideas with the potential to capture the country's imagination—such as deregulation, educational equality for all, or greater economic opportunity—and translate them into legislation fulfilling that promise. Rarely do these entrepreneurs conceive of these ideas themselves.

Such entrepreneurs can be found anywhere in the policy community—in elected or appointed positions or interest-group or research organizations. "But their defining characteristic, much as in the case of a business entrepreneur, is to invest their resources—time, energy, reputation, and sometimes money. That return might come to them in the form of policies of which they approve, satisfaction from participation, or even personal aggrandizement in the form of job security or career promotion."[63] Examples of people doggedly engaged in the politics of ideas are Ralph Nader pursuing "big business" through his network of public-interest groups, Representative Bill Archer pushing tax reform, and Bill Bennett arguing for "traditional family values."

Policy entrepreneurs not in the formal congressional power structure began to emerge in larger numbers, according to Burdett Loomis, in the mid-1970s. These "new pols" hooked their careers to ideas, issues, and problems—and prospective solutions. In doing so, they demonstrated a flair for policy issues and for relating them to the media. Consequently, reporters clearly related to these members in terms of their skills and abilities, and the congressional leadership, too, had to since these folks "will find a way to affect the debate and have an impact."[64] These entrepreneurs master a policy area through long hours of committee and subcommittee work, by taking full advantage of computerization, more extensive library resources, and the other products of the information age. In addition they often publish articles or books pushing their issue. Such information is usually aimed at the small audience that reads such national newspapers as the *Washington Post,* the *New York Times,* or the *Wall Street Journal* (whether it be the hard copy or on the Web), news magazines, or political books. In 2000, entrepreneurs aspiring to the presidency—such as Vice President Al Gore, emphasizing his proactive position on the environment, or Republican senator Richard Lugar, stressing his long involvement with foreign policy—seized on an issue and used it to reach a wider audience.

The Politics of Ideas

So ideas count, and they are contested in politics in much the same way that the economic marketplace puts competing products to the test. In the political marketplace, too, the assumption is that competition will determine the superior product. Even when the policy community has coalesced around an issue, the competition in politics continues through *public* debate. Members of Congress, presidents, and aspirants for their jobs take these ideas to the people and adjust them further in light of public reaction. The point would scarcely seem worth emphasizing were electoral turnout higher and political cynicism lower.

How can one argue that self-interested politicians will promote a politics of ideas? The question sounds odd in a country apparently at peace with the notion that self-interested business executives are providing the best available products thanks to marketplace discipline. Why cannot the political marketplace, too, produce ideas in the public interest—even if policy entrepreneurs are "self-interested"? (provided, of course, that their ideas move through a political process compelling similar discipline).

The Competition of Ideas and the Democratic Process

Criticism of the public interest, rightly in my view, points to the difficulty in defining which *substantive* policy viewpoint is in the public interest. But the means of reaching an effective decision presumably are in the public interest if the serious ideas of "high politics" are taken through a *process* that demands responsiveness both to the concerns of majority opinion and of a policy community conversant with the issue's technical problems. It is this process leading to the decision, and the adjustments made during the subsequent implementation period, that allow for the collective decision making at the heart of democracy.

And it is ideas that largely galvanize that process. Robert Reich similarly talks of "civic discovery as an opportunity for the public to deliberate about what is good for society."[65] The ultimate substantive policy decision is important, but it is this public dialogue that democratizes the process and thus legitimizes the final decisions.

Seeking the Public Interest Through Public Dialogue

Evidence that politician and citizen alike strive for a transcendent meaning beyond self-interest, even while taking into account such instrumental concerns, is manifest in the safety and health legislation and the Clean Air Act amendments—all staunchly opposed by wealthy, well-organized producers.[66] The key political-economy legislation of this century, Social

Security, with its vital social insurance principle, represents another example.

Because *public programs and regulations* impact on so many individuals and institutions, they attract a crowd as well as serious public dialogue. The tugging and hauling of high politics through the medium of "issue networks" is done by numerous powerful formal and informal political actors who jockey aggressively for position. These issue networks are sizable and complex, and a major task of the public entrepreneur is to stimulate a public voice loud enough to be heard above the din.

The Compelling Idea of Deregulation

Where an industry is at odds with a prevailing idea, the usual interest-group numbers and campaign contributions may not suffice. For example, deregulation demonstrates what can happen when an industry finds itself at odds with an idea that has captured the imagination of elected officials from both parties and an informed public. The trucking industry (supported by its teamster ally) was not confronted by competing business groups but rather, as Paul Quirk explains, by somewhat diffuse consumer public-interest groups, by strong backing from economic theory and practice, and by political agreement for once on both sides of the ideological spectrum—from conservatives anxious to reduce governmental control and liberals who wanted to attack business privilege and benefit consumers.[67] The industry proved unable to mount arguments justifying regulated rates on the basis of the general interest, and Congress passed legislation largely deregulating the industry.

Issue Networks

In the case of issue networks interested in economic regulation, powerful business and other actors are frequently pitted against one another on business policies with far-reaching implications—sometimes with and sometimes without public involvement. In the case of telecommunications, the key actors included the Federal Communication Commission, Congress, contending major telephone companies, their domestic and foreign competitors, and the unions.[68] The resulting AT&T breakup into a long-distance company and seven regional Bell operating companies in the early 1980s, coupled with subsequent events, shows how the composition of an issue network can change when the number of interest groups increases and the fate of literally tens of billions of dollars rests on public-policy decisions. The Microsoft conflict in 2000 was similarly a product of issue-network conflict.

The control of bigness and living with technologies moving more rapidly than our predictive powers is difficult enough. The even greater challenge is how to enable issue networks—the policy mechanisms designed to deal with high politics—to achieve effective public programs and regulations. Most of these issues, as they have for much of U.S. history, involve public/private partnerships. The problem now is that the private partner in some important cases is outgrowing the public sector, as its actions increasingly occur beyond the scope of its issue network and beyond the information and other resources available as a counterweight to other government actors and the citizenry.

William Greider suggests the problem's nature and scope in describing the political, public-relations, and economic resources at the disposal of what he wryly terms "Citizen GE." General Electric Corporation consists of numerous divisions: aircraft engines, appliances, broadcasting, industrial products and systems (e.g., transportation systems), materials, power generation, technical products and services (e.g., medical systems), and GE capital services (by itself, one of the largest bank and specialty-insurance companies in the world). The company's revenues totaled $112 billion in 1999—the equivalent of the gross state product for the entire state of Arizona; and $11.8 billion in cash flow enabled it to make 134 industrial and financial acquisitions in 1999 alone. Like numerous other Fortune 500 companies, its activities span numerous issue networks.

Thanks to GE's financial prowess and this involvement in so many governmental decisions, it becomes sensible to invest in as many resources as it takes to reach decision makers in as many ways as possible. The substantial resources cataloged by Greider comprise lobbying by two dozen Washington representatives; the maintenance of an active PAC; philanthropy dispensed through tax-exempt foundations and purportedly statesmanlike books published through respected think tanks; sponsorship of television's McLaughlin Group; membership on the Business Roundtable, dozens of separate trade associations, and ad hoc coalitions often designed to handle political damage control; and agenda-setting initiatives through apologist corporate organizations masquerading as good-government groups such as the Committee on the Present Danger (defense—they're for it) and the Center for Economic Progress and Employment (product liability—they're against it).

Carrying "Political Overhead"

Once assembled, these resources are available year-round. As such, they become, in effect, the corporation's political overhead. These resources can be used to convey not only GE's economic corporate image of "bringing good things to life," but also a strong political corporate image as a good citizen. To the extent that the public buys into GE as good citizen, the political brand image translates into a bargaining advantage when dealing with a particular issue network or the policy community.

Greider argues that GE has deployed its resources so extensively and systematically that in effect the conglomerate functions informally "as a modern version of the old political machine."[69] This constant and tenacious political operation operates at two levels. First, GE acts as a multifaceted interest, affected by and affecting decisions in legislative bodies, courts, regulatory agencies, and the bureaucracy. Second, GE has become a mediating institution that speaks on behalf of others, including its workers, consumers, shareholders, and subcontractors, and, it tries to convey, for the well-being of the public-at-large. The strategy makes good sense since powerful corporations like GE "have both the money and the economic incentive to play politics at both levels—bargaining outcomes in obscure places that manipulate laws and mobilizing ideas and opinions to influence the visible public contest."[70]

The Global Corporation—
Not the Political Party—as the Mediating Institution

It is the assumption of this mediating role between its attentive publics and the public-at-large and Washington that demonstrates just how deeply a number of the Fortune 500 companies have insinuated themselves into the political process. This role historically was played by political parties in translating citizen ideas into public policy. The demise of this mediating link between local and state parties and Washington created a political vacuum. In speaking for these groups, GE and other companies are purporting to express the views of these groups and conveying them to Washington and the public. The action is inauthentic in the sense that "the connective strand only runs one way."[71]

The difference is profound for two reasons. First, the interests of these citizens are assumed to be inextricably intertwined with the corporation's interests. GE stockholders are for maximizing profits, regardless of how many workers are fired or how little is done to ease their transition into subsequent employment. For their part, employees are prepared to undertake whatever steps are necessary to grow revenues and profits and to assume personal responsibility even if evidence subsequently implicates the corporation in illegal or immoral activities. Second, and even more significantly, the citizen has no voice in these actions and is thus represented by the corporation without ever having been consulted or mobilized. The corporation thus plays the role of political representative without ever consulting the represented. Indeed, GE executives even assume the views of their own corporate actors. The stockholders are not asked under what conditions they might sacrifice short-term profits for long-term considerations.

Nor does the company seek to learn employee reactions to illegal or immoral corporate activities.

The Ultimate Form of Political Influence

The nature of this political problem extends beyond PACs and discrete campaign contributions and beyond the larger amounts of money spent by corporations and other powerful interest groups on lobbying. The promise of policy issues pertaining to *public* programs and regulation lies in their stimulation of visible and newsworthy debate that engenders conflict and reduces the likelihood of ultimate PAC or individual contributor influence. Powerful corporations, interest groups, and other actors often serve in this regard as checks and balances upon one another, thereby making conflicts visible and compelling major institutions to act in a more open fashion. Decisions then are more likely to be above board because, like mushrooms, cozy political arrangements grow best in the dark.

The danger, however, is that if numerous corporations continue simultaneously to preempt the political process and to expand globally, they will ultimately overwhelm the balance of more of these issue networks and undercut the competitive process that periodically defines and redefines the public interest. We cling to but a slender reed if we gamble that, thanks to the multiplication of interest groups, these large corporations can each be expected to neutralize the other's power. Corporate interests and agendas converge on such topics as lower taxes, the social redistribution of income, and limiting government regulation, even while they diverge in other issue networks. The sizable agenda of Boeing's lobbyists, for example, includes tax law, the budget, telecommunications, health care, land use, utilities, environmental policy, labor law, international trade, and foreign policy.[72] It is the combined weight of numerous large corporations simultaneously pursuing the GE model, such as "citizen MMM," "citizen Exxon-Mobil," and "citizen Merck," that, in the presence of citizen noninvolvement, could distort the system.

Piggy-Back Pork

Public dissatisfaction with politics sometimes arises as a result of the numerous subsidiary issues that surround a public program or regulation. Thanks to the media's preference for sensationalism over substance, these subsidiary issues often hog the limelight. Such hogging is understandable since many of these issues comprise what might be termed *piggy-back pork*. High politics thus attracts wealthy contributors, interest groups, and geographical constituencies seeking favors who, while not the central players, are involved in these peripheral arrangements.

Cozy politics enters the high-politics calculus where coalitions become necessary to build political support and then placate the losers. Even where items are generally beneficial to the society, someone always loses. The bargains struck in promoting a public program or regulation sometimes are designed to provide sufficient time for the losers to adapt to the new rules of the game (as in the Tax Reform Act of 1986) or to enable a geographical constituency to adjust to the loss of government installations, programs, or other support (as in the case of military-base closings). Other times the apparent losers, because of their political and financial value to key actors, are able to extract most advantageous concessions. These concessions are often more expensive than either the winners or the alleged losers would like to admit or even realize. They represent not traditional pork items, but sometimes expensive or difficult-to-defend concessions granted in light of new or amended public programs and regulations or commitments to per-petuate cozy political arrangements associated with such programs. As such, they are more accurately termed piggy-back pork.

Far less visible than the issue at the heart of the public debate, this type of pork involves the side payments made to build a winning coalition, to compensate the losing competitors, or simply to reward deserving friends. Take, for example, the 1993 North American Free Trade Agreement (NAFTA). This agreement to lower trade barriers between the United States and its Mexican and Canadian neighbors represents a serious effort to repo-sition our economy in the direction of producing more goods and services where we have a comparative advantage, importing more from efficient producers abroad, and moving our companies and labor force away from artificial tariffs that protect them from foreign competition. We needed strong worker-retraining programs and effective government assistance for industrial conversion to accompany legislation with such far-ranging impact. What we got instead was small steps in that direction coupled with an infusion of piggy-back pork. Special deals were made, for example, for U.S. manufacturers of bed frames and headboards, orange-juice processors, and makers of flat glass.[73] The White House also promised to provide hun-dreds of millions of dollars for defense and other projects to congressional districts in exchange for NAFTA votes.[74] While some of the projects pro-tected individuals and companies affected adversely by the agreement, however, it appears that others were simply the usual congressional responses to geographical and second constituencies.

Piggy-Backing on Regulatory Legislation

Public regulations enjoying wide support, nonetheless, also serve as oppor-tunities for such gaming. While the overarching principles in such legisla-tion are sound, piggy-back pork is in the details. In order to preserve market share for producers of high-sulphur coal, the Clean Air Act of 1970 was subsequently amended to require that utilities install smokestack scrubbers even where the power plants burn low-sulfur coal. The producers in three Eastern states were the primary beneficiaries of this political maneuver, while the Western states already producing cleaner fuel were compelled to relinquish their competitive advantage. This unnecessary drag on productivity in the electric-utility industry forced ratepayers to bear the cost of the regulatory subsidy to Eastern coal.[75]

Conclusion

Since the 1970s, three trends have increased the amount of cozy politics in three pathways to Congressional decisionmaking. First, constituents expect their representatives and senators to deliver more federal grants and contracts regardless of their centrality to district or state needs. Second, policy subsystems are under increasing pressure to create "policy niches" that make no pretense that they relate to the subsystem's policy intent. Third, numerous fat-cat members of the second constituency now expect something more tangible than "access" in return for the increasing number and size of their contributions. The predominant form of pork found in each of three pathways to congressional decisionmaking—geographical pork, pet programs, and campaign-fund inducements—has thus grown in size. Even the pathway with the most legitimate decision-making process—public programs and regulations—is increasingly saddled with piggy-back pork and threatened by the political power of global corporations.

The porkophiles can, indeed, argue that each of these pathways to Congress contains a defensible version of the public interest: districts and states sometimes require federal assistance to cope with palpable geographical needs; policy subsystems are better able to take account of intense and specialized policy concerns than popular mandates; and second-constituency needs encompassing regional and national considerations can often be addressed only by the national policy system. But porkophobes are cataloging waste and corruption in a wide range of policy areas that cannot be justified by any of these public-interest versions.

Difficulties in defining the public interest and its boundaries notwithstanding, at a minimum all claims on the public treasury should presumably involve a process whereby "open covenants are openly arrived at." Furthermore, each of these pathways contains criteria against which its decisions can be judged. Over a period of time, the several grants and contracts distributed on a geographical basis should be fair to all population segments. Subsystems should adopt policies that reflect professional standards and national needs. Support to a second constituency should not materialize unless beneficiaries other than the campaign contributor can be identified.

The amount of pork now generated through the four pathways to congressional decisionmaking identified here is palpably not in the public interest. The public has demonstrated its capacity to recognize blatant self-interest and cozy political arrangements. The size of this informed public is reflected in the growing popularity of TV "news magazines" that periodically run stories exposing such cozy politics. If present trends continue, we run the twin risks of allowing further corruption of congressional decision-making and of undercutting still further the public's confidence and trust in the political system's capacity to make the vital decisions.

PART 3

FROM
COMPROMISED GOVERNANCE
TO DEMOCRATIC BALANCE

6

Agency Compromise and Privatization

Cozy political arrangements are serious enough in that they pork up legislation, provide contributors with overly generous returns on their investments, courtesy of the taxpayers, initiate superfluous programs, and perpetuate outmoded activities. Less understood is the resulting undercutting of agency effectiveness and the capacity to govern. Virtually every federal administrative agency is affected to some degree by cozy political arrangements. Some of these arrangements are new, while others have hung around longer than Civil War veterans. This chapter begins with how cozy politics affects agency missions and then turns to privatization, the reform that touts the promise of public/private partnerships for numerous federal agencies.

The Politics of Agency Compromise

Federal administrative agencies are expected to work with members of interest groups and members of Congress in formulating and implementing policies. Political agreements are the stuff of such working relationships. Where the agency can establish a close relationship with the groups that benefit from its activities, both the agency and group have much to gain. The interest group or corporation often then will support the agency's requests to Congress and the president for authorization of legislation that expands the agency's powers, for appropriations, and for political actions that counter threats to the agency's survival or growth. The agency's allies are often in a more strategic position to take such steps than the agency itself. Thus Senator Barry Goldwater, a former U.S. Air Force general, observed that the aircraft industry has probably done more to promote the Air Force than the Air Force has done itself.[1]

Agency Capture

The danger arises when, in seeking to cultivate political support, an agency comes to rely too heavily on political support from an ally. An interest group, for example, may then be able to exercise a veto over critical agency decisions. The Department of Education thus has been criticized on the grounds that it has failed to tackle such critical issues as running rigorous teacher-training programs (insulting the teachers), evaluating work done at federally funded research labs (offending education researchers), and using college work-study students for off-campus tutoring (angering universities that do not want to lose a portion of their federally funded labor pool).[2]

At its worst, the result of cultivating such political support may be that the outside interest group captures the agency. Under these circumstances, "the relationship degenerates into the transfer of public authority to private groups that use it to advance their own interests at the expense of the general public. An executive agency then becomes simply the governmental outpost of an enclave of private power able to exercise its public authority only at the sufferance of private groups."[3] Ranchers thus were able to capture the Division of Grazing (which later, as the Grazing Service, was folded into the Bureau of Land Management) with the passage of the Taylor Grazing Act in 1934. The first director, a rancher and lawyer named Farrington Carpenter, supported the principle of "home rule on the range" and appointed local advisory boards in each grazing district to manage the program. To assure such home control, Carpenter deliberately limited the number of division employees and the size of the budget. These boards set the low grazing rates and decided who would receive the permits. Grazing-fee applicants had to be, already, owners of comparable private property or water rights ("only ranchers need apply"). The National Advisory Board Council president in the 1940s underscored rancher control over the agency in reporting "that the revised (Federal Range) Code was written in its entirety by livestock men at the first meeting in Denver. The Grazing Service even asked if we would rather they weren't there."[4]

True to form, in 1998, ranchers were still paying $1.61 per AUM (animal-unit-month—the amount a cow and a calf eat in a month) to lease land from the Bureau of Land Management (BLM) and the Forest Service, while the state of Idaho charged $5.15 and private Idaho rangelands $10 per AUM. Many ranchers take advantage of this discrepancy and sublease their federal lands at up to three times that amount. Karl Hess, of the CATO Institute, estimates that the grazing program loses more than $200 million per year. This loss cannot be justified on the grounds that it maintains small ranchers. According to studies done by the GAO and National Wildlife Federation, 75 percent of the BLM's grazing land is controlled by fewer than 10 percent of the leaseholders.[5]

Agency Compromise

More commonly, the need for a sufficiently large political coalition to launch or sustain a program results in agency compromise. Unlike agency *capture,* where the agency surrenders its sovereignty to the corporation or interest group that it is intended to regulate or serve, agency *compromise* is defined here as the sacrifice of an agency's ability to run a program effectively in exchange for congressional political support. Such agency compromise results either from demands from a large number of congressional districts or states or demands by a second constituency, supported by members of Congress, that an agency cannot reject without threatening the program's survival. The second-constituency demands may entail political favors or may extend into the realm of cozy political arrangements.

Building a political coalition poses few problems when the program will actually or potentially bestow benefits widely, as in the case of Social Security, cancer research, or the provision of school lunches to disadvantaged youths. Alternatively, a program may flourish if Congress regards it highly, as in the case of the Treasury Department; if it enjoys widespread public popularity, such as the Fish and Wildlife Service; or if it receives both strong congressional and public support, as in the case of the Soil Conservation Service.[6]

The Struggle for a Viable Political Coalition

While a few programs possess such political support, and hence enjoy greater autonomy, most do not, and the agency's struggle to construct and maintain a viable political coalition is real. Agency bureaucrats cooperate with sympathetic members of Congress in the hard work of building sufficient congressional support in the necessary committees and on the floor in the House and Senate. When confronted with a questionable request from a member of Congress, the White House, or a second constituency enjoying congressional or presidential support, the bureaucrat is faced with a Hobson's choice. Either one can agree, thereby undermining the program to avoid the alienation of coalition members, or refuse, thereby running the risk of preserving agency integrity at the expense of its political support.

Trading Program Design for Votes

In describing the fate of the Model Cities program in the 1960s, R. Douglas Arnold demonstrates how the strong preference of members of Congress for "parochial" programs that deliver goods and services to their geographical constituencies complicate the task of running programs designed to serve a limited number of jurisdictions. The Model Cities program was originally designed to benefit a limited number of communities. Its program designers intended Model Cities to provide a demonstration of what federal funds could achieve if sufficient funds to make an impact were concentrated in five to ten urban areas across the country, if social as well as physical urban problems were considered together, and if its urban "coordinators" could integrate all federal programs active in these inner-city areas. Such a program held little appeal for those members of Congress who saw no benefit for their home jurisdictions. The eligibility criteria were subsequently redesigned so that a larger number of congressional coalition members could share in the benefits. By the time the Johnson administration, congressional leaders, and bureaucrats had made the necessary promises to build a winning coalition, it was agreed that the funds would be spread among 151 cities and that federal coordinators would play a limited role in deference to congressional concern for local control. Though bureaucrats made efforts to include some merit as well as political criteria, forty-eight of the initial forty-nine city grants were awarded to coalition supporters.[7] Regardless of how hard bureaucrats worked to implement Model Cities, the program was doomed when the funds for a demonstration program intended for concentration in a few cities were dissipated in 151 cities.

Similar agency compromise occurred in the case of the Water and Sewer Facilities Grants program administered by the Department of Housing and Urban Development (HUD) from 1965 through 1974. The program, designed for rapidly growing communities, provided subsidies to encourage construction of large water and sewer facilities that could be expanded, thereby preventing the need for expensive duplication of such facilities in subsequent years. In order to build a sufficient coalition to pass the bill, however, the sponsors in this case enlarged the program's geographic scope to include *all* communities, regardless of whether they were growing, stable, or declining in population.[8] The program thus became just another federal construction subsidy, and the incentive for rapidly growing communities to do long-range planning was lost. Furthermore, when such grandly conceived programs emerge in a form ensuring that they cannot meet their objectives, another result is to feed doubts that the federal government can do anything well. Individual members benefit, but at the expense of the reputations of their party and Congress more generally.[9]

Once compromised, an agency can, nonetheless, continue indefinitely, if that is in Congress's interest. When President Johnson launched the Great Society, he did so on the ramshackle porch of Tom Fletcher's three-room tar-paper shack in rural Kentucky. Fletcher was then a thirty-eight-year-old father of eight with a second-grade education. Johnson promised, in 1965 while signing into law the Appalachian Regional Commission (ARC), that it would enable the region "to support itself through the workings of a strengthened free-enterprise economy." Though the bill's intent was to overcome stubborn poverty in the coal counties of eastern Kentucky and Tennessee, southern West Virginia, and southwestern Virginia, building the necessary political coalition expanded eligibility to 399 counties in thirteen states. Not a single county has ever lost eligibility, and the list includes the Atlanta suburbs and the aerospace industrial area in Huntsville, Alabama. Such comparatively wealthy areas obtain the industrial parks and additions to their colleges, community colleges, and libraries. But two-thirds of the funding is spent on roads. The original plan directed the ARC to build 2,350 miles of road at a cost of $840 million; Congress now estimates that the highway system will cost nearly $9 billion to construct and will not be completed until 2060. Even this expanded program will not achieve the agency's mission. The county seats get the highways, explains Ron Eller, of the University of Kentucky's Appalachia Center, "That's where the political power is strongest. Communities in central Appalachia—the more rural, the more impoverished—do not have the political clout." In 1993, journalist Dale Van Atta retraced President Johnson's steps and visited Tom Fletcher. Now sixty-seven, Fletcher still lived in the same shack. None of his eight children had advanced past eighth grade. Unemployed most of his life, he survived on Social Security checks.[10]

Undercutting the Agency Mission

Congress in the 1980s and 1990s similarly ignored the original intent of the Intermodal Surface Transportation Efficiency Act of 1991 (ISTEA) and its descendants—agencies charged with creating demonstration transportation projects to encourage state and local officials to look beyond traditional road building and experiment with innovative solutions to transport problems. Too often, the projects "demonstrate nothing other than the ability of a new or larger road to carry more traffic."[11] In the case of some ill-conceived ISTEA and subsequent projects, the result has been when ill-conceived projects are adopted, to tar with the same brush not only the federal agencies but also their state and local agency partners and Congress. In 1995, Norm Mineta, ranking Democrat on the House Transportation Committee, thus proposed a twelve-mile commuter rail line linking two cities in his district, Milpitas and Mountain View, California. The Federal Transit Administration estimated that for the $500-million project, "it would cost up to $33 to attract each new rider—five times as much as the agency says is acceptable."[12] Insistence on geographical dispersion by powerful legislators is the death knell for programs whose intent is to reach specific constituencies or achieve unique purposes.

Even *traditional* pork can have a surprising aggregate impact on an agency's mission and on how it conducts itself if the pork projects flow in sufficiently large numbers and if the agency's budget is comparatively small. While the total National Park Service (NPS) budget in 1998 stood at

$1.2 billion, salaries, visitor services, and maintenance account for $900 million. It is the remaining $350 million, available to purchase new park land and build new facilities, that attracts the most congressional attention and controversy. The members of Congress who sit on the House Interior Appropriations Subcommittee have added budgetary items that virtually compel NPS agreement and thereby undercut its professional judgment in implementing its budget. The committee chair in 1994, Ralph Regula, thus added nearly $20 million to buy and add land for a park in the Cuyahoga Valley National Recreation Area adjacent to his district; that amount is equal to what the nineteen federal parks in New England received during this time period. Representative Joseph McDade won $8.3 million in land-acquisition and construction money for the Delaware Water Gap National Recreation Area in his district; this amounted to more money for these purposes than the amount received, in total, by several "crown jewels" of the park service—that is, the amount for the following parks all added together: Yellowstone, Grand Teton, Glacier, and all the other national parks in Idaho, Wyoming, and Montana. Thanks to the presence on strategic committees of three Alaska members of Congress, the NPS committed to paying $8 million toward a convention center for Seward and to placing offices and visitor facilities in the new building. "I try to be fair," contended Regula; the 1998 budget includes some projects "that are not in districts of members of the Appropriations Committee *or even the Natural Resources Committee.*"[13]

Former NPS director Roger Kennedy estimates that more money is now spent on "congressionally identified" initiatives than on projects recommended by the NPS.[14] In the face of this political spectacle, professionals become gun-shy: "I support [former NPS staffer Dwight] Rettie's projected national park system with independent, professional procedures for identifying, accepting, and managing new units for all time. But . . . can an objective evaluation be accomplished without opening the system to an economic and political gutting?"[15]

Substituting Federal Dollars for Customers

This brings us to Steamtown U.S.A. It was presumably that sad saga that led one former Interior Department policy analyst to conclude that "national parks have become a political payoff mechanism for putting together deals with members of Congress looking to it as a vehicle to promote local economic development projects."[16] Steamtown U.S.A. began as a private railroad museum with some unimpressive old engines and cars, but when customers did not troop to Scranton, Pennsylvania, in sufficient numbers, the city in 1986 turned to its congressman, Joseph McDade, a member of the Interior Appropriations Subcommittee, to bail it out. The city had long since shrunk from 150,000, when it was the nation's anthracite coal capital, to 80,000; it badly needed an economic stimulus. Scranton had no particular connection with railroads but could think of no preferable alternative to luring travelers off the interstate system to visit a tourist attraction. So McDade, comfortable astride his appropriations perch, asked NPS if it would like to take control of Steamtown, even though acquiring the property in this manner totally circumvented the NPS's elaborate historical review process and came at the expense of several more established museums.[17]

Given little alternative, NPS agreed, and Steamtown became a national historic site. Over several years, McDade put through annual appropriations until, finally, he accumulated the $100 million needed to complete the project (NPS would then pay $6.5 million each year to administer the site). Thanks to its cost, visibility, and far-fetched premise, Steamtown has become a symbol of waste, "a third-rate collection in a place to which it has no relevance."[18] Unlike traditional pork, this visible project, an object of satire in several publications, has directly sullied the agency's reputation.

Treating Expensive Construction Projects as Pork

Congress has also intervened in the selection of expensive construction projects for agencies, sometimes insisting on unneeded construction and other times violating agency procedures designed to protect an equitable and cost-effective bidding or selection process. The Senate Environmental and Public Works Committee in 1992 underscored the logrolling involved in its public-works projects when it managed to review only seventeen of fifty-seven federal buildings across the nation in a meager six hours of hearings. To complete the task, aides circulated to the senators "polling cards" with a list of all the projects. They were to initial the projects meeting their approval. The remaining forty projects, at a total cost of $788 million, thus were authorized without any hearings and in a manner where the senators could scarcely have known what they were signing.

Each year in a somewhat less cavalier but similar fashion, a generous number of courthouses and other questionable federal building allocations move through the Congress. Again, however, the victims include not only the taxpayer but also agency procedures—this time, those of the General Services Administration (GSA). Former senator William Cohen thus bitterly lashed out at GSA for building "buildings we don't need, leasing space we can't afford and making decisions that no one in the private sector with a speck of common sense would make." After reviewing 208 congressional building authorizations from the previous year, the GSA administrator had to concede that "every one of them is suspicious," but it was difficult to see just what he could do about it.[19]

Putting the Forest Service Mission into Play

The relationship of political influence to agency mission is more difficult to distinguish in the case of the Forest Service because already, at the turn of the century, its progressive director Gifford Pinchot had argued that the three main principles of conservation should be "development, preservation, and the common good." For Pinchot, development meant "the welfare of this generation first, and afterward the welfare of the generations to follow." Ultimately "conservation means the greatest good to the greatest number for the longest time." This definition of the public interest entailed the notion that the forests should be professionally managed, not simply preserved. Such forest management—and the representation of an agency's mission—would thus represent something of a balancing act among competing values. But Pinchot was under no illusions as to how some within the private sector would relate to the professionals in the Forest Service: "Their [public servants'] care for the forests, waters, lands, and minerals is often the only thing that stands between the public good and the something-for-nothing men, who, like the daughters of the house leech, are forever crying, 'Give, Give.'"[20]

The Forest Service's eventual relationship to these leeches, however, might have come as a surprise even to the realistic Pinchot. The agency now manages 730 million acres of public land, located mostly in the West. Its 155 national forests attract twice as many visitors as the more visible national parks, and the 373,000 miles of road within forest boundaries run for eight times as many miles as the federal interstate system.[21] The impetus for constructing many of these roads lay in enabling private timber-cutting companies to gain access to remote forest areas. In this fashion the Forest Service could also gain favor with Western senators who controlled the natural-resource committees and who emphasized their strong support for rural economic development. In return for facilitating these locally popular and allegedly profitable timber sales, Congress provided the Forest Service with an increasing budget to assist with planning and administration for these sales, and, rather than requiring the agency to send its timber-sale receipts to the federal treasury, provided it with discretionary authority over an ever larger chunk of these funds for its budget, staff, and operations.[22]

The road-credit program is what makes logging on public lands so profitable. The companies receive "road credits" from the Forest Service in exchange for building the roads into the timber areas. They can then use these credits to purchase the timber that they cut in those areas. The credits are supposed to cover the company expenses, but the GAO has found that the price determined by the Forest Service is often more generous than the actual cost and usually includes a 10–15 percent profit margin.[23] The Forest

Service reports of profitable sales result from some highly unusual accounting procedures (including depreciation of the roads over a hundred-year period), underestimating the timber's value, and agency assumption of the costs of presale surveying and postsale replanting. Consequently, as economist Randal O'Toole puts it, "In terms of assets, the (Forest Service) would rank in the top five in *Fortune* magazine's list of the nation's 500 largest corporations. In terms of operating revenues, however, the agency would be No. 290. In terms of net income, the Forest Service would be classified as bankrupt."[24]

As the environmental movement grew, tension increased between tree huggers, as some people called them, and the Forest Service and its congressional and corporate allies: the full extent to which development had outdistanced preservation and Pinchot's public good was becoming clear. By the 1970s, environmentalists had prevailed on Congress to pass laws requiring the Forest Service to promote nontimber uses of national forests and to prevent the extinction of forest wildlife. Soon, the agency's own scientists, while exploring the "overstocked" forests, found a myriad of animals such as the northern spotted owl that depended on "overmature" trees. Other agency studies showed that federal forests had for decades been cut faster than they could grow. It was then that U.S. District Court Judge William Dwyer barred the Forest Service from selling Northwest trees until the agency could demonstrate scientifically how logging and owls could coexist.[25]

While the spotted-owl controversy caused a sensation, later in 1998, when the same Seattle federal court determined that the Forest Service was not safeguarding a population of endangered cutthroat trout from the impact of logging in Washington's Umpqua River Basin,[26] this ruling caused little stir in the national press. Congress, too, had become uncomfortable with "timber salvage" operations allegedly aimed at dead and dying trees that cut down healthy trees. By now, the Clinton administration also had opted for varied forest use and had appointed a director who sought to reinvigorate the agency's mission by declaring a temporary moratorium on building roads in virgin forests.[27]

But the agency's mission will remain in play until well after the moratorium. More private reforested trees have now come on-line, and the amount of timber sold by the Forest Service has declined from about 10 billion board feet in 1990 to about 3 billion in 1996. However, timber profits are particularly high for large, mature trees. A number of Forest Service regional employees are rumored to be uncomfortable with the new agency policy and anxious to restore the good old days.[28] Nor are they the only ones. The two hundred member companies of the American Forest and Paper Association (AF&PA) received $104 million in Forest Service purchaser road credits between 1991 and 1997, during a period when its soft-money contributions grew from roughly \$350,000 in 1991–92 to \$1.5 million in 1995–96, plus several million more in PAC contributions and lobbying expenses. The AF&PA could, therefore, still boast in its 1996 annual report that "advocacy for our members' interests paid huge dividends."[29]

Many of these contributions went to senators from Western states such as Idaho, Washington, and Oregon. These members like to argue that rural economic development and jobs are at stake, but many of the sawmills and logging operations providing those jobs went out of business during the recession in the early 1990s. During the 1991–97 period, \$1 million or more in credits went to only eighty-five companies, accounting for \$354 million in road credits. Hence, fewer than 10 percent of the fifteen hundred corporate recipients received 75 percent of the credits.[30] The bulk of the money thus goes not to rural development but to big companies and their congressional supporters.[31] Such a cozy political arrangement is difficult to relinquish. As one public-land expert explained, "Politicians find (government) agencies to channel resources to industry, and industry channels some of the proceeds back to politicians."[32] In this case, politicians took the agency mission along with the resources.

Political Contributions and Agency Programs

These forms of cozy political arrangements are more subtle than the more direct political influence stemming from political contributions that has raised havoc with other programs and agencies. While such influence can rarely be proved to be a quid pro quo for political contributions, it is perceived as such by agency officials and thus often achieves its likely purpose. It is presumably no accident that the only two-term presidencies since the 1950s—the Republican administrations of Nixon and Reagan and the Democratic Clinton administration—have provided the most apparent tales of campaign-related interference with administrative agencies. Party label seemed less important than the prodigious fund-raising accomplished by these presidents and their entourages. The cast of characters in all three administrations included the president, vice president, and some cabinet and national-party officials. Indeed, while most of the actors are partisan, some contributors apparently managed to contribute money to these successful presidents, regardless of party affiliation, and thereby managed to benefit from the exercise of Republican and, later, Democratic influence on their behalf.

A. Bruce Rozet thus gained the enmity of three HUD secretaries—Jack Kemp, Henry Cisneros, and Andrew Cuomo—for injecting cozy politics into substandard Section 8 housing. As Cisneros put it, Rozet "got filthy rich off of this program and he left filthy places behind for people to live in." A 1992 HUD audit accused Rozet of improperly using federal subsidies and leaving insufficient money to pay for repairs and maintenance in some of his units. A few years later, several tenants died in a fire at one of Rozet's Chicago properties. Despite the opposition of these secretaries from both parties, Rozet continued to average $71 million in federal subsidies each year. When HUD officials from these three administrations were asked why funding for these 235 properties continued under these circumstances, one former HUD official apparently spoke for them all in explaining that "he's got friends in high places."[33] Rozet's contributions went to representatives on the housing committees on both sides of the aisle. Despite bitter public protestations from key HUD executives, its procedures were thus stymied for a decade by this widespread use of political money.

Cabinet Secretaries and Political Influence

Several Clinton cabinet secretaries and members of the White House staff were tied to sleazy 1996 campaign activities that spilled over into their agencies. Some did not result in agency scandals, but all of their actions left the appearance of possible agency compromise. Massachusetts nursing-home mogul Alan Solomont gave $160,000 to the party, helped raise $1.1 million more from nursing-home owners, and then successfully lobbied Health and Human Services Secretary Donna Shalala and Bruce Vladeck of the Health Care Financing Administration to ease nursing-home rules on quality standards and residents' rights. Vladeck later told *Time* that although Solomont's lobbying had some influence on his decisions, he would "comfortably defend each change on its merits."[34] When Commerce Secretary Ron Brown was killed in a plane crash, he was under investigation for, among other things, favoring corporate campaign contributors on lucrative, agency-sponsored trade missions. Not all agency political appointees acquiesced to such requests: Donald Fowler, the former Democratic national chair, testified in a Senate investigation that when he asked Trade Representative Mickey Kantor to include a business supporter on a Commerce Department trade mission to Bosnia, Kantor replied that "he didn't think I should make such a recommendation. I guess he thought it was improper."[35]

Both Bruce Babbitt, as interior secretary under President Clinton, and Harold Ickes, the White House deputy chief of staff, were implicated in an agency decision that compromised a federal agency and came uncomfortably close to a campaign-funds-for-political-influence quid pro quo. The Chippewas wanted to build a dog track and casino in Hudson, Wisconsin. For the first time, the Interior Department in 1995 overruled a decision by its regional office; it quashed the proposed casino after the project was bitterly opposed by seven other tribes—Democratic Party contributors—that owned existing casinos. When an old friend from college days and lobbyist for the Chippewas met with Babbitt, he asked why Democratic donations by tribes should be relevant in such a decision. Secretary Babbitt replied that "these tribes" had contributed "on the order of half a million dollars, something like that." The *Wall Street Journal* found that almost all of these funds were contributed *after* the casino application was rejected. A fund-raising letter from lobbyists for the Saint Croix and Oneida tribes suggests the impetus for the contributions: "As witnessed in the fight to stop the Hudson dog track proposal, the office of the president can and will work on our behalf when asked to do so."[36]

The Vice President and Political Influence

In frantically seeking to collect enough money to finance a strong 1996 campaign and impress the media, Vice President Al Gore did not break any laws, but he too contributed to agency compromise. His relationship with Peter Knight, the 1996 Clinton-Gore campaign chair, exemplifies the problem. While a $7,000-a-month lobbyist for Molten Metal, a wastewater cleanup technology firm, Knight landed the first of several federal grants that eventually totaled $32 million (more than the combined total distributed to all other eighteen companies in this small experimental program). During this same period, he persuaded the company's president, William Haney, and other executives to contribute $132,000 to President Clinton's reelection effort.

Even though there is no law against combining such activities, it did seem a bit of a stretch to have Vice President Gore describe the company's unproven hazardous waste cleanup technology as "a shining example of American ingenuity, hard work and business know-how."[37]

Even though Molten Metal on two occasions had received additional federal grants from the Department of Energy (DOE) within days after making campaign contributions, the timing was described as nothing more than coincidence.

Even though several DOE scientists objected to further government grants to Molten Metal, it presumably was difficult to keep close tabs on all of DOE's 780 new technology programs.

Even though Molten Metal president Haney gave $20,000 to Peter Knight's thirteen-year-old son two weeks after his father was appointed chair of the Clinton-Gore reelection committee.

Even though the then DOE assistant secretary, Tom Grumbly, dined with Knight and Molten executives and had telephone contact with them a surprising number of times, neither he nor Gore violated campaign laws. Besides, a month before the election, when criticism was mounting, DOE did ultimately reduce the Molten Metals contract from $20 million to $8 million.[38]

Whatever the legalities, perhaps there should be a campaign limit on the number of acceptable *even thoughs*.

Pipeline to the White House

Congressional hearings and media reports have explored in detail the ties of foreign money and influence peddlers to the Clinton candidacy and public-policy making. Lebanese businessman Roger Tamraz, though, perhaps captured the loss of innocence among immigrants as well as U.S. citizens. Not for him that symbolic first vote so valued by immigrants of an earlier era. When asked by a Senate committee investigating campaign finance why he never registered to vote but contributed $300,000 to the Democratic Party, Tamraz replied, "Well, I think this is a bit more than a vote."[39] Tamraz, an international oil financier, was seeking administration support for a controversial, multibillion dollar oil pipeline that he wanted to build from the Caspian Sea to Turkey. Several routes were under consideration in this high-politics decision because it involved stimulating more oil production and gaining cooperation among such traditional enemies as Armenia and Azerbaijan. With the assistance of State Department officials and the U.S. ambassador to Armenia, Tamraz met with Sheila Heslin, the Central Asian specialist at the National Security Council (NSC). He outlined his pipeline proposal and asked for assurances that, at least, the Clinton administration would not oppose it. Heslin rejected the possibility of an endorsement and recommended to her superiors that Tamraz have no such further meetings.

After this rebuff, Tamraz went fishing for political influence through the medium of $177,000 in campaign contributions, hooking the then Democratic National Committee chair, Donald Fowler, who telephoned Ms. Heslin and asked her to drop her opposition to the pipeline. He also indicated that Tamraz had helped the CIA in the past and that agency would send her a paper on him. Fowler, who had no CIA clearance, arranged for the paper to be sent, and Heslin reported the incident to the NSC legal counsel as "highly irregular." NSC's deputy director, Nancy Sodeberg, now telephoned Fowler, and in the words of NSC officials told him to "knock it off."[40] The exchange triggered internal investigations in the CIA and NSC as to how a political official could reach deep into the security apparatus and extract a paper to help a campaign contributor.

NSC's director, Anthony Lake, was not told about the sequence of events, since until the paper surfaced it was thought that the issue was dead after the Sodeberg conversation. Nonetheless, the revelations later damaged him in 1997 on the eve of his scheduled CIA-director confirmation hearings before the Senate, when investigative reporters Michael Frisby and

David Rogers broke the story. The Tamraz incident served as the catalyst for the withdrawal of Lake's nomination as CIA director.[41] While fishing for a pipeline with his blatant cash-for-access scheme, Tamraz got his line tangled in a major foreign-policy appointment.

Democratic Illegalities vs. Bipartisan Sleaze

One might argue that there are two levels of legal conduct: honorable and sleazy. Honorable political behavior encourages agency integrity; sleazy political behavior ultimately insures agency compromise. Senator Fred Thompson, a veteran of the Watergate hearings and chair in 1997 for the Senate campaign-finance hearings, initially decided to investigate not only illegal activities but also sleazy, improper ones. Although in doing so Thompson was invoking the same criterion used in assessing the Watergate political behavior, he was bitterly attacked by Majority Leader Trent Lott and other Republican conservatives this time around for not focusing on illegalities. Furthermore, the irregularities were to be Democratic ones, rather than the product of bipartisan approach that characterized the Watergate hearings.[42]

Privatization and Cozy Politics

Over the last twenty-five years, privatization has enjoyed increasing popularity, thanks largely to some success at the local level when applied to such services as solid-waste collection, fire protection, and transportation.[43] Privatization is also increasingly being proposed as an appropriate remedy for overgrown federal programs.

But if privatization is to fulfill its promise, the conditions necessary for market competition must be in place; administrative means must not become entangled with programmatic goals; agencies, even as they shrink, must be able to monitor contracts effectively; and, most importantly, cozy politics must not be allowed to jeopardize agency goals or client needs. Achieving successful public/private partnerships thus requires a clear sense of the promise and pitfalls of privatization, a higher quality of politics and administration than is often practiced, and the avoidance of pseudoprivatization.

Defining Privatization

The difficulty in understanding privatization begins with its definition. E. S. Savas views privatization as "the act of reducing the role of government, or increasing the role of the private sector in an activity or in the ownership of assets."[44] This definition, however, incorporates elements of three markedly different ideas, ideas that often are confused in public dialogue over privatization.

The first meaning addresses a shift in the ownership of assets from the public to the private sector. In much of the world, privatization has meant such a shift. This situation is rarely the scenario in the United States, where historically most utilities, modes of transportation, and other organizations have operated in the private sector. The second element refers to the act of shrinking the size of government. In the hands of most academic advocates, emphasis is placed here on shifting the policy-implementation role from the public bureaucracy to private and nonprofit administrative agencies. Governmental functions thus would continue to be carried out. In the popular debate on TV talk shows and in newspaper accounts, though, privatization is seen largely as the act of reducing the government. The ends of government—its appropriate size and role—along with the means of policy implementation thus become entangled in a reductionist "privatization equals shrinking" equation. The third strand refers to *how* we should deliver goods and services and *who* should do it, rather than *whether* the goods or service should be delivered at all.[45] This public/private choice then depends essentially on who will pay for the service and who will deliver it.[46] Privatization is thus touted simultaneously as a remedy for solving state and national problems, as a vehicle for shrinking the size of government, and as a means of policy implementation.

Privatization supporters view competition as a handy stick for prodding recalcitrant public agencies to achieve administrative reform. Conservatives differ in theory from neoliberals:[47] conservatives want to make government smaller, while new Democrats want to make it better. In practice it is sometimes difficult to distinguish the two. Vice President Gore's *Report on Reinventing Government,* for example, boasted that it would make the federal government better even as it removed 250,000 federal employees from the payroll.[48]

The Conditions Under Which Privatization Is Appropriate

The big payoff from privatization is clearly thought to be greater efficiency. The benefits of competition can come from pitting public units against one another, but the big advantage will come through public/private partnerships to which the private sector can bring its greater technical know-how, vigor, and commitment to the bottom line. The question then boils down to those conditions under which privatization (usually achieved through contracting out) can be successfully achieved. Ideally, the discipline of competition would be sufficient to produce prices in accord with supply and demand. Adherents and opponents of privatization have long agreed, though, that a relatively efficient market can only function where monopoly and other forces inimical to successful markets can be eliminated or at least neutralized. Under these circumstances, the administrative agency, despite imperfect competition and incomplete information, must be a "smart buyer."[49]

In the public sector, these limitations to contracting out are complicated by several problems: the government agency's goals are uncertain; the product is difficult to monitor; switching from one contractor to another in midstream is difficult; and the government agency itself knows considerably more about the best means to accomplish the goal.[50] State and federal agencies are particularly prone to difficulties in defining public goals. It is hard to draw up a contract with sufficient specificity when we know so little about, for example, how to rehabilitate prisoners, define "normality" in mental health, or break the cycle of welfare dependency. Under these circumstances, the government must be heavily involved throughout the process of implementation. This involvement enables the agency and its staff to learn how to deal with these difficult issues and how to build that knowledge into reformulated goals and strategies through its policy-formulation role.

There is also the festering problem of inadequate contract monitoring. Privatization proponents and critics agree in theory that more monitoring and evaluation are needed to gauge how well alternative strategies are dealing with these complex issues.[51] It is, therefore, disappointing that, even as privatization arrangements have continued to grow, monitoring and evaluation activities have declined at the federal and state levels. For example, after focusing on implementation of the community-health system, one study characterized the federal government as a "hollow state," lacking the personnel to perform its programmatic role. Its monitoring and evaluation capability were assessed as "very low to nonexistent."[52]

The Attraction of Political Influence

There is also a political dimension to privatization that has received comparatively less attention from scholars. Public/private partnerships are basically collaborative arrangements between a number of businessmen and some Republican and new Democrat politicians and political executives. These groups seek to "avoid political interference" even as they draw on private-sector know-how and funds to tackle complex economic and social problems. Politics in this sense has negative connotations for these actors. It refers primarily to the power of public employees, government monopolies, and career-conscious politicians seeking to develop programs at the expense of the taxpayer, as well as to the machinations of bureaucrats and bureaucracies able to manipulate the rules and an agency's mission for their own, rather than the public, interest.[53] Privatization, seen in this light, becomes a healthy antidote to big government. Political interference should not be allowed to hinder the adoption of the contracting-out mechanism.

Distaste for the "politics of politics," however, does not prevent some actors in the public and private sectors from turning privatization to their own political purposes. Cozy politics comes into play when such goal-displacement occurs. Cozy political arrangements enable companies or nonprofit agencies to win public-agency contracts through political influence rather than technical competence. The result is that those designated to provide the goods and services, along with their legislative and political executive allies, benefit at the expense of the intended program beneficiaries. On occasion, the public agency itself may become involved in such illegitimate contracting-out agreements.

For the comparatively weak public agency, the point of distorting its policy is to bring greater political power to the aid of its cause. Seeking such power becomes particularly necessary when the agency has an "impossible job."[54] Such jobs involve attempting to achieve programmatic gains with a difficult clientele, where legitimacy with the public is low, and the professions constituting the heart of the agency possess relatively low status. The number of large, complex agencies with such impossible jobs is considerable; it includes agencies concerned with social welfare, mental health, public safety, and corrections. Cozy politics also manifested itself in the 1980s and 1990s in situations where an agency was under pressure to produce quickly or when the political burden of proof was on the agency to perform in a manner acceptable to a jaded citizenry.

Private- and nonprofit-sector partners, with their greater power and status in the society as a whole and increasingly in both political parties, become valuable allies in achieving an agency's ends as well as determining its means. Thanks to the prevalence of contracting out among agencies, privatization is frequently already on the scene when the opportunity for cozy politics knocks. Where public agencies are working under pressure, such an alliance offers private or nonprofit organizations a particularly welcome opportunity to provide valuable political support when these contractors cannot meet all of the implementation conditions.

Contracting Out Without Competition

Large private and nonprofit organizations prefer to avoid the price discipline of the competitive prescription. While competition is good for the economy as a whole, individual companies understandably seek to insulate themselves from it. To the extent that they succeed, reality becomes distinctly at odds with orthodoxy. The discipline of the corporate bottom line, after all, provides much of the justification for privatization's potency as a reform movement. It is in two senses here that reality departs from theory. First, numerous conditions are necessary to achieve reasonable competition. On the basis of case studies of contracting out complex tasks in large organizations, even limited competition seems all too rare. Second, the problem becomes more convoluted in this era of privatization and political action committees. In dealing with their public-sector allies, these private actors in the political process are often well positioned either to influence the terms of the competitive bidding process or to arrange later for more profitable adjustments to the contract. Neither companies nor nonprofit organizations have been bashful in taking advantage of such access.

While studies of privatization in complex public organizations generally identify some advantages to contracting out, saving money is rarely one of them. Ruth DeHoog concluded that contracting out did not result in significant cost reduction in her two state agencies even though they used outside experts as monitors. She did find that contracting out led to greater political activity, particularly by those suppliers dependent upon government contracts for their very survival.[55]

Steven Smith and Michael Lipsky found that the resulting contracts often led to beneficial client services; indeed, they found that when states contracted out it led to a more robust service sector. But claims of cost saving could not be substantiated largely because producing human services of high quality on a sustained basis is markedly different from producing standardized products at a fixed price.[56] Nonprofit firms also enter into mutually beneficial relationships with the state, but they do so because their financial future depends on winning these contracts. Hence they, too, join the fray more as "players in a political process rather than as sellers of services."[57] Cozy politics has thus resulted from such contracting-out arrangements playing into the hands of state legislatures that are notorious for their attempts to make themselves indispensable to companies, nonprofit agencies, and interest groups.

These public/private partnerships—for example, in highway construction and defense projects—are often long-term, mutually beneficial, and somewhat productive, even if they do not reduce costs. Often there is no alternative to such partnerships. There is little justification for the duplication of existing private or nonprofit organizations when implementing public policies. The boundary line, however, between such close relationships and cozy politics is a fuzzy one.

The Opening for Political Corruption

Corruption does indeed exist in a number of contractual relationships. It generally seems to stem more from the actions of politicians and political executives than from those of civil servants. Privatization is involved because the corruption would not be possible without the cooperation of both partners and because privatization as a political movement has weakened public bureaucracies. U.S. citizens are exceptional in the extent of their antagonism toward government, and "third-party government" is one of the forces that has exploited this view.[58] Bureaucratic expertise is now largely replaced by advice to policymakers from other actors, and partisan political perspectives permeate more bureaucratic layers even while private and nonprofit agencies are increasingly responsible for policy implementation. Furthermore, adherents of the privatization movement do not evince a belief in any version of the public interest. Goal distortion of an agency and even political corruption thus seem less reprehensible and certainly less shocking.

As more systematic studies of federal government scandals emerged in the 1980s and 1990s, it was remarkable how many involved public/private partnerships. Kenneth Meier argues that where privatization occurs, evidence of corruption is pervasive. He points to the exploitation by the Wedtech Corporation of the Small Business Administration's minority-business program and to "privately owned vocational schools (that) sometimes appear to be no more than fronts to collect student loan money."[59] John Rehfuss regards "lubrication politics" as the almost inevitable price for obtaining contracts: "As long as money, geographical choices, and votes are at stake, political decisions will continue to be made about who gets contracts, for how long a period, and in which location. When the contract or project is large enough, pork-barrel politics will rule, to the detriment of program efficiency and effectiveness."[60]

Not all these cases involve small projects. The Savings and Loan debacle began in the 1980s when interest rates rose to a point where a number of S&Ls could no longer reinvest their funds into higher-yielding assets (normally residential mortgage loans). When the S&Ls could not maintain a sufficient spread between the return on their assets and the interest payments, they were obligated to pay their depositors. At that point, the solution would have been to close the weak thrifts; instead, bankers and government regulators were equally reluctant to acknowledge the problem. They allowed these "zombie thrifts" to continue, and, thanks to deregulation, to assume even greater risks with depositors money to balance their books. Bank creditors were content with this arrangement since they were protected "by the black magic of federal guarantees."[61] As one bank official who unsuccessfully sought help from the Office of Management and Budget (OMB) put it, "The administration was so ideologically blinded that it couldn't understand the difference between thrift deregulation and airline deregulation."[62]

Meanwhile, new S&L bank executives such as Charles Keating, who were willing to assume high risks, emerged, seeking political assistance when even these weak regulations became a hurdle. Developers were not to be outdone: "You give a builder a chance to build with insured deposits he can raise with a phone call whenever he needs the money, and he'll cover the earth with housing."[63] Judge Stanley Sporkin, when ruling on one of the S&L cases, condemned the "excesses of a misconceived and misapplied regulatory program along with a group of individuals . . . bent on exploiting these excesses."[64]

Academic proponents intend that the supply-and-demand requisites of competition be met before privatization can be justified. When hooked to cozy politics, however, two of its other meanings can be exploited for money. Even when the goals of greater economy and efficiency are not met, its adherents can advocate privatization for personal and corporate gain and as a relentless quest for smaller government. The result under these circumstances is what might be called pseudoprivatization—the pretense of drawing on the greater efficiency and effectiveness of the private sector, when in actuality the rationale of privatization serves merely as ideological camouflage for dramatic cases of pervasive corruption.

These cases stand out for three reasons. First, they involve actors from both the public and private sectors. Second, these actors share a political approach to privatization that fiercely condemns public bureaucracy as of such limited social utility that weakening its rule-making capacity, structure, or organizational culture is fair game. Third, the corruption is systemic and places in question the agency's integrity and purpose.

In addition to the S&L debacle, Haynes Johnson counted twenty federal administrative agencies where scandals occurred during the Reagan administration, among them the Agriculture Department, the Synthetic Fuels Corporation, and the Consumer Product Safety Commission.[65] The Department of Housing and Urban Development is an extreme case, but it demonstrates something of the problem's dimensions.

HUD: A Case Study in Pseudoprivatization

While it received its greatest notoriety during the Reagan years, HUD's fall from grace extended for twenty-five years. While this description is limited to the Reagan administration, Eugene Meehan has condemned what he called a "programmed failure in public housing" that occurred for similar reasons during Democratic administrations in the 1960s and 1970s. He bitterly criticizes the multiple goals of the policy formulators who framed "a stimulus to the construction industry, a way of assisting the cities to clear slums, and a source of needed low-income housing."[66] As for the policy-implementation stage, Meehan found the resulting public/private partnership thoroughly wanting. He characterized the HUD bureaucracy as "blundering, incompetent, insensitive, expensive, and unable or unwilling to learn and improve."[67] But, he observes, "local housing authorities did not design or construct apartments; those activities were carried out by architects and construction firms in the private sector, hence the mistakes and inadequacies that characterized that dimension of the program should be charged to the private sector account."[68]

When Ronald Reagan assumed the presidency, his Department of Management and Budget director, David Stockman, made clear that he intended to control and dramatically reduce the size of HUD.[69] These goals would be achieved by shifting agency control to the new Republican political appointees. This message was conveyed early by Housing Secretary Sam Pierce when he held a meeting of his top political appointees and civil servants. "This is the board of directors," he said pointing to the political appointees. "We make all the policy decisions." Nodding at the career workers, he continued, "You are to carry out those orders. And not ask questions."[70] Furthermore, the civil servants were not to be allowed to assist their superiors, drawn almost exclusively from the private sector, in learning the formidable thicket of HUD regulations.

These new appointees were unusually young and inexperienced. The powerful position of executive assistant to the passive Sam Pierce fell to twenty-eight-year-old Deborah Gore Dean. Her prior experience consisted of tending bar, while spending eight years obtaining her college degree, and working in a minor position in Ronald Reagan's presidential campaign. More significant was her wealthy family's connection to John Mitchell, the former attorney general.[71] As Dean and the other political appointees centralized power, ignored advice from housing experts, and pursued their own agenda, they became known as the "Brat Pack" and the "Kiddie Corps."[72] Over the six years (before the scandal dwarfed budget-cutting efforts), HUD's budget was reduced by 57 percent, and by 1986 the number of employees had fallen from 16,323 to 11,470. Whole divisions of HUD were eliminated, including the Office of Organization Management and Information responsible for surveying the effectiveness of HUD field offices. In the view of a long-time HUD observer, in its place HUD sent out people "who did not know what they were doing"; the attitude became, "Don't rock the boat, don't criticize the staff."[73] This combination of circumstances weakened the resolve of HUD civil servants to try to curb the corruption. "You could hear it all over the place," said one senior executive, "Why worry? I may not have a job next week."[74]

There were others with more direct, institutional responsibility for monitoring and oversight who failed to carry out their duty. Congress has little incentive to conduct hearings under normal conditions since there are more productive ways for a House member or a senator to invest time politically. Key committee chairs later admitted that they were unaware of the problems. This ignorance need not have been the case, since General Accounting Office reports strongly criticized HUD during this period. HUD's own inspector general took HUD's management to task but did not criticize HUD's top echelon. Furthermore, even when several subsequent inspectors general did warn of breakdowns in the system, they did so in hushed tones or, as conservative columnist James Kilpatrick wryly observed, "pianissimo."[75]

Oversight failed in part because of the absence both of internal and external pressure. Congress, with its Democratic majority, could have acted, but it was under little pressure. Because "the money (had) dried up,"[76] the mayors, home builders, mortgage bankers, and housing advocates who, as the HUD lobby, had traditionally fought for the agency lost interest. The OMB could have acted, but, as one of Reagan's budget directors later admitted, "OMB was preoccupied with trying to terminate some of the programs at HUD rather than trying to police it."[77]

Oversight would have proved particularly useful because, early in the game, HUD's executives, by their own subsequent accounts, abandoned the agency's mission (as well as any ethical compunctions). Instead, they turned to using the agency's money to reward developers who contributed funds to the president's campaign, powerful Republicans in the administration and in Congress, and, last but not least, themselves. In the mind of Dean, Pierce's administrative assistant, HUD at this point "was set up and designed to be a political program," and "I would have to say that we ran it in a political manner."[78] A former consultant to the Reagan White House put it more colorfully: "The Administration was pursuing a deliberate 'antipolicy' with regard to housing. That created a feeding frenzy in which some HUD officials believed it was OK to take the crumbs."[79]

This illegal activity was aided and abetted by the newly centralized nature of the HUD bureaucracy and by the abandonment of the key regulations that underlay the traditional decision-making process. HUD's secretary, a man of some stature—at least, before coming to Washington—could have provided some guidance for his administrative assistant, but, with some notable exceptions, he apparently took little interest in daily activities. In his absence, Dean "was the ward heeler . . . the political expediter," a role made easier since she apparently had access to Pierce's autopen whenever she chose to use it.[80] She attended meetings with what her aides called "Debbie's list," consisting of about thirty projects on a clipboard. "As Dean would announce what projects were to be funded, the aides would leaf through the notebooks, hoping to find an application from the community involved. If no letter could be found, the aides would call the communities the following day and urge them to submit an application."[81]

The "Scandal Scorecard," as one observer termed it, was long and deep, but a few examples give the idea. New York senator Alfonse

D'Amato received significant campaign contributions from Puerto Rican developers and, recalled a HUD political appointee, "took a very real interest in housing programs in Puerto Rico." Indeed, within HUD, Mr. D'Amato was known as "the senator from Puerto Rico."[82] Frederick Bush, deputy finance chairman for President George Bush's election committee in 1988, worked with two partners in a consulting firm formed to win subsidies for apartment construction. The partners brazenly submitted to HUD a typed description of the firm indicating that it had succeeded in developing "an extensive network throughout the White House and most federal agencies" as well as with Congress. The firm stressed that its "unique assets" included its "access to government officials."[83]

More resourceful than most, the firm stood ready to deal with Democratic as well as Republican administrations since one of its officials maintained close relations with the Kennedy family. Indeed, perhaps that partner had already swung into action before Reagan even appeared on the scene. According to the *Boston Globe,* "70 percent of the money [President Jimmy] Carter raised in Massachusetts in 1979 came from HUD contractors, each of whom received a new project in return."[84] Included among the other Reagan influence peddlers, each of whom was paid $75,000 or more, literally to make a few telephone calls, were former Department of Interior Secretary James Watt, President Gerald Ford's Housing secretary Carla Hills, former Republican senator Edward Brooke, and even bandleader Lionel Hampton.[85]

Particularly because of the lost public trust and confidence in Washington's leadership, the price paid as a result of these revelations was high. Even higher, however, was the price paid in total programs crippled by the revelations. By the end of this period, HUD officials admitted that "at least 28 of the department's 48 programs and activities had 'significant problems' attributable to fraud, mismanagement, and (political) favoritism."[86]

Conclusion

Such pervasive corruption over an extended time underscores how difficult it is to insure that privatization does, indeed, meet its objectives even while protecting the public sector from the dangers of cozy politics. "The bureaucracy," as well as the involved elected officials and civil servants, suffers substantial damage from a scandal of the magnitude of that at HUD (though the private sector interestingly does not seem to suffer comparable public condemnation for its role). Furthermore, the agency for years thereafter remained a fear-based chain of command wherein employees in HUD's headquarters and in the field constantly checked on one another to avoid improprieties that could lead to more bad publicity, indictments, and convictions. HUD Deputy Secretary Terrence Duvernay explained in 1993 that because of this fear HUD employees felt that they "had to cross every 't' twice and dot every 'I' three times. So people who dealt with HUD saw (the agency) as an impediment, an obstacle."[87] As is evident from this chapter, however, HUD is simply the most glaring example of cozy political arrangments that are now found in numerous federal agencies—accompanied sometimes by public/private partnerships and other times resulting from the direct exercise of political influence by members of congress or the president on public bureaucracies

There are several conclusions relating to agency compromise, cozy politics, and privatization that are relevant here. First, for better or worse, the political push for privatization will likely continue in coming years. Meanwhile, as a result of downsizing and the funding needs of entitlement programs, much of the federal government will decrease in size and power. In attempting to "do more with less," the federal and state governments will enter into even more public/private partnerships. It thus becomes imperative that governments at all levels protect their agencies' integrity and the public interest by maintaining their monitoring and evaluation capability even while they downsize.

Such positions may be perceived as "staff overhead" and thus as prime candidates for elimination. This attitude must be countered. These are the line officials responsible for contract enforcement and for monitoring the competitive environment in the contract state. In the Wedtech, HUD, and, most notably, S&L corruptions, government auditors not only were insufficient but also were subjected to cutbacks mandated precisely when their programs were most vulnerable.[88] When agencies support their auditors, they can make a significant difference. The Small Business Administration (SBA) eventually backed its Office of Inspector General in pressing the Wedtech investigation and subsequently supported legislative reforms that led to greater competition among qualified firms for large SBA contracts.[89]

Second, the danger of cozy politics and public/private partnership excesses can only be alleviated by bolstering government before more extensive privatization occurs. The conditions necessary for the success of privatization require a more widespread appreciation among the governing and governed alike of the need for, not necessarily "big," but definitely strong, government. A vacuum in the capacity to govern produces cozy politics whether the villains be Clinton Democratic devotees of Whitewater real estate or Reagan Republican cabinet devotees of HUD housing projects. Lip service to "steering," while bashing public bureaucracies, is not sufficient. Those favoring a reduction in the size of government must accept public accountability as a precondition to effective privatization.

Other conditions likely to foster success in implementing privatization must also be nurtured. Presidential and agency leadership from the top, necessary to cope with political pressure and to lend backbone to an agency's culture, enable it to implement contracts in accord with its mission. The Carter and Reagan administrations did make serious efforts to put teeth into an A-76 program requirement that every federal agency review its commercial activities and transfer to the private sector those activities that it could perform at a lower cost. While these reforms were not sufficient, the program was able to achieve some unquestioned cost savings.[90]

Third, the federal government has largely limited its concern with ethics to individual acts that violate conflict-of-interest statutes. Illegal payments by a lobbyist to a member of Congress or to a staffer that lead to agency compromise, for example, also must be investigated.[91] Governments at all levels must also transcend the level of individual legal transgressions and devote more attention to the agency rot that leads to cozy politics. James Kilpatrick captured HUD's institutional and moral climate well when he described such influence peddlers as "cats that came for the cream" who "lapped up" fat consultancy fees "in exchange for a wink, a nod, a nudge, and a couple of phone calls. Nothing illegal. Nothing even unethical. It was the 'system'."[92] High-echelon line executives from every agency involved in public/private partnerships must sponsor, and themselves participate in, training sessions to increase the likelihood that these *institutional* ethical concerns will become part of the administrative agency's culture. Dennis Thompson seems on the right track in arguing for new standards of ethics in which we would "see more concern about the mixing of private profit and public service, more attention to the merits of constituent claims, and more worry about the effects of practices of individual representatives on the broader process of democratic representation."[93]

Fourth, the danger of privatization run amok and related corruption stemming from interest group and PAC demands and its impact on the public interest underscore that the nation has an urgent stake in some type of campaign reform. Candidate needs for growing amounts of campaign funds every two, four, or six years has created innumerable opportunities for developers, corporations, and interest groups to influence policy. While some politicians are scrupulous in defining under what conditions they will accept such contributions, these scruples are under increasing pressure every year as the price of each TV minute and direct-mail letter rises. Public and private providers of public services need to clean up their acts and the systems of political financing and high-level spoils in which they are entangled.[94] It is imperative to prevent an instant replay of the HUD disgrace elsewhere by reforming the political system.

Finally, advocates of privatization, civil servants, political executives working in the administrative agency, and private and nonprofit contractors must recognize that they have an obligation to the agency's clientele. HUD's capitulation to cozy politics and resulting vulnerability to criticism, for example, brought on partially by this debacle, has left its unorganized, relatively worse-off clients utterly defenseless politically. For those earning too little to qualify for unsubsidized apartments built by the private sector and unable to obtain public housing, the result is more inadequate, unregulated dwellings. Perhaps the next time, instead of being required to pay light fines or take brief sabbaticals to white-collar prisons, those caught engaging in cozy politics and compromising our public agencies should be sentenced to live under the same conditions as the clients they defraud.

7

Reinventing Political Parties

M ore attention must be paid to our political system in order to counter cozy politics. Politics in the United States simply cannot work effectively when 60 percent of U.S. citizens are disengaged from more than minimal participation. In observing the resulting political disaster area of cynicism and lack of political knowledge, some critics have observed that we as a nation, and particularly the disengaged, deserve what such citizen lethargy begets. But ours is a nation where we learn by doing. Citizen ignorance and cynicism partly reflect this lack of involvement—and party leaders and officeholders share responsibility with the citizenry for the shabby condition of our political system.

The Consequences of Tepid Citizen Participation

Periods of rapid economic expansion often disproportionally benefit the haves at the expense of the have-nots, skewing income distribution toward the better-off. The danger posed by this condition is increased by the lack of more widespread citizen involvement in the new economy. Fortunately, good times in some ways benefit everyone in the United States, as well as the national wealth. It is, however, time to stop pretending that the majority of people in this country have benefited significantly from the stock-market explosion of the 1990s and admit that the true cost of realizing the American dream—as measured by the Future Opportunity Index (see Chapter 2)—has risen.

While these inequities are unlikely to cause major problems during comparatively good times, they will become more visible during bad times. Although the optimistic long-term projections of government agencies and some economists imply the abolition of the business cycle and preach the rhetoric of a soft landing, new economy companies and service organizations also depend on product cycles. In addition, recessions result from oil crises, wars, terrorism, and other unpredictable events. Some veteran stock analysts like to talk about the need for prudence when making investments;

futurists of various stripes seem to have purged this word from their vocabularies.

Similar prudence would suggest the advisability of stemming the rising tide of cozy politics. Instead, questionable political influence has thrived in a society already beset by "bad-news" events and institutional gridlock. The price paid by a politically disengaged society is an increase in the number of cozy political arrangements. Single-purpose interest groups, corporations, and wealthy individuals move in to fill the power vacuum. The consequence is a political system characterized by greater reliance on campaign funds and more personally expedient decisionmaking.

The changing nature of political campaigns may be seen most dramatically in the return of soft money—bigger and bolder than before Watergate—and in the rise of a second constituency willing to exploit a growing number of campaign loopholes. The result is uncontrollable campaign costs confronting needy, nervous politicians—ripe pickings for cozy politics. Citizens are left with the impression that elections, too often, are for sale. The political currency of democracy in too many minds is thereby transformed from votes into money.

And yet, if cozy politics poses such a danger to democracy, where is the public outcry? For years, a handful of public-interest groups, such as Common Cause, the Center for Public Integrity, and the Center for Responsive Politics, have sounded the call for reform. While John McCain and Ralph Nader used the issue effectively in 2000, these calls are not heard in the malls, sports stadiums, cultural and other entertainment arenas, and TV network channels where most of the population continue to hang out. Some writers have claimed that people are angry or hate politics—and that is certainly the case when economic adversity or a significant government regulation strikes them personally—but the majority of citizens seem impervious to concerns about the health of the body politic in an age when affluence dribbles down and around.

It sometimes appears that the U.S. populace simply does not care about politics and government. And yet, when national misfortune strikes, people expect government to act. When the terrorist attack occurred on September 11, 2001, a public outcry arose as to why the federal government had not anticipated this surprise attack and what actions it should take in response. When Hurricane Andrew wreaked havoc, the question was not whether the Federal Emergency Management Agency (FEMA) should intervene but why it was not moving faster. When a crop fails, farmers of all political stripes demand that a disaster declaration be issued so that they can apply for emergency loans; the same media that instinctively bash bureaucrats and bureaucracies then righteously demand action. The same politicians who screamed for a less heavy-handed federal government—and therefore provided less money to enable regulatory agencies to operate effectively—

then scream for government action. Without ever acknowledging the inconsistency in their approach, the criticism becomes: How could the federal government have allowed this to happen?

Some critics have noted this tendency to rely instinctively on the federal government and condemned it as yet another trip by groups viewing themselves as *entitled* to special treatment at the federal trough. But victims of natural catastrophes, a random sample of unlucky consumers, and farmers are hardly a shiftless and lazy bunch. Rather, we are living in a specialized society where, though it may occasionally change, the degree of dependence on one another is not fully appreciated. This complexity is captured nicely in the public/private partnership that it takes to bring even a single "low-tech" commodity, gasoline, to market. In addition to the roles played by the oil operator, refiner, and retail distributor, local government prevents the theft of oil or destruction of equipment, state and federal governments preclude interference with the transport of the oil and enforce the sanctity of contracts, and the three levels of government work together to build and maintain the necessary highway and local road systems.[1] While pipelines have partially replaced trucks since this description of our mixed economy was written in 1939, the roles of federal, state, and local governments remain essentially unchanged.

The Missing Connections in U.S. Politics

The only time citizens—and most politicians, too—pay attention to this complex delivery process is when it does not work, and then the eternal refrain arises: What is the federal government going to do about it? Many citizens assume that the government will be there no matter how cavalierly it is treated by the people and the political system. Even while they criticize the government and bitterly condemn and even undermine it, they seemingly continue to take it for granted. These same citizens do not see how their action—or inaction—has much to do with how effectively politics and government work. This is not surprising, since other than telling people that it is their duty to vote, no one tells them that the government really *needs* their participation—and periodically their sacrifice—to function.

Perhaps it should not be surprising that U.S. citizens are so casual about their government. How could it be otherwise, when so many of them know so little about what government does and often confuse which level of government does what? Congressional and state legislative case work staffers make their living partly by rerouting constituent inquiries to the level of government or nonprofit agency that can solve their problem. This lack of awareness of government's role in our society is also reflected in a 1997 poll. Younger adults, aged eighteen to thirty-four, were asked who—

government, business, or nonprofits (including universities)—deserved the most credit for a list of notable achievements over the last thirty years. Although government had played a large role in all of them, barely half of the young adults credited the government with improving health care for seniors, boosting financial aid to college students, or reducing air and water pollution. Only one in five credited the government with medical break-throughs or technological developments such as the Internet.[2] But even the federal government these days comes out smelling like a rose compared with politics. A citizen survey earlier in the same year revealed the opinion that politics posed a greater hindrance to serving the public well than did government waste.[3]

It will be dangerous if citizens continue to view the government as irrelevant to their lives and the political system as corrupt. If people then persist in opting out of the political system in growing numbers, their expectation will become a self-fulfilling prophecy. In reality, numerous decisions, along all four pathways to congressional decisionmaking (see Chapter 5), are still made in accord with the public interest. Numerous poli-cies still move through a visible, representative, and responsive policy process that, depending on the policy, seeks to translate public needs through district or state support, policy subsystems, second-constituency support, and public programs and regulations into public policy. Grassroots' influentials, information, and popular ideas, as well as money, remain driving forces behind such policies.

As citizen participation has slackened, however, one result is that all four legislative pathways are becoming clogged with extensive and expen-sive pork. The statutory and regulatory payoffs made in exchange for sec-ond-constituency support and the piggy-back pork attached to public pro-grams and regulations are especially worrisome. The nation's wealth and its political capital, particularly in the form of lost democratic credibility, are being squandered.

The impact of cozy politics on the policy process might be less disturb-ing if members of Congress and the president seemed more intent on reduc-ing such political influence on policymaking and less intent on deflecting criticism from current political practices by making a public show of whip-ping the administrative agencies into shape. But too often, politicians of both stripes blithely push agencies into more policy positions that compro-mise their missions and more cozy political arrangements that compromise their reputations. For the many Congressional Republicans who continue to subscribe to the ideas highlighted in Newt Gingrich's Contract with America (CWA), the problems of government will be solved essentially by shrinking its size and regulations. For the New Democrats in the Clinton administration too, politics was perceived as disconnected from administra-tive problems. When President Bill Clinton announced his Reinventing

Government initiative, he emphasized that it "is not about politics. Programs passed by both Democratic presidents and Republican presidents . . . are being undermined by an inefficient and outdated bureaucracy."[4] To underscore this separation of politics and administration, the backdrop at this White House announcement consisted of a forklift sagging under the weight of reams of agency regulations. Bureaucrat bashing is a time-honored tradition in Washington, D.C., and the Reinventing Government movement and the Contract with America approach are essentially variations on this political theme.

Even when they vote, U.S. citizens now express cynical attitudes toward our political leaders and democratic institutions. Some suspicion of politicians and bureaucrats is healthy for a democracy, but pervasive cynicism interferes with the necessary connection between the citizen and governance. Historically political parties have linked the citizen and the political system. However, the hijacking of traditional party roles by interest groups and social movements has edged many citizens farther away from such political participation.

Citizen-Based Political Parties

The most critical political challenge facing the United States today is how to connect or reconnect 60 percent of our population to the political system. Only then will the citizenry regain sufficient power, confidence, and political knowledge to support their political institutions and leaders on a sustained basis. This national support is a prerequisite to serious congressional and presidential action on meeting health care needs, sustaining the environment on a global basis, funding social security, and coping with the military demands on a superpower. And these issues will require national support and sacrifice.

Reinventing Citizen-Based Parties

Meeting this challenge will require nothing less than reinventing grassroots, citizen-based parties. These reconstituted parties will have to do more than merely emulate the so-called heyday of the late nineteenth century grassroots parties when it certainly was easier to reach the eligible voters through a partisan press, partisan rallies, and vigorous voter mobilization by the party faithful that resulted in high electoral turnout.[5] Furthermore, party organizations were more powerful in that they chose candidates, decided the election agenda, had dominant control of electoral resources, and influenced governmental appointments after the election.[6] It is a nice question, however, as to just how democratic such parties were when less than half of the electorate was eligible to vote and parties were riddled with boss rule and patronage.[7] Whatever the pros and cons of those parties, for a nation whose politics today must somehow parallel the world-class bigness of its global corporations, a return to such old-style self-governance is impossible.[8]

Parties need not develop full-blown ideologies, but they must communicate loose-knit belief systems that differentiate their party's aims, values, and programs. Their platforms must capture the imaginations of party workers as well as voters. In addition, they must run candidates concerned both with meeting voter demands and offering programs designed to lure nonvoters back into the voting booth. Ambitious politicians should be tempted by this possibility, since the candidate attracting numerous disaffected voters would swamp an opponent seeking merely to target its share of the current, comparatively small electorate.

Making Mobilization Work

A revival of parties today would require drastically altering politics as usual. Traditional locally rooted political parties have experienced serious decline thanks to the onslaught of television advertising, polling and focus groups, political consultants, nationally based lobbying groups, computerized modes of data analysis, direct-mail technology, and grassroots-based national interest groups.[9] The resulting actualization enables national political and party leaders to exploit fully the remarkable impact of such technologies—particularly television. Mobilization on a person-to-person basis is never going to replace these technologies.

But relying almost exclusively on media and other technologies is a strategy born partly out of weakness, since *both actualization and mobilization work*. Television is a potent political weapon, but even the impact achieved by running numerous television and radio ads eventually reaches a point of diminishing returns. So the party that can draw extensively on both actualization and mobilization strategies should enjoy a significant competitive advantage over the party compelled to rely solely on actualization for lack of available campaign workers or on mobilization for lack of sufficient campaign funds.[10]

Indeed, when used most effectively, the media and social interaction are mutually reenforcing. Some of the earliest survey researchers thus found that victory would go to the party that found the best ratio between money spent on formal media and money spent on organizing the face-to-face influences, the local "molecular pressures" that stimulate both the media and citizens. Such social interaction in their view would invigorate the formal media by injecting "more personal interpretation and the full richness of personal relationships into the promotion of the causes which are decided upon in the course of an election."[11] Voting ultimately is an individual act, but the events that lead to voting and other forms of political participation are social. The explanation of participation must include family, friends, neighbors, and co-workers, plus politicians, parties, activists, and interest groups.[12]

Television is an even more powerful medium when melded closely with the social nature of political life. This may help to explain the strong national interest in the New Hampshire primary. While still the first of the direct presidential primaries, New Hampshire is a small, unrepresentative state, quickly followed on the campaign circuit by an increasing number of larger states. Its continuing attraction may lie in its appealing emphasis on the "retail politics" of mobilization rather than relying solely on the "wholesale politics" of actualization. New Hampshire's citizens attend town hall meetings, coffee klatches, and presidential debate forums. The media cover these activities, and seeing people respond to the candidates and active in the political process perhaps make formal media reports more compelling and the interpretations more authentic, even for voters in other states.

Retail politics also brings the parties and their workers to the fore. Jim Boyle, a New Hampshire Democratic Party official, explains that in the retail stage, the presidential candidate has to "meet the people who make the party work at the grassroots, talk to them, get them excited about backing you."[13] The candidate must also win ideological activists to the cause, and convince party veterans that it would be wise to get on the bandwagon early and enthusiastically.

In the past, parties have served as the most effective catalyst between the citizen and the political system. No other political organization holds out the promise of representation to every ward and precinct within the jurisdiction of Congress and the presidency. Only revitalized political parties can supply once again that firm public support and partisan backing and serve as vehicles for the two-way communication of voter preferences and policy.[14] Conversely, a "world without parties" is one where special-interest groups, PACs, celebrity candidates, incumbents, television, and political consultants gain.[15]

The Parties as Organizational Paradox

The parties thus are faced now with the dual challenge of operating at the grassroots level to mobilize and motivate the citizenry and enable voters to participate in a two-way dialogue with their political leaders even while they build national coalitions that can support ambitious public policies and counter the narrow concerns of interest groups and the wealthy. Only the two parties—if and when they reflect public views and possess public confidence—can construct and sustain the majorities necessary to deal more than symbolically with such major political economy issues as funding social security, reconstituting medical care, and widening educational opportunity.

The model of the global corporation may point the way. Decentralized middle managers in the corporate world work near the consumers, wherever they are, and adapt the corporation's products to local differences. So, too, must the party activists listen to citizen concerns, which they then report to the state and national party, which in turn interpret the party's program and issues for party supporters and independents. These workers must thus engage, educate, involve and mobilize citizens, and enable the flow of policy ideas in two directions. In doing so, these middle managers of the parties, vested with considerable local organizational authority, become the building blocks for more decentralized parties. The organizational paradox at the heart of such efforts is captured in the aphorism, "Think locally, act globally." It is no accident that some politicians now use this saying. Note that this precept stands in marked contrast to Tip O'Neill's outmoded, but still frequently quoted, advice that "all politics is local."

These middle managers in political parties must also confront the problem of voter motivation by enlisting more local opinion leaders on a neighborhood-by-neighborhood basis and involve them in engaging larger numbers of citizens in political dialogues both during and between elections. Such two-way dialogues would provide information to a wide range of voters, engender lively debates, and create conditions where political deliberation and action become a part of everyday life.[16] These dialogues would also reestablish a deliberative process through which people resolve disputes, find remedies, and move forward on local issues, over which they have control, even while they are exercising their share of influence on national issues.

Ironically, many corporations are now concerned with the lifetime value of consumers and, in effect, treat them more like citizens, even while opportunistic practitioners of the politics of actualization are treating citizens more like customers. In promoting sustained two-way dialogues, state and local party activists would be assuming responsibility for their supporters. Actualization strategies that use people expediently to gain a short-term victory would be replaced by mobilization strategies that make an institutional commitment to remain loyal to their supporters' concerns and stay with them between as well as during elections. This would provide a forum for democratic conversations, a place to say things about public concerns and a place to teach about them, a structure around which political consensus could develop its power. Ultimately, it would also have to promise something larger—"a viable channel by which these voices could be carried upward in the structures of power and taken seriously."[17]

Striking a New Balance Between Parties and Other Political Organizations

By reconnecting the citizen bonds to the political system, assuming responsibility for party supporters, and reviving the goal of a public interest, political activists will also be enabling their parties more effectively to counter other national grassroots political organizations that too often hold a veto power over the decisions of the Democratic Party, the Republican Party, or both. There is certainly no problem in having such interest groups, social movements, and third parties promote their own frequently valuable views. Many such organizations once pushed for radical ideas that are now well accepted within the political system, such as expanding health-care coverage, strengthening the Pentagon, preserving the environment, or increasing civil rights.

The burden, however, for selecting among these competing ideas and, where possible, finding common ground—or at least grounds for compromise—has continued to fall on the political parties. But these institutions are now more ideological themselves and in their weakened state are less able to mobilize and link citizens to government, convert the needs of the unrepresented as well as represented into policies, build a winning electoral and programmatic coalition, and promote collective responsibility for policies.

As growing numbers of unaffiliated citizens abandon the parties and the political system, the parties have increasingly become coalitions of interest groups. Furthermore, the balance of power between the parties and these groups has shifted. It is now more difficult, as David Walker has noted, for parties to force "interest groups through rules, procedures, and program review both in the governmental and political arenas to moderate their parochial demands and strident rhetoric."[18]

The parties also used to provide more of a geographical counterweight to the pressures of national grassroots interest groups. But the parties now have difficulty engaging in such mediating, ameliorating, and filtering activities. In part, this is because so many interests have already infiltrated the parties and thus can stage coups in caucuses, primaries, and committee rooms.[19] Furthermore, the weakened parties increasingly need the electoral support of not only their traditional interest-group allies but also the unaffiliated interest groups whose endorsements and workers they crave. The balance of power between parties and interest groups has thus now tilted toward the grassroots interest groups organized nationally around specific substantive issues. These interest groups apply uncompromising "litmus tests" in deciding how far to support a particular candidate or party. Parties, therefore, can tackle integrative functions only if they can attract a sufficient number of new members of their own to restore their power at the ballot box.

While the wish for such active parties and engaged citizens may sound unrealistic, there are a number of politicians who have shown the way. In 1988, the Republican Party tried a sophisticated experiment to reconnect voters: it matched an Illinois target county with a similar county that served as a control group. Simple, people-intensive voter-registration and turnout programs were organized in the target county, run by the local party organization, and staffed by volunteers. These workers, among other things, registered potential voters on campus, at shopping malls, in grocery stores, and door-to-door in precincts, and participated in a massive get-out-the-vote effort that included these potential new voters. Survey evaluations subsequently conducted in both counties revealed that registration and turnout rose significantly in the target county. The program appeared to meet its objectives and did not entail great expense.[20] The Indiana Democratic state chair who in 1998 similarly recruited volunteer precinct chairs for virtually every neighborhood, "empowered every one of our 4,800 chairmen as the campaign manager for his or her precinct."[21] These efforts did not involve dramatic innovations; their success lay in effective implementation.

Significantly, these party efforts do not ignore new technologies; instead, they parlay them into broader efforts to reach constituents. So, for example, the Indiana Democratic Party headquarters mails to party activists computer printouts or CD-ROM "walking lists" of the voters to see in their precincts. Each list identifies the precinct constituents by party inclination and issue interests and includes a suggestion of talking points to use in urging them to vote. And the Republican National Committee in 1993 formed a Republican Exchange Satellite Network: in one of its programs, 350 "neighborhood meetings" of local party activists saw a cabinet secretary, a governor, and a mayor field calls from viewers concerned with creating a skilled workforce and new jobs. The Democratic National Committee chair, for his part, was trying to launch an "activist network" that would seek a "full scale dialogue between people and their government, and people and their party."[22] Emerging technologies such as satellite town meetings, electronic mail, informative Web sites, chat rooms, and talk-show politics have all expanded the opportunities for civic participation. They provide invaluable additions to traditional communications, but "neo-intermediaries" organized into "virtual communities" are no substitute for a party vehicle through which concerns enhanced by old as well as new information sources can be voiced at the state and national levels.

Identifying Incentives to Participate

It remains to be seen whether a sufficient number and sufficiently wide range of incentives can be assembled to attract the necessary number of party activists who in turn will mobilize the voters. People join and remain active in organizations for many reasons. In a culture that devalues politics as much as ours does, parties must employ every reasonable incentive to attract citizens.[23] People will be motivated by such traditional reasons as the opportunities for social contact, involvement with candidates or other interesting opinion leaders, a sense of civic duty, or the chance to get to know their neighbors better. Newer motivations might include, among others, the presence at the county headquarters of a reliable babysitting service or the nagging hunch that a steady diet of television may be bad for one's health; and local parties might provide transportation to the work site for older volunteers pleased to have an opportunity to be useful and have contact with younger people. Other activists might be interested in such activities as providing assistance to community groups in writing grants and making contact with government agencies, in promoting political education in schools, or in monitoring government services or the voting records of elected officials.

There is also an integral relation between strong local parties and exerting influence on the nomination process. Candidates and elected officials must come to feel that "the one thing [they] must have from their political parties is their nomination."[24] In recent decades, parties, thanks to the adoption of the direct primary, have largely lost the power to control candidate selection. Recapturing that power is the key to reestablishing local party activists to their rightful place as the middlemen/middlewomen of U.S. politics. If that were done, public officials would "find ways to reward party-building activity, just as they now find ways to reward their personal (i.e., nonparty) workers and supporters."[25] The channeling of more money and other resources to the local level also would do much to unleash such ingenuity.

Party Workers at the Local and State Levels Need Help

The chronically low turnout that we see today in most primary elections does have something good to say for it. If the parties were to mount a sustained organizational effort, they could recapture control over the nominations process simply by entering and supporting their designated candidates and winning those direct primaries. They could then build on that momentum, election by election. It appears that the local and state activists currently working in the parties would support such a grassroots strategy. When Southern activists from both parties were asked whether they would prefer to build the parties from the top down or the bottom up, three-quarters of the activists from both parties preferred the decentralized approach.[26] County chairs also see their efforts as most significant in "grassroots activity emphasizing ties to local people," such as organizing campaign events and getting-out-the-vote drives."[27] There is, then, a glimmer of hope in the persistence of party organizations and the continued existence of some, though few, activists. If state and local parties were truly hopeless, candidates and the national parties would not continue to invest resources in them.[28] Party organizations at the state and local levels, staffed by volunteers, remain in place. Were they to receive more support, these organizations could become the catalysts for revitalizing our political system.

If the people are to engage in collective decisionmaking, these local party organizations must send instructed delegates to the state-party conventions, and the states must send instructed delegates to the national-party convention. There, together with state and federal candidates and officeholders, they must deliberate on the party platform. Interest-group allies and large donors should also be represented, but they should not continue to dominate the national conventions. Deliberation predominantly by party activists and candidates will increase the likelihood that stands on abortion, gay rights, and many other divisive issues will be reached with "adequate attention to electoral feasibility."[29] The party's capacity to make more effective collective decisions would also reduce voter incentive to support individual candidates and provide more incentive to support or oppose the party as a whole.[30] For their part, members of Congress, now more closely linked to strong local and state parties, would share a greater incentive to support more substantive, and less symbolic, legislation.

While there are precedents and exciting possibilities for revitalized, decentralized parties, their future health remains in doubt. Already in 1983, political scientist Nelson Polsby wrote of "the chronic occurrence of depressed political participation and mobilization among ordinary Americans . . . with its steady replacement of face-to-face, primary and geographically proximate interest groups with distant, symbolic and noninteractive mediation mechanisms."[31] A few years later, three relatively optimistic observers of the political scene, after observing the damage done to the political landscape by the continuing shift from mobilization to actualization strategies, anguished that "the parties, including their hard-working activists, may be willing to endure public contempt so long as they win elections, but how long will the public tolerate such parties?"[32] Despite some promising signs, this disturbing trend has not yet reversed. Party workers at the local and state levels need help.

Three Modest Proposals to Jump-Start Party Reform

After the Watergate scandal, Congress put in place a carefully crafted reform system for privately financing congressional campaigns with limits on the amounts that parties, interest groups, wealthy individuals, and candidates could contribute or spend. Since then, loopholes have developed, undermining this attempt to keep contributions and expenditures within reasonable boundaries. By the 1996 election, with the growth of issue advocacy, express advocacy, issue advertising, and soft money, the amounts spent outside the boundaries of the campaign-finance system had mushroomed to the point where the regulatory system finally collapsed.[33] The record-setting amounts spent in support of Democratic and Republican parties and candidates in 2000 confirmed these trends.

While numerous fund-raising and expenditure mechanisms involve substantial sums, the Achilles heel of the campaign-spending system is soft money. In immense laundering operations, tens of millions of dollars travel back and forth between those states with lax campaign-disclosure and regulatory requirements and the national committees of both parties. These funds are contributed by fat cats, corporations, and labor unions who, prior to the soft-money loophole opened by the 1979 FECA amendments and FEC advisory opinions, were not permitted to make direct campaign contributions. TV and radio, while far from the only campaign expenses, are the largest single budget item. The rules governing soft money specify that such funds are intended for party-building activities, but only 15 percent of issue ads even mention a political party—whereas 99 percent give a candidate's name. Furthermore, these national party–financed ads are much more likely to be negative than those funded by the candidates themselves.[34]

Putting Humpty-Dumpty Together Again

Any new campaign-reform system will look markedly different from its 1970s predecessor as a result of the changing nature of campaigns, the philosophical concerns of all three branches of government and the electorate, the goals of reformers, and the clashing self-interest of incumbents, challengers, political parties, and interest groups for whom power remains the ultimate aphrodisiac. Campaign reformers must accept that congressional and presidential races in an age of the media, targeted mailings, and high-powered political consultants will remain expensive—particularly if insurgents are to amass sufficient funds to challenge incumbents. Reforms must not violate freedom of speech or the legitimate reelection aspirations of the president and members of Congress. The reforms must move the nation closer to equality in the voting booth, regardless of income; meet philosophical concerns about funding elections with taxpayer money; and make allowance for differences among congressional districts and states, different styles of campaigning, and disparate media costs. The system must take into account the differing needs of incumbents, challengers, those competing in open-seat elections, minor as well as major parties, and "longshot" as well as "serious" candidates.[35] Reform in the role of political money also must fulfill our belief in the integrity of elections, the openness and fairness of the contest for public office, the integrity of elections, and the actions of elected officials.[36]

Institutional Barriers to Campaign Reform

Campaign reformers run a gauntlet of obstacles. Members of Congress are sometimes surprisingly open in opposing reform proposals. While many incumbents from both parties are content to quietly kill reforms that would reduce the advantages of incumbency, some have no compunction about going on record. When asked in 1997 if Congress would consider a proposal to ban soft-money contributions, Senator Mitch McConnell, then the chief Republican fund-raiser, promised, "We'll debate it, and then we're going to kill it."[37]

Nor is the FEC in a position to lead the reform charge. From its inception in 1974, Congress has kept a tight rein on the commission vested with the responsibility for monitoring its reelection campaigns. Unlike other regulatory commissions, it does not receive multiyear budgeting authority.[38] The FEC must go to Capitol Hill every year, hat-in-hand for funds. In 1994, the commission had an aggressive chair, Trevor Potter, who pushed for change. Congress promptly cut the FEC's budget to $24 million, $3 million less than the administration proposed and $8 million less than the agency requested.[39] The agency was thus compelled to purge 166 pending cases from its docket—a move somewhat akin to the Italian post office burning the mail when it fell behind in its deliveries. Furthermore, by law, the six commissioners are evenly divided by party, three Republicans and three Democrats, which means that members of both parties must agree on frequently controversial issues. Commissioner nominations are supposed to originate with the president and be confirmed by the Senate, but an informal understanding gives Congress control over who is nominated.[40] The FEC is thus unique among regulatory commissions in that, literally on the day that it was born, it was captured by the politicians and national parties it was created to regulate.

The one exception to congressional and presidential intransigence on campaign reform has been their willingness to support full disclosure of who gets what contributions, when, and how. Congress has allowed the FEC to compile invaluable data, and journalists, reformers, academics, and the politicians, parties, and interest groups rely on it heavily. Such disclosure is a prerequisite to actual reforms, and it at least enables informed voters to compare where candidates get their money and how they vote. But even publication of one vote after another, revealing where campaign contributors appear to have had their way with a member of Congress or the president, eventually becomes a mixed blessing. As the number of coincidences between the direction of member roll-call votes and the identity of their contributors mounts year by year, the unchecked abuses year after year make patently clear to voters the political power of special interest and fat-cat money.

The Supreme Court, through its interpretation of free speech, has given fat cats and interest groups greater campaign-finance latitude than even the beneficiaries themselves might have demanded. Any solution must deal with the Supreme Court contention that a restriction on the amount of money a person or group can spend on political communications during a campaign restricts freedom of speech by reducing the number of issues discussed, the depth of such discussion, and the size of the audience.

Furthermore, the road for most proposed reforms runs through Congress, where passage unfortunately depends on the members' statesmanship and willingness to assume political risk. Regardless of a proposal's merits, that road seems a dead end. It may also be noted that since the 1970s, no president, at least when in office, has taken a vigorous stance in support of campaign reform.

Meeting the Conditions of Campaign-Finance Reform

Sifting through the legitimate concerns and the self-interest of politicians, institutions, and interest groups to find a campaign finance–reform solution is so complicated that public indifference to the resulting debates, which are often technical, is understandable. Interestingly, both incumbents and their challengers with only a few exceptions favor growth in the campaign-fund money supply—incumbents because they can collect more of it and insurgents because a substantial amount is necessary to compete in the political marketplace. Challengers, though, worry less about the size of an incumbent's campaign chest than reaching a sufficient level of funding to communicate their own views, experience, and reputation to the voters.

Reformers must, therefore, live with the political reality that the amount of money spent on campaigns will continue to grow. The challenge will be to structure the system and its incentives in such a way that more of those funds are provided with no strings attached. Reform is likely to come not through curtailing how much money is collected but by focusing on who is contributing, what contributors can expect in return, and how the money is spent.

Just as the currency of business is money, so the currency of politics is power. Community activist Saul Alinsky liked to say that "bureaucracies learn with their rears, not with their ears." It is only the sustained exercise of power that can change the political system—and campaign reform is all about politics. In this case, only large numbers of voters eventually exercising power through *their* nationwide organization—decentralized political parties—can enforce and sustain these democratic rules of the game while pursuing their goals and opportunities. Any reform proposal must, therefore, be sufficiently clear-cut that it can attract popular support. It must also help to lay the groundwork for a more democratic political system—one more firmly rooted in popular sovereignty and representative parties.

The Road to Reform:
Reducing Cozy Politics and Strengthening Decentralized Parties

I therefore make the following three proposals for achieving long-term campaign reform—at the same time being most willing to accept alternatives, provided that they meet the following test: such proposals must either reduce cozy politics, strengthen decentralized parties (thereby reengaging the people in politics), or both. Reducing cozy politics means limiting those types of political exchanges in which the more money the candidate collects, the more political debts the candidate accumulates and the more political favors must then be bestowed at the cost of sound governance. The challenge is to reduce the amount of what might be termed *suspicious money* and increase the amount of *constructive money*—those campaign funds spent in a manner likely to promote greater public participation and voting. Elimination of suspicious money entails "prohibiting those forms of campaign fund-raising that have little or no relation to legitimate persuasion."[41] Reform proposals must also be politically realistic in that they rely on the self-interest and professional goals of their supporters and of cooperating institutions rather than depend on that most slender of political reeds—the public-spiritedness of Congress and the president in restructuring the rules governing their political survival in order to foster more competitive elections.

My three proposals are:

1. Free television and radio airtime and reduced postal costs should be provided to political candidates by the networks and other major media companies for the primaries and the general election as one of the contractual conditions for receiving new space on the broadcast spectrum.

The total amount of television and radio time and the postal subsidy should equal the average amount spent in the three prior presidential or off-year elections. The stations should commit the same prime-time and other time slots as those made available in comparable prior years. While political advertising is of critical importance to the political system, it represents little more than a blip when compared with corporate advertising. According to the Television Bureau of Advertising, an industry association, the $400 million spent by local, state, and federal candidates in 1996 represented only about 1 percent of all TV advertising that year.[42]

This provision of free airtime and reduced postal costs could be structured in such a manner that the media companies would continue to be reimbursed for their airtime. The Federal Communication Commission is vested with the responsibility for auctioning broadcast frequencies. These auctions are critical to media companies that have developed high-density television. These pictures possess far more lines and are therefore much crisper. Through these auctions, the FCC periodically replaces portions of the spectrum now used by outmoded analog transmissions with digital transmissions. Furthermore, in the spectrum space now used by one analog channel, a broadcaster can transmit not just one high-definition image but five or six digital television signals. Last but not least, it can use those extra signals not just for television pictures but also to carry Internet computer files, two-way paging systems, electronic mail, and much more.[43] No one really knows how much money will be generated from these auctions, but the demand for these channels is substantial (estimates run from $10 billion to $100 billion). Verizon Communications, the nation's leading wireless company, has estimated that in ten years it will need twice the space it now has to expand into wireless, Internet, and video services.[44]

Some free-TV proposals have drawn the wrath of the National Alliance of Broadcasters on the grounds that its members would lose millions of dollars. If the money is drawn from the auction proceeds, however, it will not cost the winning bidders a penny more than the commercial value of their license. Part of the government's proceeds would simply be designated to compensate the radio and television stations for political advertising. While "free" for the candidates, the stations and the post office would receive their usual fees. A campaign trust fund comprising a small proportion of these auction proceeds could last for decades.

Critics have also objected that media costs represent less than half of a candidate's budget. Nonetheless, it remains the largest single campaign expenditure, and the proportions spent in competitive races are considerably higher. The public-interest group Study for the American Electorate found that, in 1992, media costs in competitive House races totaled 45 percent and reached 60 percent in competitive Senate races.[45] Given the substantial amounts spent on direct mail, particularly in House races, it seems likely that a provision reducing mailing as well as television and radio costs would account for more than half of the expenditures in congressional as well as presidential budgets.

The FCC has a statutory obligation to deposit such funds in the federal treasury, and Congress would have to authorize passing the money through to the stations. However, presumably the money is not yet obligated within the federal budget since the amount is uncertain, and additional spectrum space will be auctioned in the future. Furthermore, by using a set formula based on the total spent on radio and television in the prior presidential or off-year election (with an adjustment for inflation), the funding allocation would, in effect, become automatic and would not require a government mandate by either Congress or the FCC. The costs of political ads are rising more rapidly than inflation, but the formula would not capture these increases until the next election, when it would be reflected in the new total spent on radio and television ads. The commission would handle the administration of radio and television payments, but the allocations would be predictable and transparently clear to the broadcasting industry and tax-payers. While some free radio and television proposals have sought to impose conditions on the quality of programming, this proposal would leave control of the advertisements entirely in the hands of the candidates and parties and thereby avoid objections on the grounds of excessive gov-ernment interference or fears concerning violation of freedom of speech. Even civil-liberties purist Nat Hentoff agrees that since broadcasters are licensed, that "gives the state the power to make sure stations don't bump into each other's frequencies."[46]

Another advantage of a proposal that spares the government rod is its potential to build a larger coalition of support. The National Association of Broadcasters (NAB) has condemned efforts to make broadcasters pay for politicians' airtime as "blatantly unconstitutional." But court precedent sug-gests that broadcasters' use of the airwaves does carry with it a public-interest obligation.[47] NAB's contention is that compliance in meeting this obligation should be voluntary. In 1996, despite pressure from good-gov-ernment groups, the networks provided comparatively little airtime volun-tarily. They offered a one-hour special, some candidate appearances on their evening news shows, and occasional invitations to candidates to appear on programs such as *Dateline NBC* to address viewers directly on key issues.[48] As with all volunteer efforts, opinions vary sharply as to how much is enough, but NAB might deem a funding requirement acceptable that only affects those companies choosing to bid for digital licenses—and does not in any event increase the cost of their licensing bids.

Such media concessions might also attract other support. Some media entrepreneurs have already offered considerably more free airtime than their competitors, presumably to improve their personal and corporate image—not only with the public but also with regulators and agencies pos-sessing potentially valuable tax breaks.[49] Another suggestion has come from the Free TV for Straight Talk Coalition: since 1996 it has encouraged networks voluntarily to provide free airtime to presidential candidates but has met with minimal success. Two former presidents, Republican Gerald Ford and Democrat Jimmy Carter, have endorsed such a proposal. Most importantly, the general public, usually unenthusiastic about public fund-ing, is more receptive to free airtime. Some people are philosophically opposed to funding elections with taxpayer money since this would entail supporting candidates whose views are contrary to their own. In a 1996 *Time*/CNN poll, however, 63 percent believed that free TV time would make for a better race.[50]

2. *Taxpayers should be allowed to earmark up to $400 each for a contribution to go into a presidential and congressional campaign fund simply by marking the appropriate box in their 1040 Individual Income Tax Return.*

Taxpayers may currently each designate $3.00 for use in campaign funding. Despite the smallness of the amount, the trend in the number of such contributions is downward. Voters, disillusioned with the political system, are refusing to contribute, even though the contribution, as a tax credit, does not affect the individual voter's tax account. The giver in effect makes this donation at no personal cost, but nevertheless, such is the breadth and depth of political cynicism today that an increasing number of people refuse to contribute.

Presidential candidates have the option of accepting or rejecting these matching public funds in exchange for limiting their total expenditure—an option that applies both during the primary season and in the general election. During the 2000 primaries, George W. Bush raised the unprecedented sum of $80 million; because he rejected public funding that would have specified a lower expenditure limit as a condition of acceptance, he was free to he spend all of it. In the general election, however, both he and Al Gore drew on public funding.

While a relatively small proportion of all taxpayers might take advantage of the proposed larger tax earmark, the total in such contributions would be dramatic. If, for example, just five million taxpayers contributed $400, that would equal the entire amount spent on campaigns in the 1996 election. A line well below that point would, of course, be drawn as to how much such public funding should be included in elections, but, without much difficulty, the amount could be sufficiently large to make public funding a better financial deal for candidates than going it alone. Indeed, there would then be sufficient money to extend the system to congressional elections. The bottom line is that a way must be found to make swallowing the bitter pill of reform appear inevitable to the many incumbents who currently enjoy much greater access to private funding and thus a competitive advantage over their challengers.

It is true that the government would bear the tax loss resulting from such contributions. But if, for example, the amount of such public funding were as much as $1 billion, that would still represent less than one-tenth of 1 percent of the approximately $1.8 trillion budget. The price of public funding can be absorbed in a $10-trillion economy. What the nation cannot afford is the price that cozy political arrangements extract in the form of blatantly compromised governance and lost citizen trust.

Such a tax earmark would enable many citizens among the 60 percent who are now largely outside the political system to make an impact with their contributions. Their numbers would then become important not only as voters but also as political contributors. After all, even a taxpayer with an income (after taking the personal-exemption and standard deduction) as comparatively low as $9,050 must pay a tax bill of $302. Most people at every income level would continue not to contribute, but a relatively small number could make the difference. These donors would be truly empowered because their money would go a long way toward neutralizing the political power of the second constituency.

In addition, because this source of funds would come without any tacit quid pro quo or promise of access, the number of cozy political arrangements would be reduced. Such arrangements would hardly disappear in a nation that has endured government swindles since the Revolutionary War, that has known robber barons who have owned members of Congress, and, not to mention political machines, has even had a president or two that for many people continue to symbolize the meaning of politics and parties. But even as the amount of political money would continue to rise in political elections, the funds would no longer pose the same threat to the nature of the U.S. democratic system. It is the money's source, rather than the amount, that causes so much of the mischief.

This public funding would be distributed by a formula based on prior electoral expenditures. Members of Congress, national party leaders, and probably the president would continue to resist funding that would flow from a source over which they would have comparatively little control. Nonetheless, incumbents would retain some advantage since it would be easier for them to raise the private matching-fund contributions necessary to establish their eligibility for public funding. Nothing would prevent them from collecting at least some additional funds independently, but there would be some expenditure limits and challengers would receive at least a sufficient amount of funds to mount a competitive campaign. But how can members of Congress be persuaded to choose the public interest at the expense of their most compelling self-interest—*reelection*?

Where the politics of ideas leads to a palpable and sustained public outcry on a major issue, politicians feel compelled to respond. No such piercing outcry on campaign-finance reform has yet arisen, but, as Gerald Seib has written, "a massive public outcry still can overcome even the biggest pot of campaign cash."[51] Tax earmarking is straightforward and to the point.

Campaign-finance debates have not captured the public imagination partly because they involve detailed discussions about such arcane topics as coordinated and independent expenditures, issue and express advocacy, where freedom of speech begins and ends, and what the Supreme Court held in its landmark, 246-page campaign-finance decision, *Buckley v. Valeo,* 424 U.S. 1 (1976). The pathway to public funding by the people lies through a nationwide debate that ignores several comparatively smaller, questionable campaign activities, and focuses, instead, on those key issues where victory restores campaign integrity. Unless the public imagination is seized by such key issues and pressure mounts, campaign-finance proposals will continue to wither away in the Oval Office and Senate conference committees. However, the visibility achieved in the 2000 presidential election by two candidates who, with comparatively few resources, built their campaigns around the issue of campaign-finance reform—John McCain in the early Republican primaries and Ralph Nader in the general election— suggests that the issue is slowly gaining greater voter recognition. Even some members of the second constituency who benefit from the current political rules of the game are starting to wonder, given the transparently cynical campaign-fundraising antics to which they feel compelled to lend their names.[52]

Whatever the fate of public funding, the largest form of private contributions, soft money, is likely to remain a potent and dangerous force—dangerous because the identity of the donors, the unprecedented size of their contributions, and their great expectations are so transparent to officeholders and to citizens. Hence, the need for one more recommendation that, unlike most reform approaches, argues not for the abolition of such funding but for a change in how such contributions are used.

3. A lawsuit should be brought demanding that soft money not only be channeled through state parties but also that it be spent—as the 1979 FECA amendments intended—at the state and, particularly, the local level.

The intent of the 1979 Federal Election Campaign Act (FECA) amendments was to simplify reporting requirements for candidates and committees under the Federal Election Campaign Act and to encourage grassroots participation through political parties in federal election campaigns. In reporting out the bill, the Senate Committee on Rules and Administration pointed to several provisions that enlarged the scope of voluntary activity within political parties. The 1974 act had "encouraged individuals to volunteer their services in support of particular candidates, but not necessarily political parties." Furthermore, in the 1976 election, "state and local party committees were also virtually prohibited from giving any significant support to their presidential nominee in the general election. This amendment would "permit a State or local committee of a political party to pay the costs of certain campaign material used in connection with volunteer activities on behalf of candidates . . . so long as party funds were not earmarked for a particular candidate."[53]

In the 1976 election, the national parties and candidates had struggled to avoid exceeding the campaign-expenditure limitations specified in the FECA. Local and state voluntary party activities had consequently suffered as party leaders and candidates had assigned a higher priority to television and radio ads and, to a lesser extent, professionally run mailings and telephone banks. While such strategies might be more efficient in the short run, members of Congress were anxious to encourage local-party involvement, and so they specified that such grassroots activities would not fall within the act's expenditure limitations. "Contributions" to such activities could be unlimited in size, but this aroused no concern because the amendment was explicit in specifying grassroots areas where large-scale expenditures were unlikely. Party committees could pay for grassroots campaign materials such as bumper stickers and yard signs, the distribution of such electoral materials as sample ballots, and, most significantly, voter registration and turnout drives.

There were, however, certain limitations in how such grassroots funds could be used, and members of Congress carefully underscored them for their colleagues on the floor of the House and Senate and in the House *Report*. The test for determining voluntary activities would be based, explained the Committee on House Administration, on "how the campaign funds are used and by whom."[54] Since the premise of this exception (in the FECA) is that volunteer activities are a party-building function, the costs of commercial vendors should not be covered. Phone banks would only qualify for the exemption if staffed by volunteers, and media advertising, mass mailings, and campaign materials purchased by the national committee of a political party and delivered to a state- or local-party committee would not be exempted. The nature of a "contribution" under this amendment was also carefully limited: "The basic test for determining whether a contribution has been designated is whether the contributor retains control over the funds. Since the purpose of this exemption is to promote party activity, the party, not the contributor, must make the final decision as to which candidate or candidates will receive the benefits."[55]

The amendment's legislative history, while limited in length, is replete with enthusiastic statements by members of Congress from both parties on the importance of such grassroots citizen participation. Senator Mark Hatfield strongly concurred on the need to ease "the restrictions which have so severely curtailed grassroots involvement in federal campaigns."[56] Representative Bill Frenzel emphasized "the increased flexibility and encouragement given to our State and local party committees" and viewed these committees as "the broadest based units of political involvement in our election system. [The 1979 amendments] will permit them, in fact, encourage them to once again play an important role in electing federal candidates."[57]

No one anticipated the significance that the amendment's funding would assume when the amendments passed. While contributions technically were unlimited for the amendment's grassroots purposes, the expenditures qualifying for exemption from normal campaign-funding rules were carefully limited. Indeed, the term *soft money* does not appear in the hearings. Then the Federal Election Commission handed down an advisory opinion on an issue that arose as a result of the 1979 amendments. Party organizations are involved in a number of "nonfederal" elections such as gubernatorial races, state legislative contests, and campaigns for major local offices. These state-party committees, though, frequently work closely with federal committees. How, then, should a state committee allocate its nonfederal and *federally regulated* funds in paying its general overhead and operating campaign expenses?

This seemingly technical question of distinguishing nonfederal from federally regulated funding was important because state campaign-finance laws are often much more permissive than the federal law. For example, most states, unlike the federal government, allow parties to accept corporate and labor-union contributions, and one-third of the states, as of 1992, placed no limits on the amounts that could be donated by wealthy individuals. One state allowing unlimited corporate and union contributions, Kansas, asked the FEC this question and was told in 1978 that the state party could use its unlimited corporate, union, and other contributions to finance a share of its voter drives so long as it allocated its costs to reflect the federal and nonfederal shares of any costs incurred. This decision opened the door to the use of nonfederal money on election-related activity conducted in connection not just with a state but also with a federal election. In a presidential or congressional off-year election, there will normally be more state and local than federal races; hence, the practical effect of this ruling was that most of the costs of voter drives could now be financed from monies collected and spent in amounts not permissible under federal law.

So two streams of regulatory change now converged. The 1979 FECA amendments for the first time, under carefully defined circumstances, allowed party organizations to spend unlimited amounts of money within the federal rules. And the FEC in its 1978 ruling was allowing state parties to pay a share of such costs with funds not subject to federal limits. These two streams in effect opened the soft-money floodgates. Since then, the FEC has made some efforts to stem the tide of soft money, but national parties have found additional ways to spend such money.

The success of these efforts is reflected in the soft-money amounts now collected and spent. In 1996, the Republican national-party committees solicited $138 million and the Democratic committees collected $123.9 million.[58] These substantial sums are now raised in the name of party-building activities. Virtually none of this money, however, makes its way to grassroots political-party activity. Instead, it is moved from states with lenient rules as to who may contribute (corporations and wealthy individuals from anywhere welcome here) and how much (the sky's the limit) to the national parties. They, in turn, disseminate the money to presidential and congressional candidates or spend it themselves in supporting those candidates.

If a political bonanza is to be harvested through soft money, why not compel the donors and national parties to distribute the funding in accord with its 1979 statutory intent? Better that the funds should go to the local political parties than the candidates and be used for grassroots activities that mobilize citizens rather than merely enable the candidates to expand the politics of actualization that continues to turn off voters. Such activities would then include face-to-face, two-way communication among the voters, party workers, and candidates. The activities would reflect the personal preferences of local voters and activists as expressed through yard signs, campaign buttons, bumper stickers, and the like. In exchange for accepting soft money, the parties and candidates would agree to limit their use of such funds to the purposes specified under the 1979 amendments. Enforcement of the statute would, therefore, not infringe on the donors' freedom of speech by placing limits on the size of soft-money contributions; but it would encourage spending their maximum contribution in support of the party of their choice. Furthermore, candidates would remain free to use all funds that they collect under federal "hard money" regulations on whatever campaign activities they deem appropriate.

Reformers have taken a different tack—trying without success to persuade the Supreme Court to stem the tide of such soft-money funding, but the justices have rejected such overtures on the grounds that they interfere with the donors' freedom of speech. Allocating the funds in accord with the 1979 FECA amendments would not only provide the donors with the opportunity to express their views but also give local party members and citizens the opportunity to do so as well. These local parties could then use the money in their counties, districts, and precincts.

Such a solution is not without its problems. The national opponents to decentralizing control of such funds are well organized. For their part, local party leaders and workers would be cross-pressured between seeing the exciting potential of pumping such resources into grassroots activities and the opposition of their national and state leaders to such change. Nor would the additional workers and volunteers who might be lured into politics with such funds yet be on the scene to lend their voices to such party decentralization.

Emphasis on steering soft money toward local parties, however, might enlist the support of a powerful ally. While the Supreme Court may well view campaign-finance reform as a "political thicket," it has felt compelled to rule on a number of controversial cases, particularly with regard to freedom of speech. The Supreme Court as an institution has come under bitter criticism for its string of campaign-finance decisions. The justices might welcome a judicial alternative that would not interfere with freedom of speech, but that would also not be so transparently at odds with citizen government.

The Supreme Court normally prefers to leave decisions on political questions in the hands of the two branches of government elected by the people.[59] There are some interesting parallels, however, between an earlier case in which the court intervened in an important political and constitutional question and the current impasse over campaign-finance reform. In 1962, the court held that unequal citizen participation in the selection of lawmakers was a denial of the "equal protection of the laws" clause of the Fourteenth Amendment. As a remedy for this inequality caused by gerrymandering, the Supreme Court in *Baker v. Carr* 369 U.S. 186 (1962) ordered that the state legislative districts must be reapportioned and thus brought closer to this precept. The Court was under no illusions as to the political significance of its decision. Numerous friend-of-the-court briefs had emphasized the overrepresentation of rural state legislative districts at the expense of those citizens living in urban areas. More equal representation would mean less political power for rural districts.[60]

The steering of political money away from the people and into ever greater reliance on the politics of actualization is similarly undercutting the "one man, one vote" democratic precept. The remedy to correct the abuses of soft money would be to uphold congressional intent in the 1979 FECA amendments by rechanneling the flow of funds into local political parties and thereby once again broadening the scope of citizen participation. Such action does not abridge the donors' freedom of speech: it merely supports the congressional right to specify how this unique type of unlimited contributions may be spent.

As in the reapportionment case, the Court would be redistributing political power, this time by supporting the intent of the 1979 FECA amendments. Power would be shifted away from the second constituency and into the hands of the voters. The Court would thus once again be fulfilling its constitutional mission as the ultimate arbiter of the democratic rules of the game.

Redirecting soft money to the local level would have the additional benefit of facilitating reform more fundamental than even altering the national supply of political money. Success in countering cozy politics and the politics of actualization requires nothing less than reinvigorating the political parties by expanding local-party activity and funding. Reducing the impact of money on politics in and of itself will not reconnect citizens to their political system; rather, the challenge is to redirect the money.

The politics of mobilization requires that some organization—let's call it a reinvented party—must reach out and touch citizens, or, if you will, invite them to the party.[61] Such mobilization may occur through a combination of personal contact and contact by phone, fax, Internet, palm pilot, instant message, or other technological innovation. The success of such grassroots efforts would undoubtedly be uneven and would occur gradually over a number of elections. No one, however, ever accused democracy of being the most rapid political system.

Reinventing Citizen-Based Politics

The parties have now suffered through a number of bad political seasons. Over time, their members have deserted not only their organizations but also the political playing field. The substitution of the politics of activation for the politics of mobilization has expedited this process. The reduction in citizen involvement has raised the value of money in politics. Services previously provided by volunteers must now be bought, and citizens previously loyal to parties must be courted with expensive technologies and experts. It is pointless to blame wealthy individuals or interest groups for doing what comes naturally by filling the resulting political vacuum with money. Nonetheless, too much money with strings attached chasing too many politicians breeds too many cozy political arrangements with too many bad consequences for government.

The antidote to such cozy politics excesses is thus more citizen involvement. Citizens understandably want what our society has to offer both in return for their labor and through government. They are willing to work hard individually in their jobs to earn such rewards. But today they have less of a sense of what is required of them *jointly* in the political system if the government is to provide not only many other important goods and services but also leadership on critical issues. Citizen time, energy, and sacrifice are needed to counter political money from the second constituency.

No clever campaign-reform formula will substitute for committed citizens working through numerically powerful parties. At the heart of such citizen-based parties, political dialogue must occur between state and local party representatives and candidates, on the one hand, and state and national elected officials on the other. Such a dialogue must enable party activists to communicate issue preferences and information from the street-level to state and national party officials and politicians, and, in turn, enable state and national officials and politicians to sound the alarm on emerging issues that are not yet salient to the people. In the resulting give-and-take, presumably neither side would always get its way, but both sides would be engaged in weighing policy alternatives and seeking a defensible public interest. Minds in Washington, D.C., state capitals, and the precincts would all change in the process.

Interest groups and social movements must engage in such dialogues, too, but by their nature, just as self-interest compels the parties at least to seek some version of a public interest, so the self-interest of other organizations pushes them toward a more limited perspective. Only reinvented parties would seek to be giant coalitions of the people—because their self-interest in reelection would permit nothing less.

Through engaging in such a genuine political dialogue, party activists and members would gain a sense of greater political efficacy. The political currency in such a dialogue would consist not of money but rather of time and energy—and these are distributed more equally in the society. Few, even then, would have direct access to the ultimate decision makers, but thanks to their numbers and a political-party mechanism that would stretch from every precinct to the president and the Congress and would harness and communicate their views, the votes and ideas of these party members would count. Indeed, they had better count for something, or these citizens would "remember in November."

Who sleeps in the White House's Lincoln Bedroom or who flies members of Congress in a private plane on a vacation junket then becomes less important. Furthermore, while more decisions now are made at the state and local levels, the citizens in a nation where 25 percent of its gross domestic product is annually collected by the federal government can feel truly empowered only when they are engaged in thinking, learning about, and expressing their views on how that money should be spent, nationally as well as locally. Leaving such decisions to the rule of the few inside the D.C. beltway can only result in the continued hardening of democracy's arteries. We need to reinvent citizen-based political parties, whose members can then revive truly democratic governance.

Notes

Introduction

1. Leonard D. White, *The Jacksonians* (New York: Macmillan, 1956) and *The Republican Era* (New York: Macmillan, 1958).
2. Neil MacNeil, *Forge of Democracy* (New York: McKay, 1963), p. 144.
3. Paul Starobin, "Democracy's Favorite Dish," *National Journal*, September 26, 1992, p. 2222.
4. Larry J. Sabato and Glenn R. Simpson, *Dirty Little Secrets* (New York: Times Books, 1996). Sabato and Simpson make a persuasive case that corruption persists to a greater degree in U.S. politics than is generally appreciated.
5. Robert A. Dahl, *A Preface to Democratic Theory* (Chicago: University of Chicago Press, 1956), p. 84.
6. Paul Starobin, "Pork: A Time-Honored Tradition Lives On," *Congressional Quarterly*, October 24, 1987, pp. 2581–94.
7. Jack C. Plano and Milton Greenberg, *The American Political Dictionary*, 9th ed. (Fort Wayne: Harcourt, Brace, Jovanovich, 1993), p. 149.
8. James Q. Wilson, "Democracy Needs Pork To Survive," *Wall Street Journal*, August 14, 1997, p. A14.
9. Jeffrey H. Birnbaum and Alan S. Murray, *Showdown at Gucci Gulch* (New York: Vintage Books, 1987).
10. "Last Minute Squeals," *U.S. News & World Report*, October 14, 1996, pp. 17–19.
11. James M. Perry, "Full Speed Ahead," *Wall Street Journal*, June 15, 1989, p. 1ff.
12. Sheldon S. Wolin, *Politics and Vision* (Boston: Little, Brown, 1960), pp. 89–91.
13. Ferdinand Schevill, *A History of Europe* (New York: Harcourt, Brace, 1954), pp. 93–94.
14. Maggie Mahar, "It's Still Feeding Time: Despite GOP Control, Congress Keeps Its Appetite for Pork," *Barron's,* October 23, 1995, pp. 25–29.
15. Mark Zepezauer and Arthur Naiman, *Take the Rich off Welfare* (Tucson: Odonian Press, 1996), pp. 100–101.
16. Tom Schatz and Scott Denman, " . . . But Pork Barreling Isn't Dead Yet," *Wall Street Journal*, July 31, 1996, p. A14.
17. Thomas L. McNaugher, with Roger L. Sperry, "Improving Military Coordination: The Goldwater-Nichols Reorganization of the Department of Defense," in Robert S. Gilmour and Alexis A. Halley, eds., *Who Makes Public Policy?* (Chatham, N.J.: Chatham House, 1994), pp. 195–218.

18. Editorial "The Pentagon Jackpot," *Wall Street Journal*, July 10, 1995, p. A12; David Rogers, "Congress Approves Defense Bill Laden with Add-Ons for Firms in GOP States," *Wall Street Journal*, September 26, 1997, p. A2.

Chapter 1:Three-Fifths of the United States

1. W. Michael Cox and Richard Alm, *Myths of Rich and Poor* (New York: Basic Books, 1999), pp. xii–xiii.

2. Robert B. Reich, "Broken Faith: Why We Need to Renew the Social Compact," *Nation*, February 16, 1998, p. 17.

3. U.S. Bureau of the Census, Current Population Reports, P60-203, *Measuring Fifty Years of Economic Change Using the March Current Population Survey* (Washington, D.C.: U.S. Government Printing Office [GPO], 1998), p. 26.

4. Cox and Alm, *Myths,* p. 62.

5. Jared Bernstein, an economist with the Economic Policy Institute, was quoted in Jacob M. Schlesinger, "Finally, U.S. Median Income Approaches Old Heights," *Wall Street Journal*, September 25, 1998, p. B1.

6. Census Bureau, P60-203, p. 26.

7. *Economic Report of the President*, February 1998 (Washington, D.C.: GPO, 1998), p. 239.

8. Cox and Alm, *Myths,* p. 7.

9. Ben Wattenberg, "First Measured Century Tells Us a Lot about Ourselves," *Kalamazoo Gazette,* January 15, 1998, p. A13.

10. Herbert Stein, "A Lifetime of Progress," *Wall Street Journal*, October 21, 1997, p. A22.

11. The causes of productivity growth are not entirely clear, and it is difficult to disentangle the long-term trend of its growth rate from the short-term effects of the business cycle. A good portion of the superior productivity performance as well as the boom in GDP from 1996 to 1998 may have been due to cyclical factors— Alejandro Bodipo-Memba, "U.S. Productivity Surged During 1998, Hinting at Possible Escape from 25-Year Slump," *Wall Street Journal*, February 10, 1999, p. A2. Productivity growth is certainly facilitated, though, by factors that stimulate more rapid technological change and innovation, such as a high number of patent grants and healthy research and development spending. Patents in 1998 were up an impressive 29 percent from what in 1997 had been the highest number of patents ever granted. Research and development spending in 1998 rose above 2.5 percent of nominal GDP. Similarly, the amount of venture-capital funds raised between 1983 and 1995 (with the exception of the recession years in the early 1990s) ranged between $3 and $5 billion, but from 1996 through 1998 the amount steadily grew from $6 billion to more than $10 billion—Edward M. Kerschner, Thomas M. Doerflinger, and Michael Geraghty, "Paine Webber Investment Policy," *New Millennium American*, September 7, 1998, p. 11.

12. This analysis was done using data from the Bureau of Labor Statistics, *Employment and Earnings,* Vol. 48, No. 1, January 2001, pp. 228–29.

13. Bureau of Labor Statistics, "Union Members Summary," Current Population Survey, January 19, 2000, p. 1, http://stats.bls.gov/newsrels.htm.

14. Kerschner, Doerflinger, and Geraghty, "Paine Webber Policy," p. 11.

15. Paul Starobin, "The Politics of Anxiety," *National Journal*, September 30, 1995, pp. 2405–06.

16. Wayne D. Angell, "The Bubble Won't Burst," *Wall Street Journal*, February 3, 1999, p. A21.

17. Daniel Yankelovich, "Three Destructive Trends," *Kettering Review* (fall 1995).

18. See, for example, Frederick R. Strobel, *Upward Dreams, Downward Mobility* (Lanham, Md.: Rowman & Littlefield, 1993); and Andrew Hacker, *Money* (New York: Scribner, 1997).

19. Ruth Simon, "Personal Finance," *Wall Street Journal*, November 30, 1998, p. R6.

20. Edward Wyatt, "Share of Wealth in Stock Holdings Hits Fifty-year High," *New York Times*, February 11, 1998, p. A1.

21. Yochi Dreazen, "Stock Gains Help to Propel U.S. Wealth," *Wall Street Journal*, January 19, 2000, p. A2.

22. Tim W. Ferguson, "Slow and Steady Does It," *Forbes*, September 22, 1997, p. 280.

23. Dreazen, "Stock Gains."

24. Paul Krugman, *The Age of Diminished Expectations*, 3rd ed. (Cambridge: MIT Press, 1997), p. 11.

25. Alejandro Bodipo-Memba, "U.S. Productivity Surged during 1998, Hinting at Escape from Twenty-Five-Year Slump," *Wall Street Journal*, February 10, 1999, p. A2.

26. McKeon's work is cited in Greg Ip, "Why the Stock Market Isn't the Economy," *Wall Street Journal*, September 22, 1997, p. A1.

27. Quoted in Molly Ivins, "Why That Sinking Feeling?" *Kalamazoo Gazette*, August 7, 1997, p. A12.

28. Bureau of Labor Statistics, "BLS Releases New 1998–2008 Employment Projections," November 30, 1999, p.1, http://stats.bls.gov/emphome.htm.

29. Bruce Bartlett, "The Rich Get Richer, and That's All Right," *Wall Street Journal*, July 10, 1995, p. A12.

30. Mickey D. Levy, "The Economy Is Safe from a 'Savings Crisis,'" *Wall Street Journal*, February 4, 1999, p. A21.

31. Wolff's argument is cited in Ivins, "Why That Sinking Feeling?"

32. Maury Harris, "Low 'Official' Savings Rate Not Signaling Weal Consumer: It Does Signal Wealth, Low Interest Rates, and Huge Federal Budget Surplus," Paine Webber economic analysis, January 5, 1999, p. 11.

33. David Skidmore, "Economy Robust in '98," *Kalamazoo Gazette*, January 30, 1999, p. A8.

34. Harris, "Low 'Official' Savings Rate," p. 12.

35. Matthew Schifrin, "Financial Services," *Forbes*, January 11, 1999, p. 168.

36. Ellen Graham, "Dreams of Cushy Retirement Clash with Meager Savings," *Wall Street Journal*, December 12, 1997, p. R1.

37. Henry Aaron is quoted in Sheldon Danziger and Peter Gottschalk, *Uneven Tides* (New York: Russell Sage Foundation, 1993), p. 3.

38. Census Bureau, Current Population Reports, P60-200, *Money Income in the United States: 1997 (with Separate Data on Valuation of Noncash Benefits)* (Washington, D.C.: GPO, 1998), p. xii.

39. Paul Krugman, *Peddling Prosperity* (New York: Norton, 1994), p. 134.

40. Ibid., p. 135.

41. Gerald M. Pomper et al., *The Election of 1996* (Chatham, N.J.: Chatham House, 1997), p. 199. Emphasis added.

42. Census Bureau, P60-203, p. 16.

43. Ted Bridis, "Federal Report Shows Racial Divide over Technology," *Kalamazoo Gazette,* July 29, 1998, p. D5.

44. Jeannine Aversa, "FCC Chief Questions Relative Lack of Phones, Computers," *Kalamazoo Gazette,* August 10, 1998, p. A7.

45. Douglas A. Blackmon, "Forget the Stereotype: America Is Becoming a Nation of Culture," *Wall Street Journal,* September 17, 1998, p. A8.

46. W. S. Gilbert, "The Gondoliers," in *The Savoy Operas* (London: Macmillan, 1952), p. 543.

47. Lester Thurow, "Why Their World Might Crumble," *New York Times Magazine,* November 19, 1995, p. 78.

48. Jackie Calmes, "Sure, the Economy May Be Sizzling, but Some See Room for Improvement," *Wall Street Journal,* June 27, 1997, p. R2.

49. The quotation is from p. 2 of Lester Thurow's foreword to Chuck Collins, Betsy Leondar-Wright, and Holly Sklar, *Shifting Fortunes: The Perils of the Growing American Wealth Gap* (Boston: United for a Fair Economy, 1999).

50. Tom Herman, "Briefs," *Wall Street Journal,* December 15, 1999, p. A1.

51. Aristotle's views on political man and the conditions of the democratic order are cited in Seymour Martin Lipset, *Political Man* (Garden City, N.Y.: Doubleday, 1959), preceding the initial chapter.

52. Lipset, *Political Man,* p. 61.

53. This dimension in Kevin Phillips's work is emphasized by James Lardner in "The Declining Middle," *New Yorker,* May 3, 1993, p. 114. Lardner, rightly in my view, emphasizes Phillips's interpretation of the middle-class role in these societies and omits Phillips's less-satisfying explanation of elite decline that is also included in this analysis.

54. Irving Kristol, "Income Inequality without Class Conflict," *Wall Street Journal,* December 18, 1997, p. A22.

55. Jason DeParle, "'Safety Net' Social Agenda Falls Flat," N.Y. Times News Service, *Kalamazoo Gazette,* November 7, 1993, p. A2.

56. Robert Reich, "Broken Faith: Why We Need to Renew the Social Contract," *Nation,* February 16, 1998, p. 14.

57. James Galbraith, "With Economic Inequality for All," *Nation,* September 7/14, 1998, p. 24.

58. Robert Eisner, "The Economy Is Booming, So Why Are Economists Glum?" *Wall Street Journal,* July 29, 1998, p. A14.

59. John M. Berry, "Rhetoric Aside, Spurring Economic Growth Unlikely," *Washington Post,* January 29, 1996, p. A4.

60. Robert S. McIntyre, "Taxing the Poor," *New Republic,* January 30, 1995, p. 16.

61. Congressional Joint Tax Committee, *Report,* summarized in "Tax Report," *Wall Street Journal,* December 16, 1998, p. A1.

62. Arthur B. Kennickell, Martha Starr-McCluer, and Annika E. Sunden, "Family Finances in the U.S.: Recent Evidence from the Survey of Consumer Finances," *Federal Reserve Bulletin,* January 1997, p. 11.

63. Kerschner, Doerflinger, and Geraghty, "Paine Webber Policy," p. 9.

64. Kennickell, Starr-McCluer, and Sunden, "Family Finances," p. 11.

65. Ibid., p. 10.

66. "Rx Price Rise Figures Disputed by PhRMA," *Drug Topics* 143, no. 22 (1999): 7.

67. "Special Report: Relief for the Rx Blues," *Consumer Reports* 64, no. 10 (1999): 45.

68. National Association of Chain Drug Stores (NACDS), January 21, 2000, www.nacds.org/industry/facts.html.

69. "Relief for the Rx Blues," p. 39.

70. Census Bureau, *Health Insurance Coverage and Type of Coverage*, table B-25.

71. U.S. Bureau of Labor Statistics, *Bulletin 2307* and *Employment and Earnings*.

72. Census Bureau, *Health Insurance Coverage*, table HI-1.

73. Ibid., p. 3.

74. Health Insurance Association of America, "Fifty-five Million Americans Will Lack Health Insurance By 2008," press release, December 8, 1999.

75. Gary Mucciaroni, *The Political Failure of Employment Policy 1945–1982* (Pittsburgh: University of Pittsburgh Press, 1990), p. 3.

76. Bureau of Labor Statistics, "BLS Releases New 1998–2008 Employment Projections," p. 2.

77. Kathy M. Kristof, "Trouble in the Offing; Survey Finds Few Americans Know Basics of Investing," *Los Angeles Times*, May 15, 1996, D1.

78. Analysis of data from U.S. Department of Commerce, *National Income and Product Accounts for the United States*, 1929–94; and Survey of Current Business, August 1998.

79. Department of Commerce, *National Income and Product Accounts of the United States, 1929–94*, Tables 2.1, 2.7, and 3.2.

80. U.S. Department of Commerce, Bureau of Economic Analysis. Cited in Harris, "Low 'Official' Savings Rate," p. 10.

81. Collins, Leondar-Wright, and Sklar, *Shifting Fortunes* pp. 45, 50.

82. American Enterprise Institute/Roper Center chart included in Charles Murray, "Americans Remain Wary of Washington," *Wall Street Journal*, December 23, 1997, p. A14.

83. Pew Research Center, *Deconstructing Distrust: How Americans View Government*, www.people-press.org/trustpt.htm, p. 3.

84. Martin P. Wattenberg, "Should Election Day Be a Holiday?" *Atlantic Monthly*, October 1998, p. 44.

85. Cited in the introduction to Robert Kuttner, ed., *Ticking Time Bombs* (New York: New Press, 1996), p. x.

86. Charles E. Lindblom, *Politics and Markets* (New York: Basic Books, 1977), p. 205.

87. Quoted in Wattenberg, "Should Election Day Be a Holiday?" p. 44.

88. Raymond Wolfinger and Steven J. Rosenstone, *Who Votes?* (New Haven: Yale University Press, 1980).

89. Cited in Paul R. Abramson, John H. Aldrich, and David W. Rohde, *Change and Continuity in the 1996 Elections* (Washington, D.C.: CQ Press, 1998), p. 79.

90. Ibid.

91. Angus Campbell, Gerald Gurin, and Warren E. Miller, *The Voter Decides* (Evanston, Ill.: Row, Peterson, 1954), pp. 194–95.

92. National Issues Forum, *Governing America: Our Choices, Our Challenge* (Englewood Cliffs, N.J.: John Doble Research Associates, 1998), p. 41.

93. Sidney Verba, Kay Lehman Schlozman, and Henry E. Brady, "The Big Tilt: Participatory Inequality in America," *American Prospect*, no. 32 (May–June 1997): 75.

94. Campbell, Gurin, and Miller, *Voter Decides*, pp. 187–94.

95. Robert Lane, *Political Life* (Glencoe, Ill.: Free Press, 1959), p. 154.

96. In what has become the most widely used measure of such party identification, researchers asked voters to classify themselves as Democrats, Republicans, or Independents, then classified these voters on a continuum ranging from Strong Republicans, Weak Republicans, Independent Republicans ("closet Republicans" who preferred to view themselves as independent but voted quite consistently with that party), to Independents (those close to neither party), and comparable feelings of identification with the Democratic Party: Campbell et al., *American Voter* (New York: Wiley, 1960), pp. 120–23.

97. Warren E. Miller is cited in Martin P. Wattenberg, *The Decline of American Political Parties* (Cambridge: Harvard University Press, 1996), p. 11.

98. Morris Fiorina, *Retrospective Voting in American National Elections* (New Haven: Yale University Press, 1981), pp. 89–90.

99. William R. Keech, *Economic Politics* (Cambridge: Cambridge University Press, 1995), p. 148.

100. George A. Krause and Jim Granato, "Fooling Some of the Public Some of the Time?" *Public Opinion Quarterly* 62 (1998): 147.

101. Eugene Lewis, *American Politics in a Bureaucratic Age* (Cambridge, Mass.: Winthrop, 1977), p. 24.

102. Martin P. Wattenberg, "The Crisis of Electoral Politics," *Atlantic Monthly*, May 1997, p. 119.

103. Wattenberg, *Decline of American Political Parties*, pp. ix–x.

104. Fred Ebb and Bob Fosse, *Chicago: A Musical Vaudeville* (New York: Arista Records, 1975).

105. Richard Morin, "Who's in Control? Many Don't Know or Care," *Washington Post*, January 29, 1996, p. A1.

106. Benjamin Highton and Raymond E. Wolfinger, "The Political Implications of Higher Turnout," paper presented at the 1998 American Political Science Conference, p. 13.

107. Campbell et al., *American Voter*, p. 283.

108. An excellent account of how and why Ventura won may be found in Peter Fenn, "The Ventura Victory: Fluke or Future?" *Macalester Today*, May 1999, p. 48.

109. Benjamin I. Page and Robert Y. Shapiro, *The Rational Public* (Chicago: University of Chicago Press, 1992), p. 12.

110. Lonna Rae Atkeson, review of Michael X. Delli Carpini and Scott Keeter, *What Americans Know about Politics and Why It Matters* (New Haven: Yale University Press, 1996), in *American Political Science Review* 91, no. 2 (1997): 452.

111. Morin, "Who's in Control?" p. A7.

112. W. Lance Bennett, *The Governing Crisis*, 2nd ed. (New York: St. Martin's Press, 1996), p. 57.

113. Jack L. Walker, *Mobilizing Interest Groups in America* (Ann Arbor: University of Michigan Press, 1991), p. 59.

114. Jeffrey Berry, *The Interest Group Society*, 3rd ed. (New York: Longman, 1997), p. 43.

115. Robert D. Putnam, "Tuning In, Tuning Out: The Strange Disappearance of Social Capital in America," the 1995 Ithiel de Sola Pool Lecture, *PS: Political Science and Politics*, December 1995, pp. 664–66.

116. Eliza Newlin Carney, "Opting Out of Politics," *National Journal*, January 17, 1998, pp. 109–10.

117. Steven Finkel, "Reciprocal Effects of Participation and Political Efficacy:

A Panel Analysis," *American Journal of Political Science* 29, No. 4 (November 1985): 891–913.

118. G. Bingham Powell, "American Voter Turnout in Comparative Perspective," *American Political Science Review* 80, no. 1 (1986): 17–43.

119. National Commission on Civic Renewal, *A Nation of Spectators* (Washington, D.C., 1998), p. 8.

120. Gerald Seib, "Is '98's Legacy Destined to Be More Tuneout?" *Wall Street Journal*, December 30, 1998, p. A12.

121. William J. Keefe, *Parties, Politics, and Public Policy in America*, 8th ed. (Washington, D.C.: CQ Press, 1998), p. 175.

122. Wattenberg, "Should Election Day Be a Holiday?" p. 42.

123. Verba, Schlozman, and Brady, "The Big Tilt," p. 74.

124. Sidney Verba, Kay Lehman Schlozman, and Henry E. Brady, *Voice and Equality* (Cambridge: Harvard University Press, 1995).

125. Ibid., pp. 354–55.

126. David Mathews, *Politics for People* (Urbana: University of Illinois Press, 1994), p. 39.

127. Verba, Schlozman, and Brady, "The Big Tilt," p. 75.

128. The work of James Wright and Gregory Markus is cited in Seymour Martin Lipset and William Schneider, *The Confidence Gap* (New York: Macmillan, 1983), pp. 396–98.

129. William Mayer, *The Changing American Mind* (Ann Arbor: University of Michigan Press, 1992), p. 274.

130. Richard E. Neustadt, *Presidential Power and the Modern Presidents*, rev. ed. (New York: Free Press, 1991), p. 84.

131. Lipset and Schneider, *Confidence Gap*, pp. 399–400.

132. Gary Orren, "Fall from Grace: The Public's Loss of Faith in Government," in Joseph S. Nye, Philip D. Zelikow, and David C. King, eds., *Why People Don't Trust Government* (Cambridge: Harvard University Press, 1997), p. 90. See also Richard Neustadt's "The Politics of Mistrust," ibid., pp. 194–97.

Chapter 2: Why Parties Matter

1. Cornelius P. Cotter and Bernard C. Hennessy, *Politics without Power: The National Party Committees* (New York: Atherton Press, 1964), p. 8.

2. Paul Allen Beck and Frank J. Sorauf, *Party Politics in America*, 7th ed. (New York: HarperCollins, 1992), p. 10. The tripartite conception of parties originated in V. O. Key's work on political parties.

3. Ibid., p. 13.

4. Frank J. Sorauf, *Political Parties in the American System* (Boston: Little, Brown, 1964), p. 13.

5. Quoted in Robert N. Bellah et al., *Habits of the Heart* (New York: Harper & Row, 1985), p. 193.

6. William J. Keefe, *Parties, Politics, and Public Policy in America*, 8th ed. (Washington, D.C.: CQ Press, 1998), p. 70.

7. Clinton Rossiter, *Parties and Politics in America*, (Ithaca, N.Y.: Cornell University Press, 1960), p. 39.

8. Quoted in Cotter and Hennessy, *Politics without Power*, p. 229.

9. John Aldrich, *Why Parties?* (Chicago: University of Chicago Press, 1995), pp. 8–9.

10. David Broder, "Wanted: A Government," *Kalamazoo Gazette*, November 28, 1979, p. A6.

11. Quoted in William Crotty, ed., *The Party Symbol* (San Francisco: W. H. Freeman, 1980), p. 2.

12. William J. Crotty, Douglas S. Freeman, and Donald M. Freeman, eds., *Political Parties and Political Behavior* (Boston: Allyn & Bacon, 1971,) p. 499.

13. Edmund Burke, *The Cause of the Present Discontents* [1770], as cited in William Nisbet Chambers, *Political Parties in a New Nation* (New York: Oxford University Press, 1963).

14. Clifton McCleskey, *Political Power and American Democracy* (Pacific Grove, Calif.: Brooks/Cole, 1989), p. 43.

15. Robert P. Steed et al., eds., *Party Organization and Activism in the American South* (Tuscaloosa: University of Alabama Press, 1998).

16. Michael X. Delli Carpini and Scott Keeter, *What Americans Know about Politics and Why It Matters* (New Haven: Yale University Press, 1996), p. 282.

17. A number of these properties of belief systems (though not all) are drawn from Robert Lane, *Political Ideology* (New York: Free Press, 1962), pp. 13–15. The application of belief systems to political parties, however, is my own. Lane used the term in a different context.

18. Morris P. Fiorina, "The Decline of Collective Responsibility in American Politics," *Daedalus* 109, no. 3 (1980), reprinted in Pietro S. Nivola and David H. Rosenbloom, eds., *Classic Readings in American Politics*, 2nd ed. (New York: St. Martin's Press, 1990), p. 157.

19. William Greider, *Who Will Tell the People?* (New York: Touchstone, 1992), p. 261.

20. American Political Science Association, *Toward a More Responsible Two-Party System*, cited in Keefe, *Parties, Politics, and Public Policy*, p. 263.

21. Nelson W. Polsby and Aaron Wildavsky, *Presidential Elections*, 9th ed. (Chatham, N.J.: Chatham House, 1996), p. 321.

22. Jeffrey M. Berry, *The Interest Group Society*, 3rd ed. (New York: Longman, 1997), pp. 6–8.

23. Doris A. Graber, *Mass Media and American Politics*, 4th ed. (Washington, D.C.: CQ Press, 1993), pp. 4–12.

24. Berry, *Interest Group Society*, p. 240.

25. Graber, *Mass Media and American Politics*, p. 250.

26. Leon D. Epstein, *Political Parties in the American Mold* (Madison: University of Wisconsin Press, 1986), p. 38. The emphasis on common ground is made by Epstein; the quotation, cited by Epstein, is from Gerald M. Pomper, introduction to Gerald M. Pomper, ed. *Party Renewal in America* (New York: Praeger, 1980), p. 5.

27. Benjamin I. Page and Robert Y. Shapiro, *The Rational Public* (Chicago: University of Chicago Press, 1992), p. 395.

28. Alan Ehrenhalt, *The United States of Ambition* (New York: Times Books, 1991), p. 19.

29. Dwight Morris and Murielle E. Gamache, *Gold-Plated Politics: The 1992 Congressional Races* (Washington, D.C.: CQ Press, 1994), p. 36.

30. Nelson Polsby, *Consequences of Party Reform* (New York: Oxford University Press, 1983), p. 73.

31. Testimony before the Senate Committee on Armed Services, 1952.

32. Jack L. Walker, *Mobilizing Interest Groups in America* (Ann Arbor: University of Michigan Press, 1991), p. 10.

33. Greider, *Who Will Tell the People*, pp. 38–39.

34. Denise L. Baer and Martha Bailey, "NEA," in Robert Biersack, Paul S. Herrnson, and Clyde Wilcox, eds., *Risky Business? PAC Decisionmaking in Congressional Elections* (Armonk, N.Y.: Sharpe, 1994), pp. 67–68.

35. Jeffrey H. Birnbaum and Eric Pooley, "New Party Bosses," *Time*, April 8, 1996, pp. 28–32.

36. Mary Matalin and James Carville, *All's Fair: Love, War, and Running for President* (New York: Random House, 1994), p. 43.

37. Kristin Straroba, "Talking Politics, Talking Turkey," *Association Management* (November 1990): 48.

38. Guy Gugliotta and Ira Chinoy, "Outsiders Made Erie Ballot a National Battle," *Washington Post*, February 10, 1997, pp. A1, A10.

39. Fiorina, "Decline of Collective Responsibility," p. 172.

40. Gary C. Jacobson, *The Politics of Congressional Elections*, 4th ed. (New York: Longman, 1997), p. 189.

41. Jonathan D. Salant, "Christian Coalition to Boost Political Efforts after Court Win," *Kalamazoo Gazette*, August 3, 1999, p. A3.

42. R. Kenneth Godwin, *One Billion Dollars of Influence* (Chatham, N.J.: Chatham House, 1988), p. 105.

43. Seymour Martin Lipset and William Schneider, *The Confidence Gap* (New York: Free Press, 1983), p. 351.

44. Matthew Robert Kerbel, *Remote and Controlled* (Boulder, Colo.: Westview Press, 1995), p. 140.

45. Joseph S. Nye, introduction to "The Decline in Confidence in Government," in Joseph S. Nye, Philip D. Zelikow, and David C. King, eds., *Why People Don't Trust Government* (Cambridge: Harvard University Press, 1997), p. 17.

46. Garrett Hardin's argument, which originally appeared in *Science* in 1968, is nicely summarized in Elinor Ostrom, *Governing the Commons: The Evolution of Institutions for Collective Action* (Cambridge: Cambridge University Press, 1990), p. 2.

47. Stephen Ansolabehere and Shanto Iyengar, *Going Negative: How Attack Ads Shrink and Polarize the Electorate* (New York: Free Press, 1995), p. 98.

48. Martin P. Wattenberg and Craig Leonard Brians, "Negative Campaign Advertising: Demobilizer or Mobilizer?" *American Political Science Review* 932, no. 4 (1999): 891–99.

49. Kim Fridkin Kahn and Patrick J. Kenney, "Do Negative Campaigns Mobilize or Suppress Turnout? Clarifying the Relationship between Negativity and Participation," *American Political Science Review* 932, no. 4 (1999): 877–89.

50. Ibid.: 112–13.

51. David Broder, "Who's to Blame for Campaigns?" *Kalamazoo Gazette*, July 8, 1998, p. A8.

52. Robert Kuttner, introduction to Robert Kuttner, ed., *Ticking Time Bombs* (New York: New Press, 1996), p. x. Kuttner thus summarizes the Marshall Ganz essay that appears, ibid., pp. 245–60.

53. Martin P. Wattenberg, *The Rise of Candidate-Centered Politics* (Cambridge: Harvard University Press, 1991), pp. 159–60.

54. Larry J. Sabato, *Feeding Frenzy: How Attack Journalism Has Transformed American Politics* (New York: Free Press, 1993), p. 61.

55. During July 1974, House Postmaster Robert V. Rota testified that "the

hearings of the Judiciary Committee were televised nationally and we received about 3.5 million letters compared to 1,780,000 in (July) 1973"; see Steven J. Rosenstone and John Mark Hansen, *Mobilization, Participation, and Democracy in America* (New York: Macmillan, 1993), p. 111.

56. Ibid., p. 61.

57. Broder is quoted in Sabato, *Feeding Frenzy*, p. 64.

58. E. J. Dionne, *They Only* Look *Dead* (New York: Simon & Schuster, 1996), p. 243.

59. Quoted in Stephen Cain, "Experts: Negative Politics Fuel Voter Distrust," *Kalamazoo Gazette*, November 6, 1994, p. A16.

60. Jeff Greenfield, *The Real Campaign: How the Media Missed the Story of the 1980 Campaign;* cited in Dionne, *They Only* Look *Dead*, p. 244.

61. Christopher Lasch is quoted in Dionne, *They Only* Look *Dead*, p. 253. Lasch, *The Revolt of the Elites* (New York: Norton, 1995).

62. Ibid., p. 257.

63. W. Russell Neumann, Marion R. Just, and Ann N. Crigler, *Common Knowledge: News and the Construction of Political Meaning* (Chicago: University of Chicago Press, 1992), p. 112.

64. Stephen Earl Bennett et al., "'Video-malaise' Revisited: Reconsidering the Relation between the Public's Views of the Media and Trust in Government," paper presented at the 1999 Midwest Political Science Conference, p. 2.

65. Rosenstone and Hansen, *Mobilization, Participation, and Democracy*, p. 26.

66. Ibid., p. 29.

67. Ibid., p. 213.

68. Ibid., pp. 217–18.

69. Paul R. Abramson and William Claggett, "Resources, Benefits, Social Networks, and Electoral Participation: A Critique of Rosenstone and Hansen's *Mobilization, Participation, and Democracy in America*," paper presented at the 1996 Midwest Political Science Conference, April 18–21, 1996.

70. Paul R. Abramson, John H. Aldrich, and David W. Rohde, *Change and Continuity in the 1996 Elections* (Washington, D.C.: CQ Press, 1998), p. 85.

71. E. E. Schattschneider, *The Semisovereign People* (New York: Holt, Rinehart & Winston, 1960).

72. Glenn Burkins and Jeanne Cummings, "Hoffa Opposes Endorsement, Emerges as Player," *Wall Street Journal*, October 13, 1999, p. A32.

73. Steven E. Schier, "The End of Mobilization: Contemporary Party, Interest Group, and Campaign Strategies," paper presented at the Midwest Political Science Conference, April 15–17, 1999, pp. 1–3.

74. Ibid., p. 2.

75. Thomas Byrne Edsell, *Power and Money* (New York: Norton, 1988), p. 263.

76. David Mathews, *Politics for People*: *Finding a Responsible Public Voice* (Urbana: University of Illinois Press, 1994), pp. 40–41.

77. Alexis Simendinger, "Of the People, for the People," *National Journal*, April 18, 1998, p. 853.

78. Bill Bradley, "Civil Society and the Rebirth of Our National Community," *The Responsive Community* (spring 1995): 6–7.

79. Jeremy Richardson is quoted in Schier, "End of Mobilization," pp. 14–15. "The Market for Political Activism: Interest Groups as a Challenge to Political Parties," *West European Politics* 18, (January 1995): 124.

80. John C. Green, James Guth, and Clyde Wilcox, "Less than Conquerors: The Christian Right in State Republican Parties," in Anne N. Costain and Andrew S. McFarland, eds., *Social Movements and American Political Institutions* (Lanham, Md.: Rowman & Littlefield, 1998), pp. 117–18, 133–34.

81. Marjorie Randon Hershey, "The Congressional Elections," in Gerald M. Pomper et al., eds., *The Election of 1996* (Chatham, N.J.: Chatham House Publishers, 1997), p. 222.

82. Richard W. Stevenson, "A Campaign to Build Influence," *New York Times*, October 29, 1996, p. D4.

83. Peter T. Kilborn, "Republicans Are Up in Arms at Labor's Political Rebirth," *New York Times*, April 2, 1996, p. A1.

84. Hershey, "Congressional Elections," p. 227.

85. Kilborn, "Republicans Up in Arms," p. A1.

86. Steven Greenhouse, "Labor Tries New Strategy in '98 Elections," *New York Times*, May 16, 1998, p. A9.

87. Ibid.

88. Jeffrey M. Berry and Deborah Schildkraut, "Citizen Groups, Political Parties, and Electoral Coalitions," in Costain and McFarland, *Social Movements*, p. 143.

89. This Walter Dean Burnham quotation is cited in ibid., p. 155.

90. Seymour M. Lipset, *Political Man* (Garden City, N.Y.: Doubleday, 1959), p. 67.

91. John W. Kingdon, *Agendas, Alternatives, and Public Policies* (Glenview, Ill.: Scott, Foresman, 1984), p. 53.

92. Jack L. Walker, *Mobilizing Interest Groups in America* (Ann Arbor: University of Michigan Press, 1991), pp. 13–14.

93. John M. Hansen, *Gaining Access: Congress and the Farm Lobby, 1919–1981* (Chicago: University of Chicago Press, 1991), p. 230.

94. Leon D. Epstein, *Political Parties in the American Mold* (Madison: University of Wisconsin Press, 1986), p. 21.

Chapter 3: The Once-and-Future Party

1. James Q. Wilson, *The Amateur Democrat* (Chicago: University of Chicago Press, 1962).

2. Herbert McClosky, Paul J. Hoffman, and Rosemary O'Hara, "Issue Conflict and Consensus among Party Leaders and Followers," *American Political Science Review* 54 (June 1960): 424.

3. A 1980 study found comparable, dramatic differences between the party *leaders* in their degree of liberalism and conservatism; party *members* and independent voters were generally clustered toward the middle. See John S. Jackson, Barbara Leavitt Brown, and David Bositis, "Herbert McClosky and Friends Revisited," *American Politics Quarterly* 10, no. 2 (1982): 160.

4. Jeane J. Kirkpatrick, *The New Presidential Elite* (New York: Russell Sage Foundation, 1976).

5. Michael R. Kagay, "The Use of Public Opinion Polls by the *New York Times*: Some Samples from the 1988 Presidential Election," in Paul J. Lavrakas and Jack K. Holley, eds., *Polling and Presidential Election Coverage* (Newbury Park, Calif.: Sage, 1991).

6. Denise L. Baer and David A. Bositis, *Elite Cadres and Party Coalitions* (New York: Greenwood Press, 1988), pp. 203–4.

7. Dwaine Marvick, "Stability and Change in the Views of Los Angeles Party Activists, 1968–1980," in William Crotty, ed., *Political Parties in Local Areas* (Knoxville: University of Tennessee Press, 1986), p. 154.

8. Walter J. Stone and Alan I. Abramowitz, "Winning May Not Be Everything, But It's More Than We Thought: Presidential Party Activists in 1980," *American Political Science Review* 77, no. 4 (December 1983): 945.

9. Alan Abramowitz, John McGlennon, and Ronald Rapoport, "The Party Isn't Over: Incentives for Activism in the 1980 Presidential Nomination Campaign," *Journal of Politics* 45 (1983): 1013.

10. Clifford Brown, Lynda Powell, and Clyde Wilcox, *Serious Money* (New York: Cambridge University Press, 1995).

11. Jill Abramson and David Rogers, "As GOP Tries to Shrink Government, Coffers Swell with New Money," *Wall Street Journal*, February 9, 1995, p. A1.

12. Theodore J. Eismeier and Philip H. Pollock, "Following the Money: The Financial Underpinnings of the 1994 Midterm Election," paper delivered at the Midwest Political Science Association, April 18–20, 1996, pp. 13–14.

13. These *National Journal* and *Congressional Quarterly* analyses were cited in David Broder, "Differences Divide Parties," *Kalamazoo Gazette*, January 23, 1995, p. A8.

14. Eric M. Uslaner, *Shale Barrel Politics: Energy and Legislative Leadership* (Stanford: Stanford University Press, 1989), pp. 210–11.

15. David Broder, "Return Politics to Conventions," *Kalamazoo Gazette*, November 11, 1996, p. A8.

16. V. O. Key, *Politics, Parties, and Pressure Groups*, 5th ed. (New York: Crowell, 1964), p. 9.

17. Richie Ross is quoted in Marshall Ganz, "Voters in the Crosshairs: How Technology and the Market Are Destroying Politics," in Robert Kuttner, ed., *Ticking Time Bombs* (New York: New Press, 1996), p. 253.

18. Ibid.

19. John Hibbing and Elizabeth Theiss-Morse, "Popular Support for Congress: Replacing Myths with Theory," unpublished paper, 1994, University of Nebraska, summarized in Stephen C. Craig, "Change and the American Electorate," in Craig's *Broken Contract?* (Boulder: Westview Press, 1996), pp. 12–13.

20. Stephen Skowronek, *Building a New American State* (Cambridge: Cambridge University Press, 1982), p. 24.

21. William Nisbet Chambers, *Political Parties in a New Nation* (New York: Oxford University Press, 1963), p. 106.

22. Wilfred E. Binkley, *President and Congress*, 3rd rev. ed. (New York: Random House, 1962), p. 58.

23. Chambers, *Political Parties in a New Nation*, p. 106.

24. Skowronek, *Building a New American State*, pp. 24–25.

25. Samuel Eliot Morison and Henry Steele Commager, *The Growth of the American Republic*, 4th ed., rev. and enlarged (New York: Oxford University Press, 1956), p. 471.

26. Chambers, *Political Parties in a New Nation*, p. 12.

27. Key, *Politics, Parties, and Pressure Groups*, pp. 598–99.

28. Wilson Carey McWilliams, "Conclusion—the Meaning of the Election," in Gerald M. Pomper et al., eds., *The Election of 1996* (Chatham, N.J.: Chatham House, 1997), p. 255.

29. D. W. Brogan, *Politics in America* (Garden City, N.Y.: Anchor Books, 1960), p. 144.

30. Chambers, *Political Parties in a New Nation*, epigraph.

31. Ibid., p. 109.

31. Sam Hill and Glenn Rifkin, *Radical Marketing* (New York: HarperBusiness, 1999), p. 27.

33. Ibid., p. 13.

34. Ed Rollins, *Bare Knuckles and Back Rooms* (New York: Broadway Books, 1996), p. 291.

35. Ibid., p. 292.

36. Ibid., p. 290.

37 Cornelius P. Cotter and Bernard C. Hennessy, *Politics without Power: The National Party Committees* (New York: Atherton Press, 1964), p. 8.

38. Cornelius P. Cotter et al., *Party Organizations in American Politics* (New York: Praeger Special Studies, 1984), pp. 33–34.

39. Robert P. Steed et al., eds., *Party Organization and Activism in the American South* (Tuscaloosa: University of Alabama Press, 1998), p. 113.

40. William J. Keefe, *Parties, Politics, and Public Policy in America*, 8th ed. (Washington, D.C.: CQ Press, 1998), p. 40.

41. Phillips Cutright and Peter H. Rossi, "Grass Roots Politicians and the Vote," *American Sociological Review* 23 (April 1958): 179.

42. Peter W. Wielhouwer and Brad Lockerbie, "Party Contacting and Political Participation," *American Journal of Political Science* 38, no. 1 (1994): 214–15.

43. Charles L. Clapp, *The Congressman: His Work as He Sees It* (New York: Doubleday, 1963), p. 397.

44. Robert P. Steed and Lewis Bowman, "Strength of Party Attachment," in Steed et al., *Party Organization and Activism in the American South*, p. 201.

45. Jeane J. Kirkpatrick, *Dismantling the Parties: Reflections on Party Reform and Party Decomposition* (Washington D.C.: American Enterprise Institute, 1979), p. 12.

Chapter 4:
Uncontrollable Campaign Costs and Their Consequences

1. Anthony King, *Running Scared* (New York: Free Press, 1997), pp. 42–43.

2. David Broder, "Democrats Worrying," *Washington Post*, June 9, 1993, p. A1.

3. Jeffrey Berry, *The Interest Group Society*, 3rd ed. (New York: Longman, 1997), p. 24.

4. This 1998 study by the Associated Press and the Center for Responsive Politics covered the initial six months of 1997, when the figure for lobby expenditures was $600 million. The study examined the disclosure forms that the federal government now requires lobbyists to complete.

5. Jim Drinkard, "Study Unveils Costs of Lobbying," *Kalamazoo Gazette*, March 7, 1998, p. A2.

6. David Littman, Comerica Newsletter, Detroit, December 1995.

7. The 1992 data is drawn from Herbert Alexander and Anthony Corrado, *Financing the 1992 Election*, 1995, quoted in Kenneth Jost, "Campaign Finance Reform," *CQ Researcher* 6, no. 6 (1996): 124. The 1996 data is from Carroll J.

Doherty, "Inquiry on Campaign Finance: Burning with a Short Fuse," *Congressional Quarterly*, special report, April 5, 1997, p. 767.

8. Littman, newsletter, December 1995.

9. Brooks Jackson, *Honest Graft* (New York: Knopf, 1988), p. 9.

10. Kristin Straroba, "Talking Politics, Talking Turkey," *Association Management*, November 1990, p. 48.

11. Herbert Alexander, *Financing Politics*, 4th ed. (Washington, D.C.: Congressional Quarterly, 1992), pp. 87–88.

12. Rick Wartzman, "Campaign Finance Showdown Nears," *Wall Street Journal*, November 18, 1994, p. A20.

13. Adam Clymer, "For Freshmen, Fund Raising Has Yielded Big Results," *New York Times*, May 6, 1996, p. A13.

14. Adam Clymer, "Contract with America Includes Cash Bonuses," *New York Times*, February 18, 1996, E4.

15. Fred Wertheimer and Susan Weiss Manes, "Campaign Finance Reform: A Key to Restoring the Health of Our Democracy," *Columbia Law Review* 94, no. 4 (1994): 1136–37.

16. Quoted in Anthony Corrado et al., eds., *Campaign Finance Reform* (Washington, D.C.: Brookings Institution, 1997), p. 64.

17. Frank Sorauf, *Inside Campaign Finance* (New Haven: Yale University Press, 1992), pp. 9–11.

18. For an excellent discussion of the size and scope of this interest-group involvement, see Jeffrey Berry, *The Interest Group Society*, 3rd ed. (New York: Longman, 1997).

19. Rhodes Cook, "Thinnest of Margins Shows Country's Great Divide," *Congressional Quarterly*, February 15, 1997, p. 441.

20. Anthony Corrado, "Financing the 1996 Election," in Gerald Pomper et al., eds., *The Election of 1996* (Chatham, N.J.: Chatham House, 1997), p. 164.

21. For a detailed and clear discussion of this distinction and numerous other such nuances, see Trevor Potter, "The Current State of Campaign Finance Law," in Corrado et al., *Campaign Finance Reform*, pp. 5–24.

22. Joseph Cantor, "Sources of Funds—Political Action Committees from Campaign Financing in Federal Elections: A Guide to the Law and Its Operation," Congressional Research Service, November 16, 1995, p. 33.

23. Joseph Cantor, "Soft and Hard Money in Contemporary Elections: What Federal Law Does and Does Not Regulate," Congressional Research Service report distributed by the Center for Responsive Politics, October 10, 1997, p. 4. Cantor rightly distinguishes such issue advocacy from independent expenditures, since issue advocacy, if proven to have been "coordinated" with the candidate, would be subject to FEC regulation. Current campaign practices seem to suggest, however, that this means simply that issue advocacy and independent expenditures constitute two widening soft-money loopholes, rather than one.

24. Jeanne Cummings, "'Issue Advocacy' Groups to Play Bigger Role," *Wall Street Journal*, March 6, 1998, p. A16.

25. This *Los Angeles Times* article is quoted in Rebecca Carr, "Tax-Exempt Groups Scrutinized as Fundraising Clout Grows," *Congressional Quarterly*, February 22, 1997, p. 471.

26. Rebecca Carr, "Focus on Tax-Exempt Groups Puts Heat on Republicans," *Congressional Quarterly*, May 17, 1997, p. 1112.

27. Carr, "Tax-Exempt Groups Scrutinized . . . ," p. 473.

28. In order to make these contributions, a PAC had to be registered with the

FEC for at least six months, have more than fifty contributors, and have supported five or more candidates for federal office: Herbert Alexander, *Financing Politics,* p. 59.

29. Sorauf, *Inside Campaign Finance,* p. 15.

30. Alexander and Corrado, *Financing the 1992 Election,* p. 207.

31. Joseph Cantor, *Campaign Finance,* Congressional Research Service Issue Brief, December 17, 1997, p. 3.

32. Glenn R. Simpson, "'Leadership PACs' for Republicans in the House Are Popular, but Critics Warn of Voter Backlash," *Wall Street Journal,* August 29, 1995, p. A16.

33. Eliza Newlin Carney, "PAC Men," *National Journal,* October 1, 1994, p. 2268.

34. Eliza Newlin Carney, "Backdoor PACs," *National Journal* 28, no. 9 (1996): 468–73.

35. Larry J. Sabato and Glenn R. Simpson, *Dirty Little Secrets* (New York: Times Books, 1996), pp. 52–53.

36. Susan Propper, "PACless Participation," *Association Management,* November 1990, p. 52.

37. Eliza Carney, "Reform Could Strike Out Over Labor," *National Journal,* November 30, 1996, p. 2617.

38. David Broder, "Campaign Finance Reform-Lite," *Kalamazoo Gazette,* July 27, 1997, p. A12.

39. Rebecca Carr, "Tax-Exempt Groups Scrutinized as Fundraising Clout Grows," *Congressional Quarterly,* February 22, 1997, p. 471.

40. For an excellent discussion of this party soft-money process, see Joseph Kantor, *Soft and Hard Money in Contemporary Elections: What Federal Law Does and Does Not Regulate,* Congressional Research Service report, January 10, 1997, distributed through the Center for Responsive Politics, pp. 4–5, www.crp.org.

41. Quotations are found in Philip M. Stern, *The Best Congress Money Can Buy* (New York: Pantheon, 1988), p. 164.

42. Chuck Alston, "Big Money Slips Back Into Government," *Congressional Quarterly,* March 7, 1992, p. 590.

43. Bob Woodward, *The Choice* (New York: Simon & Schuster, 1996), p. 354.

44. Larry Makinson et al., *The Big Picture: Where the Money Came From in the 1996 Elections,* Center for Responsive Politics, 1997, pp. 1–4, www.crp.org.

45. Charles R. Babcock, "$100,000 Political Donations on the Rise Again," *Washington Post,* September 30, 1991, p. A4.

46. Phil Kuntz, "DNC Invites for Clinton Coffees Perked along with $25,000 Price Tag, a Businessman Recalls," *Wall Street Journal,* October 8, 1997, p. A24.

47. "The Mother Jones 400," *Mother Jones* 22, no. 3 (1997): p. 45.

48. Jennifer Loven, "Gingrich Says Colin Powell Should Speak at the Republican Convention," *Kalamazoo Gazette,* July 10, 1996, p. D1.

49. Phil Kuntz and Michael K. Frisby, "For Big Contributors, Convention's Business Isn't at the Podium," *Wall Street Journal,* August 13, 1996, p. A1.

50. Peter H. Stone, "Congress's Cash Cows," *National Journal,* October 4, 1997, p. 1957.

51. Glenn R. Simpson and Phil Kuntz, "Pennsylvania's Cones Secretly Funded Controversial '96 GOP Election Race," *Wall Street Journal,* October 29, 1997, p. A4.

52. Ruth Marcus, "GOP Keeps Fund-Raising Lead Despite Trade Group's Shift in Giving," *Washington Post,* November 3, 1996, p. A38.

53. Thomas Ferguson, *Golden Rule* (Chicago: University of Chicago Press, 1995), p. 353.

54. David E. Sanger and James Sterngold, "Fund-Raiser for Democrats Now Faces Harsh Spotlight," *New York Times*, October 21, 1996, p. A1. The nun actually was from a Texas Buddhist temple affiliated with the Buddhist temple in Los Angeles.

55. Jill Abramson and Glenn R. Simpson, "Lippo Issue Remains at Center of Presidential Race," *Wall Street Journal*, October 21, 1996, p. A24.

56. Rebecca Carr and Jackie Koszezuk, "Probe Reports Decry Abuses, but Overhaul Still Unlikely," *Congressional Quarterly*, February 14, 1998, p. 373.

57. Molly Ivins, "I.Q. of a Dust Bunny," *Progressive* 46 (September 1997): 46.

58. William Greider, *Who Will Tell the People* (New York: Simon & Schuster), 1992.

59. Phil Kuntz and Michael K. Frisby, "For Big Contributors, Convention's Business Isn't at the Podium," *Wall Street Journal*, August 13, 1996, p. A6.

60. Paul Starr, "Democracy v. Dollar," *American Prospect*, March–April 1997, p. 6. The Center for Responsive Politics data is also cited by Starr.

61. Michael Barone and Grant Ujifusa, *The Almanac of American Politics* (Washington, D.C.: National Journal, 1998), pp. 1597–98.

62. Gary C. Jacobson, "The Effects of Campaign Spending in Congressional Elections," *American Political Science Review* 72 (1978): 469–90.

63. Jack W. Germond and Jules Witcover, "In 2000, Deep Pockets May Help," *National Journal*, January 24, 1998, p. 182.

64. Elizabeth Drew, *Politics and Money* (New York: Macmillan, 1983), p. 77.

65. Robert Dreyfuss, "How Money Votes: An Oklahoma Story," in Robert Kuttner, ed. *Ticking Time Bombs* (New York: New Press, 1996), pp. 196–97.

66. Richard L. Hall and Frank W. Wayman, "Buying Time: Moneyed Interests and the Mobilization of Bias," *American Political Science Review* 84, no. 3 (1990): 797–820. The authors provide a good review of the literature on the relationship between campaign finance and roll-call votes and an excellent discussion of the mobilization of bias achieved through the systematic investment of money in politics.

67. Jeffrey H. Birnbaum and Alan S. Murray, *Showdown at Gucci Gulch* (New York: Random House, 1987), p. 288.

68. Donald L. Bartlett and James B. Steele, "How the Influential Win Billions in Special Tax Breaks," *Philadelphia Inquirer*, April 10, 1988, p. 15-A. Bartlett and Steele traced the auto-tax break, worth $8 million, to the International Shipholding Corporation of New Orleans.

69. This information from William Greider is cited in Dan Clawson, Alan Neustadt, and Denise Scott, *Money Talks* (New York: Basic Books, 1992), p. 4. William Greider, "Whitewash: Is Congress Conning Us on Clean Air?" *Rolling Stone*, June 14, 1990, pp. 37–39, 146.

70. Fred Wertheimer and Susan Weiss Manes, "Campaign Finance Reform: A Key to Restoring the Health of Our Democracy," *Columbia Law Review* 94, no. 4 (1994): 1140.

71. Larry Makinson and Joshua Goldstein, *The Cash Constituents of Congress*, 2nd ed. (Washington, D.C.: Congressional Quarterly, 1994}, pp. 36–40. The authors also document the amount in contributions given to every member of Congress. Donors must extend their giving widely to include followers as well as committee and party leaders.

72. Anita Raghavan, "Financial Firms Boost Funding to Capitol Hill," *Wall Street Journal*, March 12, 1996, p. C1.

73. Dreyfuss, "How Money Votes," p. 194.

74. Jeff Gerth, Stephen Engelberg, and Tim Weiner, "Packwood Diaries: A Rare Look at Washington's Tangled Web," *New York Times*, September 10, 1995, p. 20.

75. Amy Waldman, "Move Over, Charles Keating," *Washington Monthly* 27, no. 5 (1995): 29–30. Grogan told this episode in testimony when Cranston eventually came under congressional scrutiny for his role in the S&L scandal.

76 Jonathan Cohn, "Scandals for Dummies," *American Prospect*, no. 12 (May–June 1997): 17–19. The Woodward citation is in Cohn, ibid.

77. Quoted in Christine A. DeGregorio, *Network of Champions* (Ann Arbor: University of Michigan Press, 1997), p. 87.

78. Louise Levathes, "Easy Money," *Audubon*, 97, no. 6, November–December 1995, p. 16.

79. Charles Lewis, *The Buying of the President* (New York: Avon, 1996), p. 11.

80. Jackson, *Honest Graft*, p. 107.

81. Drew, *Politics and Money,* p. 77.

82. Ibid., pp. 78–79.

83. Richard L. Hall and Frank W. Wayman, "Buying Time: Moneyed Interests and the Mobilization of Bias in Congressional Committees," pp. 797–820.

84. Thomas Stratmann, "How Re-election Constituencies Matter: Evidence from Political Action Committees' Contributions and Congressional Voting," *Journal of Law and Economics* 39 (October 1996): 603–35.

85. Theodore B. Olson, "Clinton's Payoffs to the Trial Lawyers," *Wall Street Journal*, March 15, 1996, p. A10.

86. Samuel Morrison and Henry Steele Commager, *The Growth of the American Republic*, vol. 2 (New York: Oxford University Press), 1950, p. 263.

87. John T. Noonan, *Bribes* (New York: Macmillan, 1984), p. 625.

88. Fred S. McChesney, *Money for Nothing: Politicians, Rent Extraction, and Political Extortion* (Cambridge, Harvard University Press, 1997), pp. 30–31.

89. Gretchen Morgenson, "Look Who's Running a Protection Racket," *Forbes*, September 8, 1997, pp. 44–46.

90. *McCormick v. U.S.* 500 U.S. 257 (1991), cited in Daniel H. Lowenstein, "When Is a Campaign Contribution a Bribe?" Paper presented at the Midwest Political Science Association Conference, April 18–20, 1996, pp. 37–38.

91. Amitai Etzioni, *Capital Corruption* (San Diego: Harcourt, Brace, Jovanovich, 1984), p. 43.

92. Quoted in Jackson, *Honest Graft*, p. 48.

93. John Farrell, "'Soft Money' Diary Entry Brings Gramm Rough Patch," *Boston Globe*, September 9, 1995, section 4, p. 4.

94. Helen Dewar, "Packwood Diaries Spur Call for Campaign Finance Probe," *Washington Post*, September 14, 1995, p. A4.

95. Norbert McCrady, "Branching Will Help Fat Cats Feed Clinton's War Chest," *American Banker*, April 27, 1994, p. 17, quoted in Lewis, *Buying of the President,* pp. 58–59.

96. Drew, *Politics and Money*, p. 9.

97. Larry J. Sabato and Glenn R. Simpson, *Dirty Little Secrets* (New York: Random House, 1996), p. 14.

98. Alexander, *Financing Politics*, pp. 19–20.

99. Lewis, *Buying of the President*, p. 8.

100. Peter M. Senge, *The Fifth Discipline* (New York: Doubleday, 1990), p. 22.

Chapter 5: Pathways to Congressional Decisionmaking

1. Morris Fiorina, *Congress: Keystone of the Washington Establishment* (New Haven: Yale University Press, 1989), pp. 37–44.

2. Peter Brimelow, "Privilege-seeking?" *Forbes*, September 22, 1997, pp. 73–74.

3. James Q. Wilson, "Democracy Needs Pork to Survive," *Wall Street Journal*, August 14, 1997, p. A12.

4. John W. Ellwood and Eric M. Patashnik, "In Praise of Pork," *The Public Interest*, no. 110 (winter 1993): 21.

5. Wilson, "Democracy Needs Pork," p. A12.

6. This CAGW definition is cited in Barry D. Friedman, "The 'Efficiency Dividend': How Many New Services Can Be Squeezed Out of a Diminished Budget?" paper presented at the 1996 American Society for Public Administration Conference, p. 5

7. Tim Weiner, "Sending Money to Home District: Earmarking and the Pork Barrel," *New York Times*, July 29, 1994, p. D18.

8. Ibid.

9. Citizens Against Government Waste, *1998 Pig Book*, p. 1, www.govt-waste.org.

10. Steven D. Levitt and James M. Snyder, "The Impact of Federal Spending on House Election Outcomes," National Bureau of Economic Research Working Paper Bibliographic Entry, January 1, 1995.

11. Paul Starobin, "Pork: A Time-Honored Tradition Lives On," *Congressional Quarterly*, October 24, 1987, p. 2581.

12. David Rogers, "Accord in Congress to Boost EPA Funds Is Loaded with Items for GOP Districts," *Wall Street Journal*, September 29, 1997, p. A24.

13. Rudy Baum, "House Panel Targets Academic Pork Barrel," *Chemical and Engineering News* 71, no. 8 (1993): 5.

14. Thomas Toch and Ted Slafsky, "The Scientific Pork Barrel: Universities Have Taken to Lobbying Congress Directly for Scarce Federal Dollars," *U.S. News & World Report* 114, no. 8 (1993): 59.

15. Graeme Browning, "Colleges at the Trough: Momentum is Building in Congress to Crack Down on Academic Research Grants that Bypass Review Procedures and are Tacked on to Appropriations Bills in Classic Pork Barrel Fashion," *National Journal,* March 7, 1992, p. 568.

16. Browning drew on data from the *Chronicle of Higher Education* and *Congressional Research Service* in reaching this conclusion; ibid., p. 566.

17. Gary J. Andres, "Pork Barrel Spending—On the Wane?" *PS: Political Science and Politics* 28, no. 2 (June 1995): 207.

18. Randall B. Ripley and Grace A. Franklin, *Congress, the Bureaucracy, and Public Policy*, 5th ed. (Pacific Grove, Calif.: Brooks/Cole, 1991), p. 76.

19. David W. Rohde, *Parties and Leaders in the Postreform House* (Chicago: University of Chicago Press, 1991), p. 29.

20. Herbert Kaufman, *The Administrative Behavior of Federal Bureau Chiefs* (Washington, D.C.: Brookings Institution, 1981), pp. 91–138.

21. Eugene Lewis, *Public Entrepreneurship* (Bloomington: Indiana University Press, 1980), pp. 14–17.

22. Frederick C. Mosher, *Democracy and the Public Service*, 2nd ed. (New York: Oxford University Press, 1982), p. 117.

23. Rohde, *Parties and Leaders,* pp. 26–27.

24. Kenneth A. Shepsle, "The Changing Textbook Congress," in John E. Chubb and Paul E. Peterson, eds., *Can the Government Govern?* (Washington, D.C.: Brookings Institution, 1989), pp. 250–55.

25. William P. Browne, *Cultivating Congress* (Lawrence: University Press of Kansas, 1995), p. 16.

26. Theodore Lowi, *The End of Liberalism*, 2nd ed. (New York: Norton, 1979), pp. 68–77.

27. John W. Kingdon, *Agendas, Alternatives, and Public Policies* (Glenview, Ill.: Scott, Foresman, 1984), p. 72.

28. "Longstanding Farm Laws Rewritten," *1996 CQ Almanac* (Washington, D.C.: CQ Press, 1996), pp. 3–19.

29. Shepsle, "Changing Textbook Congress," p. 253.

30. Ibid., p. 70.

31. Ibid., p. 209. The examples in this section are drawn from various parts of Browne's invaluable study; this interpretation of the data, however, is my own.

32. John A. Ferejohn, *Pork Barrel Politics* (Stanford: Stanford University Press, 1974), pp. 251–52.

33. John F. Cogan, Timothy J. Muris, and Allen Schick, *The Budget Puzzle* (Stanford: Stanford University Press, 1994), p. 111.

34. While cozy political arrangements are difficult to measure, other, more corrupt regimes presumably distribute a higher proportion of illegitimate spoils. The federal $1.8-trillion budget, however, provides far more opportunities for enterprising politicians under pressure to express gratitude for campaign contributions.

35. George Will, *Restoration* (New York: Free Press, 1992), p. 92.

36. Robert M. Stein and Kenneth N. Bickers, *Perpetuating the Pork Barrel* (New York: Cambridge University Press, 1995), p. 90.

37. Diana Evans, "PAC Contributions and Roll-Call Voting: Conditional Power," in Allan J. Cigler and Burdett A. Loomis, eds., *Interest Group Politics*, 2nd ed. (Washington, D.C.: CQ Press, 1986), pp. 114–32.

38. Stein and Bickers, *Perpetuating the Pork Barrel*, p. 113.

39. Larry J. Sabato, *PAC Power* (New York: Norton, 1984), p. 127. Emphasis added.

40. Office of Management and Budget, "Tax Expenditures," *Analytical Perspectives*, FY 1999, *Budget of the U.S. Government*, 105th Cong., 2nd sess., 1998, p. 89.

41. Peter Kobrak and Warren Gregory, "Expanding Budget Options: Tax Expenditures and the Michigan Legislative Process," *Public Budgeting and Financial Management* 5, no. 2 (1993): 192–95.

42. "Let's Revamp the Tax Code—but How?" *Wall Street Journal*, April 15, 1998, p. A22.

43. Dan Clawson, Alan Neustadtl, and Denise Scott, *Money Talks* (New York: Basic Books, 1992), p. 95.

44. Arthur P. Hall, "The Compliance Costs and Regulatory Burden Imposed by the Federal Tax Laws," *Special Brief*, Tax Foundation, January 1995, p. 3.

45. "Let's Revamp the Tax Code—but How?" p. A22.

46. Hall, "Compliance Costs," p. 3.

47. Pamela Fessler, "Congress Urged to Scrutinize Tax Breaks That Cost U.S. Billions in Lost Revenues," *Congressional Quarterly*, January 30, 1982, p. 157.

48. Jeffrey St. Clair and Alexander Cockburn, "Teapot Dome, Part II: The Rush for Alaskan Oil," *Nation* 264, no. 13 (1997): 20–24.

49. Kirk Victor, "Takin' on the Bacon," *National Journal*, May 6, 1995, p. 1082.

50. Robert J. Shapiro, *Cut and Invest: A Budget Strategy for the New Economy*, Progressive Policy Institute Report no. 23, March 1995, p. 17.

51. Stephen Moore and Dean Stansel, "Ending Corporate Welfare as We Know It," *Policy Analysis*, no. 225, CATO Institute Series, May 12, 1995, p. 1.

52. Dean Stansel and Stephen Moore, "Federal Aid to Dependent Corporations: Clinton and Congress Fail to Eliminate Business Subsidies," *CATO Fact Sheet*, January 28, 1997, p. 2.

53. Alan K. Ota, "Criticism of 'Corporate Welfare' Heats Up in Congress," *Congressional Quarterly*, January 17, 1998, p. 121.

54. "Kasich Scores Few Wins," *Wall Street Journal*, August 8, 1997, p. A1.

55. Randy Fitzgerald, "Sugar's Sweet Deal," *Reader's Digest* 152, no. 910 (1998): 91–95.

56. Paul Glastris et al., "Hang on to Your Wallet," *U.S. News & World Report*, April 14, 1997, pp. 27–28.

57. Brooks Jackson, *Honest Graft* (New York: Knopf, 1988), p. 107.

58. Greg Hitt and Phil Kuntz, "Who Are Those People Donating to Politicos?" *Wall Street Journal*, May 28, 1998, p. A1ff.

59. Ed Gillespie and Bob Schellhas, eds. *Contract with America* (New York, Times Books, 1994).

60. Charles O. Jones, *An Introduction to the Study of Public Policy*, 3rd ed. (Monterey, Calif.: Brooks/Cole, 1984), pp. 46–49; Emmette Redford, *Democracy in the Administrative State* (New York: Oxford University Press, 1969), pp. 108–9.

61. John W. Kingdon, *Agendas, Alternatives, and Public Policies* (Glenview, Ill.: Scott, Foresman, 1984), pp. 72–74.

62. James Thurber, "Dynamics of Policy Subsystems in American Politics," in Allan J. Cigler and Burdett A. Loomis, eds. *Interest Group Politics*, 3rd ed. (Washington, D.C.: CQ Press, 1991), p. 320.

63. Kingdon, *Agendas, Alternatives, and Public Policies*, p. 129.

64. Burdett A. Loomis, *The New American Politician* (New York: Basic Books, 1988), p. 53.

65. Robert B. Reich, "Policy Making in a Democracy," in Robert B. Reich, ed., *The Power of Public Ideas* (Cambridge, Mass.: Ballinger, 1988), p. 144.

66. Steven Kelman, "'Public Choice' and Public Spirit," *The Public Interest*, no. 87 (spring 1987): 86.

67. Paul Quirk, "Deregulation and the Politics of Ideas in Congress," in Peter Kobrak, ed., *The Political Environment of Public Management* (New York, HarperCollins, 1993), p. 374.

68. Jeffrey M. Berry, *The Interest Group Society*, 3rd ed. (New York: Longman, 1977), pp. 206–15.

69. William Greider, *Who Will Tell the People* (New York: Simon & Schuster, 1992), p. 346.

70. Ibid., p. 336.

71. Ibid., p. 346.

72. Ken Silverstein, "The Boeing Formation: A Squadron of Seventy Lobbyists Prepares for Air Superiority," *Harper's Magazine*, May 1997, p. 56.

73. Michael Wines, "A 'Bazaar' Way of Rounding Up Votes," *New York Times,* November 11, 1993, p. A23.

74. Greg Rushford, "Hog Heaven for Congressmen," *Reader's Digest* 145, no. 870 (1994): 65.

75. Pietro S. Nivola, "The New Pork Barrel," *The Public Interest,* no. 131, (spring 1998): 95.

Chapter 6: Agency Compromise and Privatization

1. Francis E. Rourke, *Bureaucracy, Politics, and Public Policy,* 3rd ed. (Boston: Little, Brown, 1984), p. 57.

2. Greg M. O'Brien and Charles Peters, "Why the Right May Be Right," *Washington Monthly,* April 1997, pp. 28–33.

3. Rourke, *Bureaucracy, Politics, and Public Policy,* p. 63.

4. Christopher McGrory Klyza, *Who Controls Public Lands?* (Chapel Hill: University of North Carolina Press, 1996), pp. 109–16.

5. The Hess and GAO studies are cited in Edward A. Chadd, "How Congress Pays Industry—with Federal Tax Dollars—to Deplete and Destroy the Nation's Natural Resources," *Common Cause,* fall 1995, pp. 4–5.

6. Richard F. Fenno, *The Power of the Purse* (Boston: Little, Brown, 1966), pp. 404–12.

7. R. Douglas Arnold, *Congress and the Bureaucracy* (New Haven: Yale University Press, 1979), pp. 200, 204.

8. Ibid., pp. 129–30.

9. Gary C. Jacobson, *The Politics of Congressional Elections,* 4th ed. (New York: Longman, 1997), p. 186.

10. A more detailed account of the ARC can be found in Dale Van Atta, "You Can't Kill a Good Giveaway," *Reader's Digest* 143, no. 856 (1993): 55–59.

11. Jon Healey, "States Actively Seek a Share of 'Demonstration Projects,'" *Congressional Quarterly,* July 17, 1993, p. 1869.

12. Christina Del Valle, "Meet Bud Shuster, Prince of Pork," *Business Week,* May 15, 1995, p. 87.

13. The term *crown jewels* is used by former NPS director James M. Ridenour in *The National Parks Compromised: Pork Barrel Politics and America's Treasures* (Champaign: University of Illinois Press, 1995).

14. The comment and quotation in this paragraph are drawn from Frank Greve, "Senior Legislators Claim Park Funds for Pet Projects," *Washington Post,* December 1, 1997, p. A23.

15. Quoted in Lary M. Dilsaver, book review in *Annals of the Association of American Geographers* 86, no. 2 (1996): 357.

16. Russell Shaw, "GOP Vows to Take Pork Out of Parks," *Insight on the News* 11, no. 46 (1995): 17.

17. Brian Kelly, *Adventures in Porkland* (New York: Villard, 1992), p. 78.

18. John Marchese, "High on the Hog," *Philadelphia* 83, no. 10 (1992): 65.

19. Edward T. Pound and Douglas Pasternak, "The Pork Barrel Barons," *U.S. News & World Report,* February 21, 1994, pp. 35–39.

20. The Pinchot quotations are drawn from Klyza, *Who Controls the Public Lands?* pp. 16–17.

21. Charles Pope, "Members Go Out on a Limb over National Forests," *Congressional Quarterly,* April 18, 1998, p. 976.

22. Paul Roberts, "The Federal Chain-Saw Massacre," *Harper's,* June 1997, pp. 38–41.

23. "Carry a Big Stick: How Big Timber Triumphs in Washington," *Common Cause Report: Return on Investment,* 1997, pp. 1–3, www.commoncause.org/publications.

24. Quoted in Edward A. Chadd, "Manifest Subsidy," *Common Cause,* fall 1995, p. 5, www.ccsi.com/~comcause/news.

25. Roberts, "Federal Chain-Saw Massacre," p. 44.

26. Margaret Kriz, "Fighting over Forests," *National Journal,* May 30, 1998, p. 1233.

27. Ibid., p. 1235.

28. Ibid., p. 1236.

29. "Carry a Big Stick," *Common Cause,* p. 2.

30. Ibid.

31. Kriz, "Fighting over Forests," p. 1236.

32. Chadd, "Manifest Subsidy," p. 2.

33. Albert R. Hunt, "In Washington, the Spoils Go to the Big Contributors," *Wall Street Journal,* December 18, 1997, p. A23.

34. Mimi Hall, "Shalala, Ickes Are Drawn into Money Probe," *USA Today,* February 3, 1997, p. 9A.

35. Phil Kuntz, "Clinton Officials Scolded DNC Head for Seeking Favors," *Wall Street Journal,* August 18, 1997, p. A1.

36. John H. Fund, "The Chippewa Connection," *Wall Street Journal,* October 22, 1997, p. A22.

37. Don Van Natta, "Clinton '96 Chief under New Inquiry," *New York Times,* November 4, 1997, p. A24.

38. Elizabeth A. Amery, "Molten Meltdown," *Forbes,* April 21, 1997, p. 48.

39. Douglas Strangling, "Washington Whispers," *U.S. News & World Report,* September 29, 1997, p. 20.

40. Michael K. Frisby and David Rogers, "Businessman's Access to White House Leads to a Security Inquiry," *Wall Street Journal,* March 17, 1997, p. A6. The information on the Tamraz incident is drawn primarily from this excellent account.

41. Albert R. Hunt, "The Vice President: Mr. Clean or the Godfather?" *Wall Street Journal,* March 20, 1997, p. A17.

42. Albert R. Hunt, "What We've Learned," *Wall Street Journal,* October 9, 1997, p. A19.

43. E. S. Savas, *Privatizing the Public Sector* (Chatham, N.J.: Chatham House, 1982), pp. 89–117.

44. E. S. Savas, *Privatization: The Key to Better Government* (Chatham, N.J.: Chatham House, 1987).

45. Ibid., pp. 58–92.

46. John D. Donahue, *The Privatization Decision* (New York: Basic Books, 1989, p. 7.

47. David Osborne and Ted Gaebler, *Reinventing Government* (Reading, Mass.: Addison-Wesley, 1992).

48. Al Gore, *The Gore Report on Reinventing Government* (New York: Times Books, 1993), p. iii.

49. Donald F. Kettl, *Sharing Power* (Washington, D.C.: Brookings Institution, 1993), pp. 20–30.

50. Donahue, *Privatization Decision,* p. 45.

51. John Rehfuss, *The Job of the Public Manager* (Chicago: Dorsey Press, 1989), p. 47.

52. H. Brinton Milward, Keith G. Provan, and Barbara A. Else, "What Does the 'Hollow State' Look Like?" in Barry Bozeman, ed., *Public Management* (San Francisco: Jossey-Bass, 1991), p. 319.

53. Savas, *Privatizing the Public Sector,* pp. 17–24. Savas acknowledges the occasional danger of corruption in public-private partnerships. So do Osborne and Gaebler. In neither case, however, is there any hint that the problem may be systemic in nature.

54. Erwin C. Hargrove and John C. Glidewell, *Impossible Jobs in Public Management* (Lawrence: University Press of Kansas, 1990), pp. 5–8. Hargrove and Glidewell do not link their discussion of impossible jobs to privatization, but it is often agencies with such missions and roles that appear vulnerable to cozy politics.

55. Ruth Hoogland DeHoog, *Contracting Out for Human Services* (Albany: SUNY Press, 1984), p. 26.

56. Steven Rathgeb Smith and Michael Lipsky, *Nonprofits for Hire* (Cambridge: Harvard University Press, 1993), p. 193.

57. Ibid., p. 171.

58. Francis E. Rourke, "American Exceptionalism: Government without Bureaucracy," in Larry B. Hill, ed., *The State of Public Bureaucracy* (Armonk, N.Y.: Sharpe, 1992), pp. 226–29.

59. Kenneth J. Meier, *Politics and the Bureaucracy,* 3rd ed. (Pacific Grove, Calif.: Brooks/Cole, 1993), p. 221.

60. Rehfuss, *Job of the Public Manager,* p. 189.

61. Edward J. Kane, *The S&L Insurance Mess: How Did It Happen?* (Washington, D.C.: Urban Institute Press, 1989), p. 4.

62. Peter DeLeon, *Thinking about Political Corruption* (Armonk, N.Y.: Sharpe, 1993), p. 156.

63. Quoted in Martin Mayer, *The Greatest-Ever Little Bank Robbery* (New York: Scribner's, 1990), p. 55.

64. DeLeon, *Thinking about Political Corruption,* p. 156.

65. Haynes Johnson, *Sleepwalking through History* (New York: Anchor, 1991), p. 169.

66. Eugene J. Meehan, *The Quality of Federal Policymaking: Programmed Failure in Public Housing* (Columbia: University of Missouri Press, 1979), p. 195.

67. Ibid., p. 194.

68. Ibid., p. 206.

69. Bill McAllister and Chris Spolar, "The Transformation of HUD: 'Brat Pack' Filled Vacuum at Agency," *Washington Post,* August 6, 1989, p. A10.

70. Ibid., p. A1.

71. Johnson, *Sleepwalking through History,* p. 182.

72. McAllister and Spolar, "Transformation of HUD," p. A1.

73. Ibid., p. A10.

74. Ibid.

75. James Kilpatrick, "It's Reagan's Mess at HUD," *Washington Post,* August 11, 1989, p. A25.

76. McAllister and Spolar, "Transformation of HUD," p. A10.

77. Ibid.

78. Edward T. Pound and Kenneth H. Bacon, "Housing Subsidy Plan for the Poor Helped Contributors to GOP," *Wall Street Journal,* May 25, 1989, p. A1.

79. Carol Steinbach, "Programmed for Plunder," *National Journal,* September 16, 1989, p. 2260.

80. McAllister and Spolar, "Transformation of HUD," p. A10.

81. Ibid.

82. Pound and Bacon, "Housing Subsidy Plan Helped Contributors," p. A1.

83. Ibid., p. A12.

84. Cited in Steinbach, "Programmed for Plunder," p. 2:262.

85. "The Many Paths of the HUD Investigation," *New York Times,* August 13, 1989, p. E3.

86. Ibid.

87. Rochelle L. Stanfield, "Tall Order," *National Journal,* July 24, 1993, p. 1864.

88. DeLeon, *Thinking about Political Corruption,* p. 227.

89. Norma A. Riccucci, *Unsung Heroes: Federal Execurats* (Washington, D.C.: Georgetown University Press, 1995), pp. 160–61.

90. Kettl, *Sharing Power,* pp. 41–63.

91. A case in point is the indictment by a grand jury of Ann Eppard, long-time staffer for Bud Shuster, the House Transportation Committee chairman, for accepting illegal payments from lobbyists for assistance relating to a Boston highway construction project. Jim Drinkard, "Transportation Interests Still Knock at Indicted Lobbyist's Door," *USA Today,* April 24, 1998, p. 5A.

92. Kilpatrick, "It's Reagan's Mess," p. A25.

93. Dennis F. Thompson, "Mediated Corruption: The Case of the Keating Five," *American Political Science Review* 87, no. 2 (1993): 377.

94. Chester A. Newland, "Public Executives: Imperium, Sacerdotium, Collegium?" *Public Administration Review* 47, no. 1 (1987): 55.

Chapter 7: Reinventing Political Parties

1. U.S. National Resources Committee, *The Structure of the American Economy,* Part 1: *Basic Characteristics* (Washington, D.C.: Government Printing Office, 1939), p. 96, quoted in David B. Truman, *The Governmental Process* (New York: Knopf, 1951), pp. 53–54.

2. David Broder, "What Does Government Do Right?" *Kalamazoo Gazette,* November 24, 1997, p. A8.

3. Stephen Barr, "Americans Gain a Small Measure of Confidence in Government," *Washington Post,* March 24, 1997, p. A17.

4. Quoted in Al Gore, *Creating a Government that Works Better and Costs Less* (New York: Times Books, 1993), p. iv.

5. Walter Dean Burnham, *The Current Crisis in American Politics* (New York: Oxford University Press, 1982).

6. Steven E. Schier, *By Invitation Only* (Pittsburgh: University of Pittsburgh Press, 2000), p. 204.

7. Leon D. Epstein, *Political Parties in the American Mold* (Madison: University of Wisconsin Press, 1986), p. 5.

8. Chester A. Newland, "Realism and Public Administration," guest editorial in *Public Administration Review* 57, no. 2 (1997): iii.

9. Theda Skocpol, "Unravelling from Above," in Robert Kuttner, ed., *Ticking Time Bombs* (New York: New Press, 1996), pp. 299–300. Jane Mansbridge, "Social and Cultural Causes of Dissatisfaction with U.S. Government," in Joseph S. Nye, Philip D. Zelikow, and David C. King, *Why People Don't Trust Government* (Cambridge: Harvard University Press, 1997), p. 147.

10. Stephen C. Craig, "Change and the American Electorate," in Stephen C. Craig, ed., *Broken Contract?* (Boulder: Westview Press, 1996), p. 8.

11. Paul Lazarsfeld, Bernard Berelson, and Hazel Gaudet, *The People's Choice*, 2nd ed. (New York: Columbia University Press, 1948), p. 158.

12. Steven J. Rosenstone and John Mark Hansen, *Mobilization, Participation, and Democracy in America* (New York: Macmillan, 1993), p. 23.

13. Boyle is quoted in John Nichols, "How Al Gore Has It Wired," *Nation*, July 20, 1998, p. 12.

14. Cited in Robert J. Huckshorn and John F. Bibby, "State Parties in an Era of Political Change," in Joel L. Fleishman, ed., *The Future of American Political Parties* (Englewood Cliffs, N.J.: Prentice-Hall, 1982), p. 100.

15. Larry J. Sabato, *The Party's Just Begun: Shaping Political Parties for America's Future* (Glenview, Ill.: Scott, Foresman, 1988), pp. 20–21.

16. Thomas Ferguson, *Golden Rule* (Chicago: University of Chicago Press, 1995), p. 29.

17. William Greider, *Who Will Tell the People* (New York: Simon & Schuster, 1992), p. 265.

18. David B. Walker, *The Rebirth of Federalism* (Chatham, N.J.: Chatham House, 1995), pp. 295–96.

19. Walker, *Rebirth of Federalism*, p. 295.

20. Ruy A. Teixeira, *The Disappearing American Voter* (Washington, D.C.: Brookings Institution, 1992), pp. 176–77.

21. David Broder, "Better Days Ahead for Both Parties?" *Kalamazoo Gazette*, December 9, 1998, p. A10.

22. Laura Berkowitz and Steve Lilienthal, "A Tale of Two Parties: National Committee Policy Initiatives Since 1992," in Daniel M. Shea and John C. Green, *The State of the Parties: The Changing Role of Contemporary American Parties* (Lanham, Md.: Rowman & Littlefield, 1994), pp. 237–47.

23. Sabato, *Party's Just Begun*, pp. 184–85.

24. Clifton McCleskey, *Political Power and American Democracy* (Pacific Grove, Calif.: Brooks/Cole, 1989), p. 51.

25. Ibid.

26. Frank B. Feigert and John R. Todd, "Party Maintenance Activities," in Robert P. Steed et al., eds., *Party Organization and Activism in the American South* (Tuscaloosa: University of Alabama Press, 1998), p. 113.

27. John P. Frendreis et al., "Local Political Parties and the 1992 Campaign for the State Legislature," paper presented at the American Political Science Conference in Washington, D.C., September 2–5, 1993, p. 10.

28. Robert Huckfeldt and John Sprague, "Political Parties and Electoral Mobilization: Political Structure, Social Structure, and the Party Canvass," in *American Political Science Review* 86, no. 1 (1992): 84.

29. Kay Lawson, ed., *Political Parties and Linkage* (New Haven: Yale University Press, 1980), p. 23.

30. Morris Fiorina, "The Decline of Collective Responsibility in American

Politics," in Pietro S. Nivola and David H. Rosenbloom, eds., *Classic Readings in American Politics*, 2nd ed. (New York: St. Martin's Press, 1990), p. 158.

31. Nelson W. Polsby, *Consequences of Party Reform* (Oxford: Oxford University Press, 1983), p. 141.

32. Kay Lawson, Gerald Pomper, and Maureen Moakley's article "Local Party Activists and Electoral Linkage: Middlesex County, N.J." is quoted in John J. Coleman, "Party Organizations in Contemporary America," in John C. Green and Daniel M. Shea, eds., *The State of the Parties*, 2nd ed. (Lanham, Md.: Rowman & Littlefield, 1996), p. 375.

33. Anthony Corrado, "Financing the 1996 Elections," in Gerald M. Pomper, et al., *The Election of 1996* (Chatham, N.J.: Chatham House, 1997), p. 164.

34. While interest groups also can now interject themselves into campaigns through campaign advertising—previously illegal—an important electoral-campaign study by New York University's Brennan Center for Justice has demonstrated that soft money now pays for a disproportionate number of these ads, too. The study provided an exhaustive catalog of the twenty-one hundred political ads for congressional races that in 1998 aired more than three hundred thousand times on TV stations (broadcast and cable) in the top seventy-five media markets, serving 80 percent of the population. This study is summarized in David Broder, "High-tech Study Reshapes Campaign Finance Debate," *Kalamazoo Gazette*, May 29, 2000, p. C2.

35. Joseph E. Cantor, *Campaign Financing*, CRS [Congressional Research Service] issue brief, updated December 17, 1997, p. 6.

36. Kent D. Redfield, *Cash Clout: Political Money in Illinois Legislative Elections* (Springfield: University of Illinois at Springfield, 1995), p. 161.

37. Richard Lacayo, "The Gang's All Here," *Time*, October 6, 1997, p. 43.

38. Jackie Koszczuk, "Money Woes Leave FEC Watchdog with More Bark Than Bite," *Congressional Quarterly*, February 28, 1998, p. 469.

39. Richard L. Berke, "The Agency Congress Loves to Hate: Why Nothing Ever Changes," *New York Times*, July 17, 1994, section 4, p. 3.

40. Brooks Jackson, *Broken Promises: Why the Federal Election Commission Failed* (New York: Priority Press, 1990), p. 27.

41. Michael W. McConnell, "A *Constitutional* Campaign Finance Plan," *Wall Street Journal*, December 11, 1997, p. A22.

42. John R Wilke and Kyle Pope, "Plan for Free Air Time for Candidates Is Blasted by Lawmakers, Broadcasters," *Wall Street Journal*, January 29, 1998, p. A9.

43. Max Frankel, "Airfill," *New York Times*, June 4, 1995, magazine p. 26.

44. Jill Carroll and Leslie Cauley, "Rising Demand for Airwaves Raises Fears," *Wall Street Journal*, August 2, 2000, p. A2.

45. Eliza Newlin Carney, "Tuning Out Free TV," *National Journal*, April 12, 1997, p. 701.

46. Nat Hentoff, "Free Television Time for Campaign Spiels Hits Stations' Rights," *Kalamazoo Gazette*, March 23, 1998, p. A9.

47. Carney, "Tuning Out Free TV," p. 700.

48. Gerald F. Seib, "Advocates of Free TV Air Time for Candidates during Fall Presidential Race Make Headway," *Wall Street Journal*, June 25, 1996, p. A16.

49. Barry Diller, chairman of HSN, Inc., in 1996 publicly challenged the industry to cover the cost of all political messages since "it just isn't a lot of money." Fox network owner Rupert Murdoch offered an hour of free airtime the night before the 1996 election with "no censorship on our part, no interviews by some all-knowing correspondent," and ten minute-long "position statements" by

each candidate to air during prime time in the month before the election. He was also prepared to offer more free time if other networks joined in the effort. For Diller's quote, see Carney, "Tuning Out Free TV," p. 702; for Murdoch's quote, see Alan Bash, "Presidential Candidates to Get Free Time on Fox," *USA Today*, February 27, 1996, p. D1.

50. Nancy Gibbs, "The Screen Test," *Time*, May 20, 1996, p. 32.

51. Gerald F. Seib, "Nader's Mantra: Politics as Usual Taints the System," *Wall Street Journal*, June 14, 2000, p. A28.

52. Clyde Wilcox and Wesley Joe, "Dead Law: The Federal Election Finance Regulations, 1974–1996," *PS: Political Science and Politics*, March 1998, p. 16.

53. Committee on Rules and Administration, *Federal Election Campaign Act Amendments of 1979 Report*, U.S. Senate, 96th Congress, 1st session, September 17, 1979, p. 4.

54. Committee on House Administration, *Federal Election Campaign Act Amendments and Report of 1979*, Committee Print, 96th Congress, 2nd session, January 1980, p. 9.

55. Committee on House Administration, *Federal Election Campaign Act Amendments of 1979 Report*, U.S. House of Representatives, 96th Congress, 1st session, September 7, 1979, p. 9.

56. Senator Mark Hatfield, *Congressional Record*, U.S. Senate, December 18, 1979, p. 36754.

57. Representative Bill Frenzel, *Congressional Record*, U.S. House, September 10, 1979, p. 23814.

58. This section draws heavily on Anthony Corrado's superb essay "Party Soft Money," in Anthony Corrado et al., eds., *Campaign Finance Reform: A Sourcebook* (Washington, D.C.: Brookings Institution, 1997), pp. 167–77.

59. There is also the question whether anyone would have standing to bring such a case. The person or organization bringing the suit must be able to show some direct injury, not merely suffering held in common with people generally. The advent of "class action" suits, though, has enabled someone who is one of a considerable number who have sustained injury to bring a suit on behalf of the group. It is through such class-action suits that the Supreme Court came to rule on integration and legislative apportionment. The Court may view a question as "political," rather than justiciable, if it believes that the other branches are better equipped constitutionally to handle the matter.

60. An excellent case study of the Supreme Court's role in reapportionment may be found in Andrew Hacker, "The Supreme Court: Entering the 'Political Thicket' of Reapportionment," in Allan P. Sindler, ed., *American Political Institutions and Public Policy* (Boston: Little, Brown, 1969), pp. 231–75.

61. Steven E. Schier, *By Invitation Only* (Pittsburgh: University of Pittsburgh Press, 2000). Schier argues that parties now practice exclusive politics to which members are admitted by invitation only.

Selected Bibliography

Abramson, Paul R., John H. Aldrich, and David W. Rohde. *Change and Continuity in the 1996 Elections*. Washington, D.C.: CQ Press, 1998.

Alexander, Herbert, and Anthony Corrado. *Financing the 1992 Election*. Armonk, N.Y.: Sharpe, 1995.

Arnold, R. Douglas. *Congress and the Bureaucracy*. New Haven: Yale University Press, 1979.

Bellah, Robert N., Richard Madsen, William M. Sullivan, Ann Swidler, and Steven Tipton. *Habits of the Heart*. New York: Harper & Row, 1985.

Bennett, W. Lance. *The Governing Crisis*. 2nd edition. New York: St. Martin's Press, 1996.

Berry, Jeffrey. *The Interest Group Society*. 3rd edition. New York: Longman, 1997.

Biersack, Robert, Paul S. Hernnson, and Clyde Wilcox, eds. *Risky Business? PAC Decision Making in Congressional Elections*. Armonk, N.Y.: Sharpe, 1994.

Browne, William P. *Cultivating Congress*. Lawrence: University Press of Kansas, 1995.

Chambers, William Nisbet. *Political Parties in a New Nation*. New York: Oxford University Press, 1963.

Chubb, John E., and Paul E. Peterson, eds. *Can the Government Govern?* Washington, D.C.: Brookings Institution, 1989.

Clawson, Dan, Alan Neustadtl, and Denise Scott. *Money Talks*. New York: Basic Books, 1992.

Coleman, John. *Party Decline in America*. Princeton: Princeton University Press, 1996.

Corrado, Anthony, Thomas E. Mann, Daniel R. Ortiz, Trevor Potter, and Frank J. Sorauf, eds. *Campaign Finance Reform: A Sourcebook*. Washington, D.C.: Brookings Institution, 1997.

Costain, Anne N., and Andrew S. McFarland, eds. *Social Movements and American Political Institutions*. Lanham, Md.: Rowman & Littlefield, 1998.

Cotter, Cornelius P., and Bernard C. Hennessy. *Politics Without Power: The National Party Committees*. New York: Atherton Press, 1964.

Cotter, Cornelius P., James L. Gibson, John F. Bibby, and Robert J. Huckshorn. *Party Organizations in American Politics*. New York: Praeger Special Studies, 1984.

Cox, W. Michael, and Richard Alm. *Myths of Rich and Poor*. New York: Basic Books, 1999.

Craig, Stephen C., ed. *Broken Contract?* Boulder: Westview Press, 1996.

Danziger, Sheldon, and Peter Gottschalk. *Uneven Tides*. New York: Russell Sage Foundation, 1993.

Delli Carpini, Michael X., and Scott Keeter. *What Americans Know about Politics and Why It Matters.* New Haven: Yale University Press, 1996.

Dionne, E. J. *They Only Look Dead.* New York: Simon & Schuster, 1996.

Dolbeare, Kenneth M. *Democracy at Risk.* Rev. edition. Chatham, N.J.: Chatham House, 1986.

Donahue, John D. *The Privatization Decision.* New York: Basic Books, 1989.

Edsell, Thomas Byrne. *Power and Money.* New York: Norton, 1988.

Ehrenhalt, Alan. *The United States of Ambition.* New York: Times Books, 1991.

Epstein, Leon D. *Political Parties in the American Mold.* Madison: University of Wisconsin Press, 1986.

Ferguson, Thomas. *Golden Rule.* Chicago: University of Chicago Press, 1995.

Fiorina, Morris P. *Congress: Keystone of the Washington Establishment.* New Haven: Yale University Press, 1989.

———. "The Decline of Collective Responsibility in American Politics." In Pietro S. Nivola and David H. Rosenbloom, eds., *Classic Readings in American Politics*, 2nd edition, pp. 156–78. New York: St. Martin's Press, 1990.

Goidel, Robert K., Donald A. Gross, and Todd G. Shields. *Money Matters: Consequences of Campaign Finance Reform in U.S. House Elections.* Lanham, Md.: Rowman & Littlefield, 1999.

Graber, Doris A. *Mass Media and American Politics.* 4th edition. Washington, D.C.: CQ Press, 1993.

Green, John C., and Daniel M. Shea, eds. *The State of the Parties.* 2nd edition. Lanham, Md.: Rowman & Littlefield, 1996.

Greider, William. *Who Will Tell the People.* New York: Simon & Schuster, 1992.

Hacker, Andrew. "The Supreme Court: Entering the 'Political Thicket' of Reapportionment." In Allan P. Sindler, ed., *American Political Institutions and Public Policy*, pp. 231–75. Boston: Little, Brown, 1969.

———. *Money: Who Has How Much and Why.* New York: Scribner's, 1997.

Hall, Richard L., and Frank W. Wayman. "Buying Time: Moneyed Interest and the Mobilization of Bias." *American Political Science Review* 84, no. 3 (1990): 797–820.

Hansen, John M. *Gaining Access: Congress and the Farm Lobby, 1919–1981.* Chicago: University of Chicago Press, 1991.

Hill, Sam, and Glenn Rifkin. *Radical Marketing.* New York: HarperBusiness, 1999.

Huckfeldt, Robert, and John Sprague. "Political Parties and Electoral Mobilization: Political Structure, Social Structure, and the Party Canvass." *American Political Science Review* 86, no. 1 (1992): 70–86.

Jackson, Brooks. *Honest Graft.* New York: Knopf, 1988.

Jacobson, Gary C. *The Politics of Congressional Elections.* 4th edition. New York: Longman, 1997.

Jamieson, Kathleen Hall. *Dirty Politics.* New York: Oxford University Press, 1992.

Johnson, Haynes. *Sleepwalking through History.* New York: Anchor Books, 1991.

Kelman, Steven. "'Public Choice' and Public Spirit." *Public Interest*, no. 87 (spring 1987): 80–94.

Kettl, Donald F. *Sharing Power.* Washington, D.C.: Brookings Institution, 1993.

King, Anthony. *Running Scared.* New York: Free Press, 1997.

Klyza, Christopher McGrory. *Who Controls the Public Lands?* Chapel Hill: University of North Carolina Press, 1996.

Kobrak, Peter. "Privatization and Cozy Politics." *Public Integrity Annual*, pp.

13–22. Council of State Governments and the American Society for Public Administration, 1996.

Kuttner, Robert, ed. *Ticking Time Bombs*. New York: New Press, 1996.

Levy, Frank. *The New Dollars and Dreams*. New York: Russell Sage Foundation, 1998.

Lewis, Charles. *The Buying of the President*. New York: Avon Books, 1996.

Lipset, Seymour Martin, and William Schneider. *The Confidence Gap*. New York: Macmillan, 1983.

Makinson, Larry, and Joshua Goldstein. *The Cash Constituents of Congress*. 2nd edition. Washington, D.C.: Congressional Quarterly, 1994.

Makinson, Larry, et al. *The Big Picture: Where the Money Came from in the 1996 Elections*. Center for Responsive Politics, 1997. www.crp.org.

Malbin, Michael J., and Thomas L. Gais. *The Day after Reform: Sobering Campaign Finance Lessons from the States*. Albany: Rockefeller Institute Press, 1998.

Matthews, David. *Politics for People: Finding a Responsible Public Voice*. Urbana: University of Illinois Press, 1994.

McClosky, Herbert, Paul J. Hoffman, and Rosemary O'Hara. "Issue Conflict and Consensus among Party Leaders and Followers." *American Political Science Review* 54 (June 1960): 406–27.

Meier, Kenneth J. *Politics and the Bureaucracy*. 4th edition. Fort Worth: Harcourt College Publishers, 2000.

Newland, Chester A. "Public Executives: Imperium, Sacerdotium, Collegium?" *Public Administration Review* 47, no. 1 (1987): 45–56.

Neustadt, Richard. *Presidential Power and the Modern Presidents*. Rev. edition. New York: Free Press, 1991.

Nye, Joseph S., Philip D. Zelikow, and David C. King, eds. *Why People Don't Trust Government*. Cambridge: Harvard University Press, 1997.

Phillips, Kevin. *Boiling Point: Democrats, Republicans, and the Decline of Middle-Class Prosperity*. New York: Random House, 1993.

Polsby, Nelson, and Aaron Wildavsky. *Presidential Elections*. 9th edition. Chatham, N.J.: Chatham House, 1996.

Pomper, Gerald M., et al. *The Election of 1996*. Chatham, N.J.: Chatham House, 1997.

Price, David E. *Bringing Back the Parties*. Washington, D.C.: CQ Press, 1984.

Reich, Robert B. "Policy Making in a Democracy." In Robert B. Reich, ed., *The Power of Public Ideas*, Cambridge, Mass.: Ballinger, 1988, pp. 123–56.

Rohde, David W. *Parties and Leaders in the Postreform House*. Chicago: University of Chicago Press, 1991.

Rosenstone, Steven J., and John Mark Hansen. *Mobilization, Participation, and Democracy in America*. New York: Macmillan, 1993.

Rourke, Francis E. *Bureaucracy, Politics, and Public Policy*. 3rd edition. Boston: Little, Brown, 1984.

Rozell, Mark J., and Clyde Wilcox. *Interest Groups in American Campaigns*. Washington, D.C.: CQ Press, 1999.

Sabato, Larry J. *Feeding Frenzy: How Attack Journalism Has Transformed American Politics*. New York: Free Press, 1993.

Sabato, Larry J., and Glenn R. Simpson. *Dirty Little Secrets*. New York: Times Books, 1996.

Savas, E. E. *Privatization and Public-Private Partnerships*. New York: Chatham House, 2000.

Schattschneider, E. E. *The Semisovereign People*. New York: Holt, Rinehart & Winston, 1960.

Schier, Steven E. *By Invitation Only*. Pittsburgh: University of Pittsburgh Press, 2000.

Schwartz, Mildred A. *The Party Network: The Robust Organization of Illinois Republicans*. Madison: University of Wisconsin Press, 1990.

Skowronek, Stephen. *Building a New American State*. Cambridge: Cambridge University Press, 1982.

Sorauf, Frank. *Inside Campaign Finance*. New Haven: Yale University Press, 1992.

Starobin, Paul. "Pork: A Time-Honored Tradition Lives On." *Congressional Quarterly* (October 24, 1987): 2581–94.

Steed, Robert P., John A. Clark, Lewis Bowman, and Charles D. Hadley, eds. *Party Organization and Activism in the American South*. Tuscaloosa: University of Alabama Press, 1998.

Stein, Robert M., and Kenneth N. Bickers. *Perpetuating the Pork Barrel*. New York: Cambridge University Press, 1995.

Teixeira, Ruy A. *The Disappearing American Voter*. Washington, D.C.: Brookings Institution, 1992.

Thompson, Dennis F. "Mediated Corruption: The Case of the Keating Five." *American Political Science Review* 87, no. 2 (1993): 369–81.

Verba, Sidney, Kay Lehman Schlozman, and Henry E. Brady. "The Big Tilt: Participatory Inequality in America." *American Prospect*, no. 32 (1997): 74–80.

Walker, Jack L. *Mobilizing Interest Groups in America*. Ann Arbor: University of Michigan Press, 1991.

Wattenberg, Martin P. *The Rise of Candidate-Centered Politics*. Cambridge: Harvard University Press, 1991.

———. *The Decline of American Political Parties*. Cambridge: Harvard University Press, 1996.

Wattenberg, Martin P., and Craig Leonard Brians. "Negative Campaign Advertising: Demobilizer or Mobilizer?" *American Political Science Review* 932, no. 4 (1999): 891–99.

Wertheimer, Fred, and Susan Weiss Manes. "Campaign Finance Reform: A Key to Restoring the Health of Our Democracy." *Columbia Law Review* 94, no. 4 (1994): 1126–59.

West, Darrell M., and Burdett A. Loomis. *The Sound of Money*. New York: Norton, 1998.

White, John Kenneth, and Daniel M. Shea. *New Party Politics: From Jefferson and Hamilton to the Information Age*. New York: St. Martin's Press, 2000.

Zepezauer, Mark, and Arthur Naiman. *Take the Rich Off Welfare*. Tucson, Ariz.: Odonian Press, 1996.

Index

About the Book

Cozy politics, Peter Kobrak contends, is shredding the already fragile fabric of political rapport between citizens and their government. Exploring the insidious system that encourages elected officials to cooperate with their supposed opponents—rather than with their own constituents—he reveals the enormous power that wealthy donors and interest-group supporters wield over politicians, congressional decisionmakers, and agency agendas.

Peter Kobrak is professor of public administration and political science at Western Michigan University. He has written extensively on public spending and political decisionmaking.